Europe and German Unification

Europe and German Unification

RENATA FRITSCH-BOURNAZEL

BERG

New York / Oxford

Distributed exclusively in the U.S. and Canada by
St. Martin's Press, New York

943. 087 FRI
74889

Published in 1992 by
Berg Publishers, Inc.
Editorial offices:
165 Taber Avenue, Providence, RI 02906, U.S.A.
150 Cowley Road, Oxford OX4 1JJ, UK

© Renata Fritsch-Bournazel

British Library Cataloguing in Publication Data
Fritsch-Bournazel, Renata
Europe and German unification.
I. Title
943.087

ISBN 0 85496-979-9   (hardback edition)
ISBN 0 85496-684-6   (paperback edition)

Library of Congress Cataloging-in-Publication Data Applied For.

Printed in Great Britain by
Billing & Sons Ltd, Worcester

Contents

List of Abbreviations

ABC (weapons)	Atomic, biological, and chemical armaments
BILD	Bureau International de Liaison et de Documentation
CC	Central Committee
CDU	Christlich-Demokratische Union Deutschlands (Christian Democratic Party of Germany)
CMEA	Council for Mutual Economic Assistance (a.k.a. COMECON)
CPSU	Communist Party of the Soviet Union
CSCE	Conference on Security and Cooperation in Europe
ČSFR	Czecho-Slovak Federative Republic
ČSSR	Czechoslovakian Socialist Republic (former name of ČSSR)
CSU	Christlich-Soziale Union (Christian Democratic Party of Bavaria)
EBRD	European Bank for Reconstruction and Development
EC	European Community
EDC	European Defense Community
EFTA	European Free Trade Area
EIB	European Investment Bank
EPC	European Political Cooperation
ESA	European Space Agency
EUREKA	European Research Coordination Agency
FDP	Freie Demokratische Partei (Free Democratic Party, the German Liberals)
FEDN	Fondation pour les Etudes de Défense

	Nationale (National Foundation for Defense Studies), Paris
FRG	Federal Republic of Germany
GATT	General Agreement on Tariffs and Trade
GDR	German Democratic Republic
IFRI	Institut français des relations internationales (French Institute for International Relations)
IPW	Institut für Internationale Politik und Wirtschaft (Institute for International Politics and Economy, quondam East Berlin)
NATO	North Atlantic Treaty Organization
PDS	Partei des Demokratischen Sozialismus (Party of Democratic Socialism, successor to the SED)
RKDB	Ring Katholischer Deutscher Burschenschaften (Circle of German Catholic Students' Associations)
SACEUR	Supreme Allied Commander Europe
SED	Sozialistische Einheitspartei Deutschlands (Socialist Unity Party of Germany, the former name of the East German Communist Party)
SIPRI	Stockholm International Peace Research Institute
SPD	Sozialdemokratische Partei Deutschlands (Social Democratic Party of Germany)
USA	United States of America
USSR	Union of Soviet Socialist Republics
WEU	Western European Union

Preface

Have Europe's upheavals of the last two years provided an answer to the "German Question," or merely multiplied it into a number of new ones? While those Germans who gave absolute priority to national unification would obviously accept the former view, those who perceived the "German Question" in terms of the reconciliation of social or economic systems, or of the place of a united Germany in an unstable Europe, continue to see many question marks over the future.

So many aspects of the rapid achievement of German unity were unsettling, both for the Germans themselves and for some of their neighbors. The reasons for this, in most cases, can be traced back to the sheer speed of the events we witnessed after the Berlin Wall was opened in November 1989. How, when all the comparative studies of the two German economies and social systems had underlined their profound differences, could it possibly be safe and sensible to try to force them together in an "economic, monetary and social union" at only a few weeks' notice? If the President of the Bundesbank expressed grave doubts about the speed of this rash project, could the Federal Chancellor be trusted to know what he was doing? Again, when every study of German unification had produced a conventional wisdom, reinforced over a third of century, to the effect that Germany could only be safely united when the two Cold War blocs had coalesced into a Pan-European security system, could Europe really feel safe at the prospect of a unified German state emerging while its environment was still so unstable?

Within Germany itself, would the apparently irresistible pressure of the East Germans for unification sweep away not only all the

1

detestable aspects of the Stasi-regime, but also certain positive features of East German society: such, for instance, as solidarity with family and friends, a Protestant reserve toward the rat-racing materialism of the West, a reflective *Innerlichkeit* or "inwardness," and public welfare provision in the form of school meals and state-run nurseries?

On such questions and many others, Renata Fritsch-Bournazel's book provides an illuminating and reliable guide to the thoughts and reactions of the Germans and their neighbors. One of the most difficult tasks, for any observer of revolutionary processes like those of the last two years, is to distinguish the significant from the ephemeral and to seize the essential arguments in a fast-moving, many-sided, and intensive debate. The author's method, that of identifying the fundamental issues and then documenting the controversies and the decisions in the words of those directly involved or close at hand, gives the reader an exceptionally vivid sense of the issues at stake and how it felt as they unfolded.

The practical significance of many contemporary slogans — "a common European house," "a European peace order," "a European Germany, not a German Europe" — is explored, in their historical context, in this well-documented analysis of a dramatic moment of German and European history.

It is interesting to note how some of the witnesses quoted here — especially the non-German ones — resort, as a means of understanding Germany's present situation, to images and stereotypes from the past. A striking example is the "psychogram" of "the Germans," compiled by Margaret Thatcher's advisor Charles Powell: "The Germans . . . are not concerned with the feelings of others, are plagued by fear, are bragging and pushy but want to be loved, suffer from an inferiority complex and self-overestimation," etc. As the academic participants in Mrs. Thatcher's "seminar" at Chequers seem to have told her, and as many of the other documents in this book confirm, the German reality is a good deal more complex, and much less alarming, than this would suggest.

One important aspect of this book is that the various international organizations that form Germany's "European" framework — the CSCE, NATO, and above all the European Community — are clearly and precisely identified and described. They are all in a process of rapid and confused evolution, and the statements from some of their leaders, quoted here, give a good picture of the widespread concern of Europe's leaders (including Germany's) to provide a European framework for the new united Germany, despite all the handicaps caused by the different tempos and still unclear destinations of the various processes now under way.

Of all the comments by eyewitnesses and participants that Renata Fritsch-Bournazel has brought together in this fascinating book, perhaps the most profound is an observation made by Willy Brandt in October 1990: "the real problems, the economic difficulties and the balancing out of the differing worlds of consciousness and of experience will keep us busy for a long time yet."

This book, which reflects both the witnesses' "consciousness" of events, and also the true nature of the events themselves, will give its readers a valuable guide to the development of this complex process.

ROGER MORGAN
Professor of Political Science
European University Institute

Introduction

"The German question will stay open as long as the Brandenburg Gate stays closed." This phrase, coined in Berlin in the early 1980s, aptly described the situation of the divided German State. The revolutionary changes in the German Democratic Republic (GDR) since autumn 1989 showed clearly that the statement could not simply be turned on its head. The German question did not "close" the moment the Brandenburg Gate and the border between the two States in Germany opened. The breaking down of the Wall on 9 November 1989 certainly made a decisive contribution to the realization of East German aspirations to freedom. But only a few weeks later it was clear that this was by no means an exhaustive answer to the German question. In addition to East Germans' desire for freedom and demands for democracy, the gross disparities in levels of prosperity between the Federal Republic and the GDR were to become a decisive factor for the dynamics of German unification.

The unforeseen end in 1989 to the postwar period in Europe initially evoked a general perplexity. Under the pressure of events and a mass flight from the GDR that had persisted for months, the Germans themselves and also their allies and neighbors were soon confronted with the need to rethink existing standpoints and reformulate the connection between the German question and the system of peace in Europe. At a stroke, everything that had always seemed defined, decided, or hopeless had become immediate, uncertain, and open again. There had certainly been public reflection since the late 1970s on Germany's role in Europe, and indications had multiplied in the Federal Republic of Germany — and, in another form, in the GDR too — that the special historical, political, and psychological situation in the center of Europe had returned more strongly to the consciousness of many Germans. In Europe, however, peace was defined as stability, and stability as the status quo. This definition was, to be sure, occasionally questioned, but never with enough seriousness to make possible any attempt to estimate its consequences.

With the elections in the GDR on 18 March 1990, the die was cast for national unity. Most GDR citizens wanted German unity; a clear majority wanted it right away. At the same time, all responsible politicians in both German States pointed to the need to integrate the German unification process into the international context. Thus, both German governments were faced with the task of seeking consensus with their neighbors and with the Four Powers of 1945, Britain, France, the Soviet Union, and the United States.

The achievement of national unity for Germans is inseparable from the fate of Europe as a whole. The presumption had long been that the division of Germany could be overcome only at the end of a gradual growing together of the European continent. But the revolutionary upheaval in the GDR reversed this order. In all likelihood, it will be the solution to the German question that will generate the impulse to replace postwar power structures and world views in Europe. Germany will again become the catalyst for a new order in Europe.

In the course of the Cold War, Germany was squeezed out of its traditional position at the center of Europe and placed on the margins, for the line between the new, antagonistic power blocs now exactly coincided with the boundary between the two German States. Each of the two world powers increasingly endeavored to exploit the German potential lying in its own power sphere, and as far as possible the one in the opponent's sphere of influence too, in their struggle for world political predominance. This made the German question the core conflict of the Cold War in Europe. In this situation, all attempts to work against the political, ideological, and sociopolitical disruption of the German nation were condemned to failure. The division was based on an interest shared by the victorious powers not to let Germany either go it alone or go entirely to the other side.

This clear system of blocs has now been replaced by a multitude of uncertainties generated by the revolutionary changes in Eastern and Central Europe. The German question has suddenly become acute again, and in a highly dynamic fashion. As the ideological division of Europe comes to an end, much that once seemed out of the question is now possible. The year 1989 not only marked the irrevocable end of the postwar period, it also put an end to the notion that the ideas and ideologies of the nineteenth century could be used to solve the quite different problems of the late twentieth century.

With the process of German unity under way, there is a growing need for institutions that will facilitate cooperation between the two sides of the European continent. Alongside the military alliances and the economic communities, the CSCE is assuming a new significance, not only as a forum for East-West dialogue but also as an additional instrument for political arrangements that concern all of Germany and also all of Europe. At the start of the 1990s it is again becoming clear and is apparent to all of Germany's neighbors, that the way to German unity can be safeguarded only as a decisive step toward European unification. From this follows the special German task not to overlook, in joy and worry at German unity, their responsibility within Europe.

When in the 1950s the great German writer Thomas Mann returned from long exile in the United States, he articulated his vision of the future for the Germans in Europe. His address to the students of Hamburg still deserves our respect. He said:

> We do not fear that the operations of time may never bring a united Europe, with a reunited Germany at its center. We do not know how it will happen, how this unnaturally divided Germany is to become one again. It is obscure to us, and we must take refuge in the belief that history will find ways and means of overcoming the unnatural and restoring the natural: a Germany as a consciously serving member of a Europe united in self-awareness — not as its lord and master . . .
>
> Let us not delude ourselves over the fact that among the difficulties delaying the unification of Europe is a mistrust of the purity of German intentions, a fear by other peoples of Germany and of hegemonic plans that its vital energy may instill into it, which in their view it does not conceal very well . . . .It is for the rising German generation, for German youth, to dispel this mistrust, this fear, by rejecting what has long been rejected and clearly and unanimously announcing their desire: not for a German Europe, but for a European Germany.[1]

---

1. Thomas Mann, Address to Hamburg students on 8 June 1953, in "An die gesittete Welt," *Politische Schriften und Reden im Exil* (Frankfurt/M: Fischer Verlag, 1968), 811.

The fact that, over fifty years after the outbreak of the Second World War, the "European Germany" longed for by Thomas Mann has become a solid part of our historical landscape does not mean that the past no longer casts its shadows on this continent. On 8 May 1985, in the German Bundestag's Hour of Remembrance for the fortieth anniversary of the end to the war in Europe and to National Socialist tyranny, Federal President Richard von Weizsäcker asked that Germans recognize their special obligation not only to see the past as a burden but also to draw from it the strength for political action in awareness of responsibility:

Speech by Federal President Richard von Weizsäcker at the Hour of Remembrance of the German Bundestag for the 40th Anniversary of the End of the War in Europe, 8 May 1985 (extract)

We all, whether guilty or not, whether old or young, must take on the past. We are all affected by its consequences and have a liability for them. The young and their elders must and can help each other to understand why it is vitally important to keep the memory awake.

The point is not to overcome the past. That is not possible. It cannot be changed in retrospect or undone. But those who close their eyes to the past become blind to the present. Those who do not wish to remember inhumanity will become susceptible again to new risks of infection...

The wish to forget prolongs exile,
and the secret of salvation is recall.

This oft-cited Jewish saying we take to mean that the belief in God is belief in His action through history. Recall is the experience of God's operation in history. It is the source of faith in salvation.... For us what is important is how we remember, in thinking and feeling within ourselves.

These two statements on the historical "community of responsibility" of the Germans (to use a term from the early 1980s) make it clear that the international debate that has recently flared up again over the role and mission of the Germans in Europe is fed by two sources: from the reactions of other countries to political change in Central Europe, and from those of Germans themselves, both East and West.

This work attempts to assess the German problem in European context as the 1990s begin. It draws from a representative selection of documents and statements by many of those involved. The debate as to Germany's future poses a challenge not only to policy and diplomacy but to scholars as well. Here, too, the heartfelt sigh of one Bonn politician applies: "Some words are old before they leave your mouth!"

And so, the unification of the Germans is not just crisis and opportunity for all of Europe, it is also one specifically for contemporary historians, whose realization of the necessity of leaving the beaten track of earlier certainty goes hand in hand with awareness of the risk of being caught up with, or even overtaken by, the storms of the present.

Europe and German Unification

1

Germany on the Agenda

By the end of the 1970s, the close connection between the political, and legal, position of the Germans and the situation in Europe had become the basis for a number of ideas as to how to overcome, or at least improve, the situation of a split Germany and a split Europe. The decisive reshaping of the East-West relationship following Gorbachev's coming to power gave added impetus to these ways of thinking. But it was not until the autumn revolutions of 1989 that such ideas became real possibilities, giving political relevance to all reflection on Germany's future.

The recent radical changes in East-West relationships demonstrate how crucial this community in the center of Europe is, based as it is on one common culture and on common memories and hopes. Revolutions have shaken the Communist world and changed it past recognition. The Soviet model, transplanted to Eastern and Central Europe, never took root there, and now, after years of rigidity and stagnation, the heritage of Stalinism is being rejected by the people that took to the streets.

With all the impressive images of 1989, none was more dramatic or more hopeful than that of the razing of the Berlin Wall, that inhuman division between East and West Europe. When this symbol of a whole international order collapsed into saleable souvenirs, the Cold War system fell apart before the eyes of the world. The Germans experienced the collapse of the Wall in a way similar to the Poles during the Pope's visit in 1979: it was an epiphany, a sudden awareness that the people were in fact one people, feeling and thinking in the same way. But has this feeling of solidarity smoothed the path to German unification as the political trade union *Solidarnošč* did for Poland's rebirth as a nation? This remains to be seen.

The end of Stalinism calls for a radically new approach to what is again, with capital letters, the German Question. The division of a city, a country, and a continent came out of Adolf Hitler's war. At the end of this century, after its self-destructive civil wars, Europe is looking toward a period of promise, and hopes this time for a happy ending. Uncertainty still prevails as to the long-term consequences of this new volatile continent. The development of a new European peace system demands that the German Question be resolved in a way acceptable both to the Germans and to their neighbors. The two German States would have needed what unfortunately they were not given, in a world with greater freedoms but also greater dangers; namely, a breathing space for the calm consideration of alternatives.

A People Breaks Down Its Walls

The building of the Berlin Wall in August 1961 was a turning point in European, and indeed in international, politics. It sealed both the division of Germany and that of Berlin. It made clear that the Soviet Union was not prepared to look on passively while the GDR fell apart, and it demonstrated the West's determination to keep West Berlin within its world. For more than twenty-eight years East Germans experienced the Wall as a heavy psychological burden; many developed what one East Berlin doctor called "Wall sickness." People fell ill or committed suicide because of the Wall. West Berliners, too, were forced to adjust to a life in the shadow of the Wall, and they did so by gradually forcing its existence out of their minds. Yet, the division of the city remained an open wound, perhaps like Garcia Lorca's famous "Casida of Lamentation:"

> I have closed my shutters
> for I will not hear the wailing;
> yet from behind the grey walls
> there's nothing else to hear but the wailing.[2]

2. Federico Garcia Lorca, "Casida del Llanto" (Casida no. 2), in Federico Garcia Lorca, *Obras completas* (Madrid: Aguilar, 1955), 497.

The Berlin Wall was thus both a symbol of national division and an expression of psychological barriers. This tension between national desire to overcome division and actual experience of national acquiescence to the separation found expression in a number of novels, short stories, and poems about East-West German reality, which sought to work through this reality on an intellectual and literary level. A few months before the opening of the borders, the author Elisabeth Plessen, living in West Berlin, wrote:

> Berlin is the city in which the country's division is most perceptible, in which the two isms that dominate the world and separate the German States from each other clash. The embodiment of that is the Wall, and the Wall is the embodiment of the divided city...
>
> Erich Honecker recently stated that the Wall will still be there in a hundred years. I sincerely hope that that will not be the case, that instead the Wall will fall at a far earlier date, soon, in the spirit of glasnost, in the spirit of human rights, a part of which is abolition of the order to shoot in the heart of Europe, for the fact of the death strip is intolerable to a high civilization.[3]

At a time when national frontiers are playing a lesser role in Europe than before, the removal of this boundary between States and systems, the removal of this frontier that ran through Germany, was not only seen as an opportunity. Many intellectuals in West and East expressed their unease at a development that rendered invalid not only the external demarcation and symbols of separation, but the internal ones as well. Typical of the conflicted reactions of the West German Left is Peter Schütt's prologue to an illustrated book about the moving scenes of the night between the 9th and 10th of November, when Berlin men and women disbelievingly, with tears of joy in their eyes, went past the GDR borderguards and fell into each others' arms.

The Fall of the Wall

When the Wall fell
a stone fell
from my heart too.

3. Elisabeth Plessen, "Durch viele Deutschlands unterwegs," in Françoise Barthélémy and Lutz Winckler, *Mein Deutschland findet sich in keinem Atlas, Schriftsteller aus beiden deutschen Staaten über ihr nationales Selbstverständnis* (Frankfurt/M: Luchterhand, 1990), 49.

And the piece of
concrete that had grown into me from the Wall
right into my brain
was suddenly gone.

Yet the headache
remained. And vertigo
came on me, as I went
with no hands over the ruin
of the structure
that had so often held me up
whenever I stood
with my back to the wall.

Scared, I gazed
into the void.
Where there used to be
the icon wall
stopping all sight
now gapes an empty hole.[4]

A similar confusion of feelings can be encountered among many GDR dissidents. In a very emotional contribution to the daily paper "taz," theater director Freya Klier, who had been deprived of her GDR citizenship almost two years before the Wall came down, thus describes her own "hangover":

Breathing out is hard. Forty years cannot be stripped off with a laugh; the past overlays even the most stupendous turn of events. We fought to the point of absurdity, so that the force of the news sent me under the bedclothes rather than onto the night streets. What is going to happen? Will Maxwell be buying up the Wall now? No forecasts, anything is possible. Yet I am afraid the GDR could dissolve like an effervescent pill.[5]

With some distance of time from the razing of the Wall, theologian Hans-Joachim Beeskow, in the preliminaries to the GDR

    4. Peter Schütt, "Der Fall der Mauer," in *Berlin im November* (Berlin: Nicolaische Verlagsbuchhandlung, 1989), 6.
    5. Freya Klier, "Der Mauerfall unter der Decke," in *DDR Journal zur Novemberrevolution, August bis Dezember 1989, Vom Ausreisen bis zum Eintreißen der Mauer* (Frankfurt/M: Verlag "die taz," 1990), 114.

elections of March 1990, reached back to a famous saying of
Heine's to express the way he felt in a land without walls. Beeskow
had been among the "privileged" allowed to travel West even in
the period just before the upheaval: in April 1989 he had been
in the western part of Berlin for the first time in 28 years.

> When I think of Germany
> in the night
> I am robbed of sleep.

Thinking currently about this Heine quotation, three keywords arise
in my mind: joy, depression or sadness, and repressed hope . . .

After forty years of absolute and truly anti-popular rule by the SED,
a people now finds itself in upsurge and upheaval, brought by peaceful
means and great level-headedness. Certainly, at the moment the collapse
is greater than the upsurge. Although the "round table" and the present
GDR government would like to bring our country out of the deep crisis,
fears for the future are nonetheless spreading. Many are asking what
will be, and facing the problem of a life lived in vain.[6]

The hundreds of thousands in Leipzig, and then in other towns
too, who took to the streets for democracy and reform, forced
the SED leadership, by their nonviolent revolution, to adopt different policies and give the people's demands a hearing. Helping
in the birth of that transformation were those who publicly, at
great personal risk and before all others, pressed for change:
dissidents, rank-and-file groups, and parts of the Protestant Church,
under the aegis of which most of the latter came into being.

But many intellectuals and artists, scholars, writers, and journalists acted less commendably than the Churches. In 1956 in
Hungary, and in 1968 and 1989 in Czechoslovakia, writers and
artists lit the revolutionary torch; in the GDR they instead marched
pensively behind the revolution. Most East Germans openly joined
the expressions of political dissatisfaction only after this no longer
involved any great personal risk. Yet had there not been, in the
arts and in science, a counterculture, if only an intellectual one,
there would not have been that intellectual potential for renewal,

---

6. Hans-Joachim Beeskow, "Mit der Bibel in der Hand . . . ," in *Neue Zeit*, 10
March 1990.

and range of proposals for how renewal would take place, that actually brought the change that autumn.

When, in a document volume issued in mid-November 1989, reformers and dissidents — those who had left and those who had stayed behind, representatives of established parties and those of the opposition, scholars and writers — expressed their ideas on the future of their country, an attempt was made at a preliminary assessment of where Germany stood after this "German October Revolution." Quite strikingly, most contributions showed far-reaching agreement on one point: that the GDR should not disappear from the map and should constitute a socialist-inspired alternative to the Federal Republic's consumer society. Hubertus Knabe, publisher of the volume and study director at the Evangelical Academy in West Berlin, made the following critical remarks:

> There follows a strongly felt sense of responsibility for a stable GDR that does not shrink even before such unpopular criticism as that of the over-hasty opening of the borders. By contrast with other Warsaw Pact countries, in many GDR dissidents the anti-capitalist, left-wing orientation is so strong that one sometimes wonders why the SED fought them so stubbornly . . . But this ideological affinity with those in power also contains the danger that the new opposition groups may become alienated from the population again just as quickly as they became their mouthpiece.[7]

As the elections of 18 March 1990 were to show, the population's willingness to make itself available as guinea pigs for the utopias of intellectuals playing at politics was indeed very slight. At the end of November 1989, GDR author Christa Wolf had collaborated on the controversial appeal "For Our Country," whose initial signatories included well-known writers and artists; she later took the following stance, in a very self-critical introduction to some of her own texts from those months:

> The appeal came at the time of the revelations of the extent of abuse of power, about the true state of the economy, the old city centres, the environmental pollution; the time when many citizens of the GDR were for the first time able to see the towns and the consumer possibilities in the other part of Germany. The critics were right: for many the

7. Hubertus Knabe, ed., *Aufbruch in eine andere DDR, Reformer und Oppositionelle zur Zukunft ihres Landes* (Reinbek bei Hamburg: Rowohlt Verlag, 1989), 19f.

word "socialist" was worn out. After hours of discussion we had included it in our text only once, of course redefined: as a "socialist alternative"; it made many angry and aggressive, and they probably also feared that one single word like that could delay the urgently necessary financial assistance from the Federal Republic. They presumably wanted not to take part in yet another experiment themselves, but instead to take over what was tried and tested.[8]

Dual Germany or Single Fatherland?

The "For Our Country" appeal of 26 November 1989 was met with anger for another reason in particular. One day after its publication in the SED party organ *Neues Deutschland*, the then SED leader and GDR Head of State Egon Krenz, Council of Ministers' chairman Hans Modrow, and other members and candidate members of the Politburo and Central Committee of the SED signed the intellectuals' appeal. Additionally, its publication coincided with Federal Chancellor Helmut Kohl's spectacular speech to the German Bundestag on 28 November, in which he presented his ten-point program for overcoming the division of Germany and of Europe.

For Our Country, appeal of 26 November 1989

Our country is in deep crisis. We cannot and will not live any longer the way we have lived hitherto. The leadership of one party had arrogated to itself rule over the people and its representations; structures marked by Stalinism had permeated all spheres of life. Without violence, through mass demonstrations, the people have compelled the process of revolutionary renewal, which is coming about with breathtaking rapidity. We are left with only a little time to exercise influence over the various possibilities that present themselves as ways out of the crisis.

Either

we can insist on the autonomy of the GDR and seek with all our efforts and in cooperation with those States and interest-groups prepared to do

---

8. Christa Wolf, *Im Dialog, Aktuelle Texte* (Frankfurt/M: Luchterhand, 1990), 13f.

so to develop a society of solidarity in our country, in which peace and social justice, freedom of the individual, free movement for all and the conservation of the environment are guaranteed.

Or

we have to tolerate the start of a sell out of our material and moral values, caused by heavy economic constraints and by unacceptable conditions linked by influential circles of the economy and of politics in the Federal Republic to their assistance to the GDR, leading in the short or long term to absorption of the German Democratic Republic by the Federal Republic of Germany.

Let us take the first path. We *still* have the chance of developing a socialist alternative to the Federal Republic, as neighbours on an equal footing with all the States of Europe. We can *still* take inspiration from the anti-fascist and humanist ideals we once started from. We appeal to all citizens, male and female, who share our hope and our concern to join this appeal by signing it.

Berlin, 26 November 1989

The Federal Chancellor's ten-point plan was in part an answer to internal criticism; he had been reproached with lacking the visionary power necessary for the formulation of an appropriate response to the cumulative changes in the GDR. His announcement of his plan was also connected with the decision of his party, the Christian Democratic Union (CDU), to make unification its most important campaign issue in the forthcoming Bundestag elections. The Chancellor formulated some of the steps on the path, through economic assistance, to a kind of confederation between the two States, and finally to a united nation, as set forth as one primary objective in the preamble to the Federal Republic's Basic Law.

Ten-Point Program to overcome the division of Germany and of Europe. Speech by Federal Chancellor Kohl to the German Bundestag on 28 November 1989 (extracts)

We are all deeply impressed by the living, unbroken will for freedom that moves the people in Leipzig and many other towns. They know what they want. They want to determine their future themselves — in the original meaning of the words. In this we shall of course respect every decision that the people in the GDR take in free self-determination ...

We cannot plan the road to unity in smoke-filled rooms or with a timetable in our hands. Abstract models are of no assistance either. But we can now, today, prepare the stages that will lead to this goal. I should like to set them forth on the basis of a ten-point program:

First: Right away, immediate measures arising out of the events of the last few weeks, particularly the refugee movements and the new dimensions of travel, are necessary.

The Federal Government is prepared to give immediate practical assistance where that assistance is needed now. In the humanitarian sphere and in medical provision we shall help wherever it is wanted ...

Second: The Federal Government will as hitherto continue cooperation with the GDR in all spheres of direct benefit to the people on both sides ...

Third: I have offered to extend our assistance and our cooperation comprehensively when a radical change in the political and economic system in the GDR is bindingly decided and irreversibly set in motion. "Irreversibly" means for us that the GDR national leadership should come to agreement with opposition groups on constitutional change and on a new electoral law.

We support the demand for free, equal and secret elections in the GDR with the involvement of independent parties, including non-socialist ones. The SED's power monopoly must be removed ...

Fourth: Prime Minister Modrow spoke in his government statement of a community based on treaty. We are prepared to take up this idea.

Fifth: But we are also prepared to take one further decisive step, namely to develop confederative structures between the two States in Germany, with the object of then creating a federation, that is, a national federal system in Germany. This necessarily presupposes a democratically legitimated government in the GDR ... How a reunited Germany will finally look is something no one today knows. But that unity will come if the people in Germany want it — of that I am certain.

Sixth: The development of German internal relationships remains embedded in the overall European process and in East-West relationships. The future architecture of Germany must be fitted into the future architecture of Europe as a whole. For this the West, with its concept of a lasting and just European system of peace, has rendered yeoman service.

Seventh: The European Community's power of attraction and influence is and remains a constant factor in overall European development. We wish to strengthen it further. The European Community is now being called on to approach the reform-oriented States of Central, Eastern and South-Eastern Europe with openness and flexibility.

We see the process of regaining German unity as a European matter.

It must therefore also be seen in combination with European integration. In this sense, the European Community must keep itself open for a democratic GDR and for other democratic States of Central and South-Eastern Europe. The Community must not end at the Elbe, but must maintain openness eastward too . . .

Eighth: The CSCE process is and remains the core of this architecture of Europe as a whole, and must be pushed energetically forward. For this the existing CSCE forums must be taken advantage of . . .

Ninth: The overcoming of the splitting of Europe and the division of Germany requires far-reaching, speedy steps in disarmament and arms control. Disarmament and arms control must keep pace with political developments, and therefore as far as possible be accelerated . . .

Tenth: With this comprehensive policy, we are working towards a situation of peace in Europe in which the German people can regain its unity in free self-determination. Reunification, that is, the regaining of Germany's national unity, remains the Federal Government's political objective.

The term mentioned in point four of Kohl's initiative, a "community based on treaty," had already been used on 17 November 1989 by Hans Modrow, the new Chairman of the Council of Ministers of the GDR. In contrast to the Federal Chancellor, Modrow had called speculations about German unification "unrealistic" and had advocated reforms within the existing system.

Government statement by the Chairman of the Council of Ministers of the GDR, Hans Modrow, given before the Volkskammer in East Berlin on 17 November 1989 (extract)

Among the fundamental preconditions for stability and peace in Europe are stable, reliable relationships between the two German States and their constructive further development. With the opening up of its frontiers for free travel, the GDR has made a step in this direction that has been welcomed and supported worldwide. With the reform of our political system that is being aimed at and has indeed already begun, the path to the upholding and implementation of the process of self-determination of the people of the GDR has also been set on a new foundation. This has meant a renewal of the GDR's legitimation as a socialist State, as a sovereign German State. It is not by pronouncements but by a new reality of life in the GDR that the speculations about reunification, as unrealistic as they are dangerous, will be given clear refutation.

The two German States, for all the difference of their social systems, have a centuries-old common history. Both sides should seize the opportunity lying in this of giving their relationship the character of qualified good-neighbourhood . . . .

We are in favour of supporting the coresponsibility of the two German States by a community based on treaty, extending far beyond the Basic Treaty and the treaties and agreements concluded to date between the two States. This government is prepared to enter into talks for this.

In this way the two German States and their relationships could become important pillars for the construction and design of the common European house.

Helmut Kohl had particularly stressed the need to fit the architecture of a future Germany into the structure of Europe as a whole; he wished thus to preempt the fears, more or less clearly expressed, of a Greater Germany that could, in the course of tumultuous changes, lose interest in the European Community or leave NATO. This blueprint for unification, however vaguely and openly it was drawn, was also intended to diminish pressures from the furious, frustrated people in the GDR for immediate, radical steps toward unification. It was to them primarily that Kohl's ten-point program was directed. An American journalist working in Paris, Jim Hoagland, articulated this aspect particularly well:

The rest of Europe is missing the point about Germany. The force moving the two Germanies closer together is the mass power of the street, not governments or other institutions that can be obstructed and controlled by diplomatic footwork and faint voices drifting down from Eurosummits.

The work of the citizen armies of Eastern Europe has been glorious upheaval, knocking troglodyte Communist regimes onto the ropes. Even the opening of the Berlin Wall on 9 November was the work of the street, not a reasoned decision by the regime of Egon Krenz . . . . .

Imagine the impact and the nature, Mr. Kohl is saying in the invisible subtleties of his unity speech, of a Germany brought to a decision on reunification by street action and popular protest. That is an alternative worth shrinking from . . . . If Europe does not like Mr. Kohl's plan, it will have to tell it to the crowds in the German streets.[9]

9. Jim Hoagland, "Go tell it to the people in German streets," in *International Herald Tribune*, 2–3 December 1989.

Voices in the GDR pressing for rapid change were indeed multiplying. On 20 November hundreds of thousands of people gathered in Karl Marx Square in Leipzig and sang the verses of the unsung national anthem of the GDR: "Germany, One Fatherland." Johannes R. Becher had written the words to this song, "Reborn out of Ruin," in Soviet emigration in 1942; the song had been confirmed by the GDR Council of Ministers as the "National Anthem of the GDR" as early as 5 November 1949 — barely a month after the GDR was set up in the Soviet occupation zone. Becher's song demonstrates, through its fivefold repetition of the word "Germany," how little a policy of division was being pursued in 1949. But after the Wall was built in 1961, the text was no longer appropriate to the GDR's political calculations: Since the early 1970s the GDR anthem was no longer sung on official occasions; only the melody, by Hanns Eisler, was played. It was not until 5 January 1990 that the GDR government again broadcast the anthem on television and radio, with words included.

National Anthem of the German Democratic Republic

Reborn out of ruin
turned to the future
let us serve you as we may
Germany, one Fatherland.
All constraint to overcome
and overcome we shall together
since some day we must succeed
to make the sun as never yet
shine over Germany.

Joy and peace be with you
Germany our Fatherland.
All the world longs for peace:
reach your hand to the peoples.
If we fraternally unite
we shall beat the people's foe!
Let the light of peace shine
that never mother more
her son bewail.

Let us plough, let us build,
learn and work as never yet
and with trust in our own power
see a free generation rise.
German youth, the best endeavour
of our people united in thee,
you are Germany's new life
and the sun as never yet,
over Germany will shine.

The GDR's striving after recognition in diplomacy and in international law was undoubtedly one of the reasons for its decision in 1949 to equip itself all the more strongly and quickly with symbols of a nationality of its own.

In contrast, the Federal Republic of Germany hesitated until as late as 1952 over whether or not to declare Hoffmann von Fallersleben's "German Anthem," which had been written in 1841, the national anthem again. Like all other national symbols, the anthem had been abused and perverted by the National Socialists and been made to stand for something it was not. This free democratic song of opposition, which in its first stanza, "Germany, Germany above all else," set the unity of Germany above the multiplicity of the States of the German Federation and was never meant chauvinistically or aggressively, was already in Wilhelmine Germany being transformed into the insane illusion of complete German supremacy. Very soon after Hitler's accession to power on 30 January 1933, a decree appeared that allowed the first stanza to be sung only together with the SA song, the Horst Wessel song; when the German anthem was played or sung, the right arm had to be raised in the salute to Hitler.

It is therefore understandable that at the end of the war the Allied Control Council banned not only all the Nazi songs but also the German Anthem. National songs were understandably no longer in demand after the collapse; yet once the Federal Republic of Germany was founded in May 1949, the problem of an anthem pressed for a solution. In the spring of 1952 an agreement was finally reached to sing, on official occasions, only the third stanza of the German Anthem.

National Anthem of the Federal Republic of Germany (third stanza of von Fallersleben's Deutschlandlied)

> Unity and right and freedom
> For the German Fatherland!
> Strive we all as brothers for them
> With our brain and heart and hand.
> Unity and right and freedom
> Are happiness's pledging-band:
> Flourish in that joyful shining,
> Flourish, German Fatherland!

The fact that the key line in the GDR national anthem, "Germany, one Fatherland," was used in the political debate on German unification is remarkable in many respects. Initially this too — like the first stanza of the German Anthem in its original intention — was not a nationalist slogan. It came from the same people of Leipzig who later, in a minute's silence on 20 November 1989, demonstrated their solidarity with the Czechs, who in those days were fighting for their own liberation from Communist domination. What it initially expressed was a demand for immediate and radical change. Speakers in Leipzig — and shortly thereafter at mass demonstrations at other towns in the GDR — called for unification with the Federal Republic, above all because for them "real socialism" had collapsed, and they no longer wished to sacrifice their lives for a vague future of reform.

This late-November initiative of the Federal Chancellor was still perceived at home and abroad as spectacular, yet only a few weeks later the second wave of demonstrations in the GDR definitively and emphatically pushed German unification into the foreground. Not even the Social Democratic Party of Germany (SPD), the biggest opposition party in the Federal Republic, could remain aloof. The declaration on German policy presented to delegations at the SPD programmatic conference in West Berlin in mid-December should be seen as an adaptation to a changed situation in which the national abstinence hitherto practiced was no longer acceptable. This text, too, made reference to Modrow's concept of the "community based on treaty."

The Germans in Europe. Berlin Declaration of the Social Democratic Party of Germany, resolved at the SPD Party Congress of 18–20 December 1989 (extracts)

I. On German soil a democratic revolution is under way. Following the policy of perestroika in the Soviet Union, people in Poland, in Hungary, in Czechoslovakia, Bulgaria and the GDR are peacefully and without violence conquering their right to freedom and self-determination. Peacefully and without violence, they have overcome the Wall, compelled the opening of frontiers and ended the unnatural separation of people. This brings nearer the fulfilment of one Social Democratic dream: now what belongs together is growing together — in Germany and in Europe! . . .

IV. On the road to European and to German unity, it is important to shape the political, economic, environmental, energy, transport, cultural and disarmament policy cooperation between the two German States ever closer and more comprehensively, and without delay to give it a new quality. This can come about on the basis of the Basic Treaty, in the form of individual agreements, of a treaty-based community, of a confederation and finally also in federal State unity. The forms and speed of this process cannot be determined in detail today. We wish to reach our goal not against but with our friends and partners. The men and women in both States will decide when what steps are to be taken. . . .

VII. Concerns that the Federal Republic of Germany might now turn away from the West are unjustified. We know that the European Community has a key role in the process of general European integration. It promotes the transcendence of nation States through European cooperation. Only a strong European Community can make a strong contribution to the construction of Europe. We therefore wish in future to continue contributing to the development of the European Community into a democratic and social union and to its becoming a solid basis for ever-closer cooperation in the whole of Europe . . .

VIII. Anyone wishing to advance the process of German unification must take into account the interests of the great powers and of our European neighbours. It is on the basis of this perception that we pressed for the Helsinki process. The Conference on Security and Cooperation in Europe, in which 33 European States, the US and Canada take part, will bring about a European peace order that will incorporate the united life of Germans too.

At the same time, there was no lack of voices warning against overhastiness. In a much-discussed interview in mid-December 1989 with GDR television, Federal President Richard von Weizsäcker asked the people in the GDR for patience, argued for nonviolence, and counseled that politicians and the media in the Federal Republic maintain a reserved attitude, so as not to inflame the debate. He further recalled, emphatically, the European responsibility of Germans, making it their duty to shape the peaceful change in their own country in a way that was tolerable to Europe:

Federal President Richard Freiherr von Weizsäcker's interview with GDR television on 13 December 1989 (extracts)

It is my belief that we are one nation, and what belongs together will grow together. But it has to do just that — grow. The attempt must not be made to force it together. We need time . . . . We have three different speeds, if I can put it that way: there is a German dynamic and there is a dynamic in Europe. How is economic, scientific and cultural cooperation to be brought about here? Thirdly and finally, how are the two pacts, the two alliance systems, to provide for a security umbrella that we continue to need, under which we can peacefully encourage the dynamics relating to Europe and to Germany?

It is important for these three speeds to remain in contact with each other. As regards the wishes that we have as Germans on this side and on that, we shall be all the more able to count on a happy future the more we show our European neighbours and partners our shared concern and shared responsibility for how Europe's integration is coming along.

The Germans in European Change

In fact, the Federal Republic of Germany acted from the outset as the hinge linking the three interconnected subsystems of the postwar world: East-West relations, the Atlantic Alliance, and the European Community. Konrad Adenauer, the first architect of Bonn's foreign policy and a convinced advocate of its links with the West, had set up, in his years of office, a structure based on what Ralf Dahrendorf once called the principle of the "Russian doll." The alliance with the West allowed the overcoming of former enmity through Franco-German friendship. This concept fit seamlessly into the process of European cooperation and integration, and was not in contradiction with the Atlantic Alliance, the foundation of Federal German security and Western unity. The West would then be able, from a "position of strength," to force the Soviet Union to the negotiating table and to accepting a solution of the German question on Western terms.

The dramatic events of 1989 confirm that Adenauer's firm belief in the magnetic power of Western ideals and values was not so utopian after all. The West has now won the Cold War; the question remains, however, how peace is to be won. In the eyes of the founding fathers of Community Europe, the Community itself would be only an intermediate stage on the road to a new order for the continent. Yet, many Western Europeans today secretly wish that Warsaw, Budapest, East Berlin, and Prague had postponed their peaceful revolution until after 1992. By then the European Community would have created the internal market, the differences among its members might perhaps have been resolved, and the path to political union opened up.

The Europe of 1992, with its supranational combinations and its commitment to the idea of integration, has indeed become a magnet for Eastern Europe. The gloomy mood described not all that long ago by the words "Eurosclerosis" or "Europessimism" seems to have been definitively dispelled. There is agreement that the Community must be strengthened in order to be able to rise to the challenge posed by the self-liberation of Eastern Europe and the unification of Germany. At the European Council in Strasbourg in December 1989, it was decided that proposals for a joint economic and monetary policy be developed by the end of 1990. With its help, the Community was to develop into the core of a future greater Europe.

More than ever before, there will be an abandonment of national sovereignty within the European Community. The Western Europe that still has no clarity as to its own future has been thrown into additional uncertainty by the change in Eastern Europe. The very day the Berlin Wall fell, German-born American historian Fritz Stern sought to identify some of the questions facing Europeans now:

But what of the implicit threat of exclusion? Would the creation of a strengthened European Community condemn the East European countries, notably Poland and Hungary, to an impoverished orphan status — an economically deprived no man's land between a declining

Soviet Union and a walled-off half-continent of wealth and freedom
and renewed vitality? Or, as may be more likely, will the development
of the Eastern countries be increasingly financed by, and intermeshed
with, the economies of the Common Market countries, particularly the
Federal Republic of Germany? Or will the European Free Trade Area,
including Sweden, Switzerland, and Austria, become enlarged?

In considering such questions, some historic paradoxes are worth
noting: the Europe of 1992 is a manifestation of a declining nationalism, while the great events in Eastern Europe bespeak a revived national
pride. The Germans, in both Germanies, partake of both: the desire
for European integration and a reawakened, confused national consciousness, in which concerns about nuclear weapons and damage to
the environment have been increasingly intense.[10]

In the European Commission, as well as in the capitals of France,
Italy, and Belgium, there is concern that events in Central and
Eastern Europe may lead the Community to make a "wrong turn,"
choosing to make itself bigger, but in no way bringing it closer
together. On the one hand there is great satisfaction at the westward
urge of the former Comecon countries; on the other, the complex
task of helping and ultimately integrating the Eastern European
democracies into the European Community could delay completion of economic and monetary union, the most ambitious aspect
of the planned internal market. According to estimates from Brussels,
it will cost $22.7 billion per year in order to help the six former
Comecon countries to the same extent as the structurally weak areas
already in the Community, and equip the European Investment Bank,
as its financing agency, with the necessary capital. First, however,
Community Member States must overcome the consequences of
the political earthquake in the GDR by offering both parts of
Europe a model and a vision for the 1990s.

In a noteworthy speech delivered by European Commission
President Jacques Delors to the European Parliament in January
1990, this sort of model was sketched out. The Commission's President linked his support for President Mitterrand's proposal to create
a European Confederation with a vision of how to bring Eastern and
Western Europe together in a structure similar to the one that linked
the German States in the nineteenth-century German Confederation.

10. Fritz Stern, "The Common House of Europe (9 November 1989)," in *The
New York Review of Books*, 7 December 1989.

The German Reich in that form consisted of individual States that had a wide-ranging autonomy and that differed considerably in internal structure. The concept of "unification" played no part in regulating their relationships with each other, since they all belonged to a larger confederative entity. This Confederation idea of the pre-Bismarckian period has been discussed in the last ten years as a possible model for a solution to the German problem today. Perhaps in this way the new dynamics of the German question will benefit the goal of European unification.

Speech by European Commission President Jacques Delors to the European Parliament in Strasbourg on 17 January 1990 (extracts)

And yet recent events in Central and Eastern Europe should make us pause for thought. Why has it taken us more than thirty years to respond tentatively, with moves towards Economic and Monetary Union, to the objective of a political Community set by the founding fathers, whereas the Germans of the East, released from former constraints, have taken no more than a few weeks to re-open the Brandenburg Gate, in an act full of symbolism for the future unity of the German nation? . . .

But, first and foremost, how, in a new and shifting situation, can we not feel some anxiety and at the same time a very special hope since time is running short and events in Europe are challenging the Community to respond? . . . This immediately raises the German question. Rapprochement, or even unification, of the German people is clearly a matter for the Germans themselves. But the Community has an interest too. Let me explain why. The preamble to the German Basic Law of 23 May 1949 links the principle of German unification, on the basis of self-determination by the German people, to the issue of European unity — and may I say in passing that this text, which predates the Treaty of Rome by nine years, testifies to the perspicacity of the German leadership.

Furthermore, the Treaty of Rome itself makes reference to this issue, in the Protocol on German internal trade, in the declarations on German nationality and the status of Berlin, and in the 28 February 1957 declaration by the Bonn negotiators.

This makes East Germany a special case. I would like to repeat clearly here today that there is a place for East Germany in the Community should it so wish, provided, as the Strasbourg European Council has made quite clear, the German nation regains its unity through free self-determination, peacefully and democratically, in accordance with the principles of the Helsinki Final Act, in the context of an East-West dialogue and with an eye to European integration. But the form that it will take is, I repeat, a matter for the Germans themselves.

Once this issue has been clarified, however, new light will be thrown on our relations with the rest of the world and the future shape of our continent.

In this model of a Europe in "concentric circles," the democratic, highly industrialized West would constitute the core. The neutral countries and the former Communist countries would stay in an outer ring around this core, as associates of the European Community, until they are in a position to bear full political and economic responsibility of Community membership. The GDR is the exception here; it has been allowed to use the "fast track" into the European Community. The Community's attempt to convey to Europeans the feeling that the German question was not completely out of control might have appeared insufficient in a situation in which the law of action was determined by a headlong sequence of fast-changing events. But the very challenge represented by the promotion of German unification under a European roof could strengthen the political will to create a United States of Europe — the dream of the postwar generation.

The Russian Question

The German question certainly weighs heavily in any assessment of future prospects for reunifying the divided continent. The emerging new order of a Europe from Brest to Brest-Litovsk will decisively influence the role the Germans will play in the 1990s. Germany will again constitute the center of the European continent, and from there, instead of separating East and West, it will link them. By contrast, it is totally unclear what the repercussions of the final collapse of the model of Marxist-Leninist Socialism in Eastern Europe will be on the Soviet Union itself.

The Soviet leadership had tolerated the change in the allied countries of Eastern Europe in the expectation of a renewal of socialism, and even encouraged it with an eye to the challenge coming from successful integration of Western Europe. The collapse of the postwar order in Europe, but particularly the opening of the Wall in Berlin, came as a surprise to Moscow, too. The changes in Eastern and Central Europe are now being seen in Soviet domestic politics in exacerbated polarization between supporters of radical democratization and opponents of far-reaching reforms.

In the preliminaries to the Twenty-Eighth Party Congress of the CPSU in July 1990, criticisms of the "new thinking" in foreign policy condensed into the reproach that the loss of ideological, political, and economic control of Eastern Europe — but particularly developments in the GDR — had destroyed the foundations of the Soviet Union's status as a great power. To supporters of the old Soviet imperial policy, heavily represented in the army, the KGB, and the bureaucratic apparatus, it is Gorbachev who is responsible for the decline of the Soviet Union. He is held to have promoted excessive disarmament of the Red Army, to have looked on as the socialist regimes in Eastern Europe collapsed instead of sending in Soviet tanks, and now even to be permitting the unification of Germany instead of blocking it by military pressure. A few days before the Party Congress opened, then Soviet Foreign Minister Shevardnadze sought to oppose the campaign over the "loss" of Eastern Europe and to justify the principle of "freedom of choice of social and political system," which had, with Gorbachev's July 1989 address to the Parliamentary Assembly of the Council of Europe in Strasbourg, replaced the Brezhnev doctrine of limited sovereignty.

Article by Soviet Foreign Minister Eduard Shevardnadze "On Foreign Policy" in Pravda, 26 June 1990 (extracts)

It is painful and bitter to me to see that there are people according to whose assessments the Soviet Army did not liberate certain countries of Europe, but merely seized them as trophies of war. Chauvinistic statements insulting to the dignity of sovereign countries are being tolerated. I consider it my moral duty to apologize to the peoples of the Eastern European countries for such insulting, unacceptable effusions by some of my countrymen . . . .

What answers can be given to questions like: "Why were the changes in Eastern Europe allowed?" Or "Why have we agreed to the withdrawal of our troops?" Between the lines, it is easy to read the real idea: "Why were the tanks not used to restore order?"

Can it seriously be supposed that that sort of thing is possible, that the problem can be solved that way? Have we really learned nothing: failed to remember the lessons of Afghanistan, if we have already forgotten

1956 and 1968? Can it be that we have not had enough of funerals and
of disabled internationalists? . . .

It should be time to understand that neither socialism nor friendship,
neither good-neighbourly relationships nor respect, can be set up with bayonets,
tanks and bloodletting. Relationships with every country must be established on a calculation of mutual interests, on reciprocal advantage and
on the principle of freedom of choice. That is the way we have begun to
conduct affairs, and thanks to it enormous changes for the better have been
set going in the world. Certainly, problems have cropped up too. But things
might have ended in tragedy if these changes had been held back.

Indeed, the point was that, because of the "Gorbachev effect," the
slow melting away of the former Soviet defensive glacis, meant that
for the first time since the Red Army's victorious advance in 1945
a leading Soviet figure had become the bearer of hope for Eastern
Europeans. Gorbachev not only personified hope, but also took away
fear. It was only when fear had faded and had given way to the
impression — not the certainty — that Soviet troops would not
suppress an attempt at liberation, that the days of the Communist
regimes in Eastern and Central Europe were numbered. How could
the GDR in particular, in the fortieth year of its existence, have
asserted itself against the will of the occupying power to which it
owed its existence and on which it had always been dependent?

But the Kremlin boss has long been overtaken by the developments that he himself helped decisively to influence. Even in
December 1989, when *Time Magazine* picked Gorbachev as "Man
of the Decade," the British *Economist* saw the danger that he
might soon be "Yesterday's Man":

In the West Mr. Gorbachev is, deservedly, a hero. In calming East-West
conflict and allowing democracy into Eastern Europe, he is doing what
most people reckoned to be impossible. Now he faces another Her-
culean challenge: to remain the hero of the next, and hardest, stage
of perestroika, as the democratic revolution he has permitted in Eastern
Europe starts rolling into the Soviet Union itself . . . .

Maybe Mr. Gorbachev will manage to stay in charge and help ensure
a stable transition to democracy, as General Jaruzelski has done in
Poland. He might even win an election. But just as British voters decided
in 1945 that Winston Churchill, brilliant though he had been as a war
leader, was not the man to run the peace, so the West should be
prepared for the possibility that Mr. Gorbachev, brilliant though he has
been as a smasher of Stalinism, is not the man to introduce democracy.

Let the West remember that keeping a Soviet hero in power is a means, not an end. The end should be for the Soviet Union to become a true democracy.[11]

In a talk with American historian and Librarian of Congress James H. Billington, Gorbachev himself named Peter the Great and Alexander II as the two historical figures from the Russian past with whom he felt most closely linked in terms of his own reform program. This answer inspired Billington, author of several works on Russian cultural history, to draw the following comparison:

> Mikhail Gorbachev's determination to seek both legitimation and models for reform primarily in the West has produced a bitter nationalist reaction among many ordinary Russians — as in the past under innovative czars like Peter the Great and Alexander II....
>
> Like both of those aggressively innovative czars, Mr. Gorbachev faces a popular opposition among Russian traditionalists. He no doubt hopes that his conservative opponents will eventually simply fade away into the forest as the Old Believers did under Peter the Great. But he must have more realistic fears based on the more modern and more relevant example of Alexander II, the Anglophile reformer who freed the serfs and opened up Russia, only to be assassinated by younger radicals who did not believe he had gone far enough.
>
> Alexander II was the victim of rising expectations that he could not satisfy in the first age of mass journalism. Many fear that Mr. Gorbachev may suffer some such fate in this first age of mass television.
>
> But the more relevant lesson to be learned from Alexander's reign may be that evolutionary progress reform from above may not be possible when the society below is throwing up new extremes of right and left that feed on each other and destroy the moderate, progressive center.[12]

In the marathon twelve-day running fight of the longest Party Congress in Soviet history in July 1990, Gorbachev won a Pyrrhic victory. The CPSU proved unreformable. Despite a turbulent finale, it has remained what it has been since Lenin and Stalin: an instrument of its leaders. Admittedly, the General Secretary managed, with compromises, to tack together the structure of the age-weakened party. But because he was unable to renew it from the

---

11. "Yesterday's Man?" in *The Economist*, 16–22 December 1989.
12. James A. Billington, "Russia's Future: Alternatives for a Modern Identity," in *The Washington Post*, 24 January 1990.

bottom up, he runs the risk that those for whom change in the crisis-ridden empire is not rapid enough may follow the example of Boris Yel'tsin, President of the Russian Republic and radical reformer, and run away from him in droves. Only then, perhaps, will the process of internal fermentation really begin.

Gorbachev's political fate is therefore still very much in the balance — bound up with the success or failure of *perestroika*, in particular of the economic reform that has still not gotten off the ground after six years. Critics in the country are loudly asking why Gorbachev has achieved nothing but a situation resembling civil war in his country and why the Soviet Union is continuing to fall apart. While the Soviet President is shaping world history and shining at summit meetings with Western statesmen, while his popularity curve in the West is still high, loss of confidence in him at home has taken on alarming proportions.

Probably the biggest problems arise for Moscow from the increase in centrifugal forces within the Soviet Union. On the same day in July 1990 that Gorbachev conceded unlimited sovereignty over the future Germany to the Federal Chancellor, the Ukraine declared its own sovereignty: the second-largest Soviet Republic, the granary of the USSR, announced that it wanted to become a neutral State with its own currency and its own army. Barely two years after the German question appeared on the political agenda, and in parallel with the overcoming of the East-West German division, it looks as though the enormously more explosive Russian question will be a major issue for the 1990s. In a contribution to the collective volume "After Gorbachev," in which leading French experts take positions on the chances of survival for the Soviet Union and its present leadership, Hélène Carrère d'Encausse, who had already pointed to the explosiveness of the nationality problem in 1978 in her widely ready book *Splits in the Red Empire*, gives the following prognosis:

> Can the difficult process of democratization in Eastern Europe give Gorbachev a breathing space for his internal problems and save his program of economic and political reconstruction? The process of collapse of the Empire, which started from the USSR itself, is now being reflected in full onto that country. The problem presents itself more radically here than elsewhere, since the issue is survival of the USSR and not merely influence and power. National tensions are running so high that the leadership sees itself faced with the dilemma of keeping to its basic attitude of tolerance or else switching over to intolerance. . . .

> Gorbachev seems to prefer to these possibilities, neither of them
> favourable to far-reaching, definitive change for his country, a third
> path, that of the authoritarian transitional State, which could ultimately
> lead to a consolidated State based on the rule of law.[13]

In the midst of a deep crisis in his period of government,
Gorbachev has still found the courage to distance himself from
old sacred cows. The eve of the anniversary of the day the Potsdam
Conference opened forty-five years ago, he finally wrote off the
Yalta system. While the first six months of 1990 had still been
overshadowed by Moscow's refusal to allow unified Germany a
free, independent decision as to its future alliance membership,
the two-day meeting between Kohl and Gorbachev on 15 and 16
July 1990 brought clarity here too. The Germans received, practically
on a silver platter, what they scarcely dared to hope for, given the
earlier dogged resistance of the Soviet Union: the freedom to be
able to unite, and to become sovereign, while in every respect
belonging as a partner to the West.

For Bonn's Foreign Minister Hans-Dietrich Genscher, the outcome
of the negotiations was a brilliant justification of his political strategy
toward the Soviet Union, which had in the past caused so much
suspicion of him. At a time when the West as a whole saw Gorbachev
with unconcealed mistrust and regarded the "new thinking" as just
a skilled propaganda offensive, Genscher was already pleading for
a more differentiated approach.

In a much-discussed speech to the World Economic Forum in
Davos on 1 February 1987, he advocated a joint Western strategy
that would take Soviet policy "at its word" and respond with
initiatives of its own.

**Speech by Hans-Dietrich Genscher, Minister of Foreign Affairs of the
Federal Republic of Germany, to the World Economic Forum in Davos
on 1 February 1987** (extracts)

Are these only words to lull the West? Is this new foreign policy of
Gorbachev's merely a policy presented in a new way and enormously
better than before, more flexible and more skilled, but ultimately pursuing
the old goal of expanding the Soviet Empire and of hegemony over the

13. Hélène Carrère d'Encausse, "L'U.R.S.S. éclatée," in Jean-Marie Benoist and
Patrick Wajsman, eds., *Après Gorbatchev* (Paris: Editions de La Table Ronde,
1990), 134f.

whole European continent? Or else is Gorbachev merely seeking to gain a breathing space for a few years, to let his economy recover and then continue the policy of expansion? In a word, is the new policy ultimately no more than the old one, dressed up in new, prettier clothing? . . .

If there were today to be the opportunity of reaching a turning-point in East-West relations after forty years of confrontation, then it would be a mistake of historic dimensions for the West to let this chance slip just because it cannot rid itself of a way of thinking which when it looks at the Soviet Union can always and only suppose only the worst possible case. "Worst Case Analysis" is necessary, but it must not determine policy. If it did we would truly be incapable of policy. The proper, urgently necessary policy for the West seems to me today instead to be to take Gorbachev and his "new politics" at their word, with all the consequences.

Let us not sit with our arms folded and wait for what Gorbachev will bring us! Let us instead seek to influence developments from our side, to push them forward and to shape them. We need an active political strategy for the West. The Alliance's Harmel strategy was conceived as such a strategy.

Our answer to Gorbachev should be: If deeds follow words, then the West will be a constructive partner to such a development.

A stabilization of Central and Eastern Europe and particularly of the Soviet Union cannot be achieved by Germany alone. In the preliminaries to the three Western summit meetings of the European Community, of NATO and of the Western industrialized countries in the early summer of 1990, it became clear that there is greater willingness among Continental Europeans to help Moscow than among, say, the British, the Japanese, and the Americans. Certainly, all agreed that the Soviet Union's economic system is now a bottomless pit; opinions diverged, however, as to where and in what circumstances the basis for rational support of *perestroika* can be found. To many political observers, the ultimate point was "whether we ought to help Kohl," as Paris journalist Jean-Louis Arnaud so poignantly put it:

> It is not without reason that there has for a year now been talk of a Marshall Plan for Eastern Europe. The Soviet Union differs from its former satellite countries just because it covers almost a continent; but the problems cannot be solved separately. The Germans saw the signals from the East before anyone else, and understood them properly . . . . What is now at stake is the reconstruction and rehabilitation of the Eastern economic systems, including the Soviet one. We can see that the Europeans, with

the Germans at their head, are better able than the Americans at this time to play the part of General Marshall, and we can take it that Mitterrand has decided in favour of not leaving the regaining of European economic and political power to Kohl, alone.[14]

Not placing obstacles in the Federal Chancellor's path as to his decision to use offers of economic assistance to the USSR as a way of removing Soviet reservations against NATO membership for a united Germany and smoothing the way for the ultimate withdrawal of soviet troops from German soil, was, and still is, an elementary interest for Bonn's Western allies. Along with this insight, however, awareness is growing among neighbors and allies that the rapid accord between Bonn and Moscow also points to the growing specific weight that both united Germany and German-Soviet relations will have in the future of Europe. It is one of the most urgent tasks of German diplomacy in the 1990s to ensure that the open Russian question is approached not by Germans alone, but in a consensus shared by Germany's neighbors.

14. Jean-Louis Arnaud, "Faut-il aider Kohl?" in *Le Quotidien de Paris*, 12 July 1990.

2

Europe in Upheaval

I n 1989 world history turned on its pivots, driven by the masses of ordinary citizens more than by those in power. At the start of the 1980s there did not seem much prospect of a more peaceful world. In Europe the missile debate was making big waves, in the West as well as in the East. In Poland the Communist government was attempting to subdue the opposition by martial law and by force. European peace seemed hostage to remote conflicts.

Ten years later, confrontation and stagnation in Europe seem to be things of the past. The Old Continent is ceasing to be both defensive glacis and potential battlefield and can grow together again. It may be that only the tensions and crises of the decade, with the growing threats they entailed, could allow reason to have a chance. It may be that such environmental catastrophes as Chernobyl and the ozone hole over the Antarctic sharpened the eyes of both East and West for challenges that faced both equally. But the turning point was ultimately the uprising of men and women against their oppressors; the revolt of peoples against the rule of lies and the throttling of freedom. And with the collapse of the Berlin Wall and the opening up of the border between the two German States, relationships between States and societies in East and West Europe must be subjected to close review. They can no longer be grasped primarily according to traditional categories of ideologically rooted contradictions. Political change in Central and Eastern Europe is erasing boundaries between systems that have hitherto split the European continent. What seemed to be the determining factors of East-West relationships, what gave them such an antagonistic nature, seems to be evaporating.

In West and East, the changes in Europe are being studied with great attention to see also whether and what effects they will have on the situation in the center of Europe, and particularly on the shape of national conditions in Germany. Since the changes emerging in Europe are rapidly altering the *modus vivendi* between East and West in the direction of overcoming the continent's division, the question is thereby raised as to the Germans' place in a changing Europe.

The Social-Liberal Coalition's Ostpolitik

A divided Germany was the core of the international system that formed in Europe after the Second World War. Once the idea gained a hold among the Western Allies, and particularly in the American leadership, in the second half of the 1960s, that the barriers between East and West should be broken down, while largely accepting the political and territorial status quo in Europe, in the Federal Republic of Germany too there was intensive consideration of the question of whether and how a *modus vivendi* with the USSR and the other Eastern European countries might be arrived at.

In the Harmel Report, which was adopted by the NATO foreign ministers on 14 December 1967, the sixteen Western governments that had come together to form the North Atlantic Pact signed in Washington in 1949 defined the structural conditions for their national strategies of détente, which were as far as possible to be transformed into a policy borne by NATO jointly. The report describes détente not as a final goal but as part of a long-term process of improving relations and furthering the settlement of outstanding European issues, central among which was the question of Germany.

From this emerged the two pillars of NATO philosophy — deterrence and defense on the one hand, negotiation and détente on the other — that would form the basis of all future common policies. Lothar Rühl, then Permanent Secretary in the Bonn Defense Ministry, defined the reasons for this NATO initiative as follows:

> A number of governments had reached the conclusion, with the passage of time after the end of the crisis period 1962–63, that besides the negative task of "deterrence" of an attack on NATO territory — especially Western Europe — and the collective defense function inseparable from

that, their alliance ought also to take on a more positive role, directed toward peace. In Western Europe generally, interest grew in easing the situation of conflict in relations with the Soviet Union and Eastern Europe which had survived from the Cold War period. The idea also gained ground that European security in its widest sense would have to be organized in collaboration with the "potential enemies" in the East. To achieve either objective, the need was seen for NATO to present itself in a more positive light, not only toward the outside world, but also towards its own domestic policy.[15]

The Harmel Report took up a number of ideas previously developed by individual Western States: the idea, first raised by President Johnson, of "bridge-building" between East and West; President de Gaulle's concept of "détente-entente-coopération"; and the principle developed by the then West German Foreign Minister, Willy Brandt, of a "peaceful order in Europe". This was also the context for the Federal Republic's change of course in its relations with Eastern Europe and the GDR, decided on by the coalition of Social Democrats and Liberals in government from 1969.

Report on the Future Tasks of the Alliance (Harmel Report), 14 December 1967 (extract)

The Atlantic Alliance has two main functions. Its first function is to maintain adequate military strength and political solidarity to deter aggression and other forms of pressure and to defend the territory of member countries if aggression should occur. Since its inception, the Alliance has successfully fulfilled this task. But the possibility of a crisis cannot be excluded as long as the central political issues in Europe, first and foremost the German Question, remain unsolved. Moreover, the situation of instability and uncertainty still precludes a balanced reduction of military forces. Under these conditions, the Allies will maintain as necessary, a suitable military capability to assure the balance of forces, thereby creating a climate of stability, security and confidence.

In this climate the Alliance can carry out its second function, to pursue the search for progress toward a more stable relationship in which the underlying political issues can be solved. Military security and a policy

15. Lothar Rühl, "Die neuen Ziele im Atlantischen Bündnis und die Fortsetzung der westlichen Détentepolitik nach Prag," in *Die Internationale Politik 1968–1969, Jahrbücher des Forschungsinstituts der Deutschen Gesellschaft für Auswärtige Politik* (Munich/Vienna: Oldenbourg Verlag, 1974), 341.

of détente are not contradictory but complementary . . . .

No peaceful order in Europe is possible without a major effort by all concerned. The evolution of Soviet and East European policies gives ground for hope that those governments may eventually come to recognize the advantages to them of collaborating in working toward a peaceful settlement. But no final and stable settlement in Europe is possible without a solution of the German question which lies at the heart of present tensions in Europe. Any such settlement must end the unnatural barriers between Eastern and Western Europe, which are most clearly and cruelly manifested in the division of Germany.

NATO's newly adopted twin goals of defense and détente had more far-reaching consequences for the Federal Republic than for any other member of the Alliance. In Europe at least, this country was the first and most directly affected, with regard to its former policy objectives, by the changed international ground rules and way of thinking. Until the 1960s the Federal Republic had tried to harness every issue to the achievement of its primary goal of reunification and self-determination, thus binding East-West relations to a solution of the German question. But Bonn's function as a doorkeeper on East-West issues became obsolete when the other Western powers gave German unity second place to provisional acceptance of the status quo in Europe as a precondition for normalization.

The objectives of the government headed by Brandt and Scheel in its "new *Ostpolitik*" are described by Berndt von Staden, from 1970 to 1973 head óf the Political Department in the West German foreign office:

> Being a regional power of medium size and part of a divided nation straddling the divide between East and West in Europe, Germany had to put its relations with its East European neighbours and with the Soviet Union on a normal footing, to ensure the security and viability of Berlin, to make division more bearable by cooperating with the GDR on a wide variety of levels, to preserve the sense of belonging together of the people of both German States, and to carry all this through without giving up the claim of the German people to free self-determination.[16]

16. Berndt von Staden, "Das Management der Ost-West Beziehungen," in Karl Kaiser und Hans-Peter Schwarz, eds., *Weltpolitik, Strukturen – Akteure – Perspektivon* (Bonn: Bundeszentrale für politische Bildung, 1985), 121.

Matters to be dealt with in West Germany's relations with the Soviet Union were the inviolable nature of existing frontiers in Europe and Berlin's viability and access routes. As for Poland, the Oder-Neisse line was to be respected as the Western frontier. The key points in relations with East Germany were the recognition of the existence of the other German State and various practical issues arising from the survival of links between families and individuals in the two halves of Germany. Finally, in the case of Czechoslovakia, there were problems concerning the validity of the Munich Agreement of September 1938 and humanitarian questions.

Excerpts from the Federal Republic's Agreements with East European Countries (Ostverträge)

Treaty between the Federal Republic of Germany and the Union of Soviet Socialist Republics (Moscow Treaty), 12 August 1970

The Moscow Treaty strives for normalization and détente in Europe on the basis of the "actual situation existing in this region" (Art. 1). In accordance with the Charter of the United Nations, the Federal Republic and the USSR undertake to refrain from the threat or use of force (Art.2). From this ban on the use of force is derived the regulation on frontiers and on territorial integrity, which commits the Federal Republic to respect "the frontiers of all States in Europe as inviolable ... including the Oder-Neisse line which forms the western frontier of the People's Republic of Poland and the frontier between the Federal Republic of Germany and the German Democratic Republic."

The Western powers in an exchange of Notes regarded their "rights and responsibilities in relation to Berlin and to Germany as a whole [as] not affected."

Treaty between the Federal Republic of Germany and the People's Republic of Poland on the basis of the normalization of their mutual relations (Warsaw Treaty), 7 December 1970

In the Warsaw Treaty the Federal Republic and the People's Republic of Poland state "in mutual agreement that the existing boundary line ... shall constitute the western State frontier of the People's Republic of Poland." Both partners "reaffirm the inviolability of their existing frontiers now and in the future" and declare "that they have no territorial claims whatsoever against each other and that they will not assert such claims in the future" (Art.1).

In a Note to the three Western Powers, the Federal Republic refers to the fact that "it can only negotiate in the name of the Federal Republic" and that the Treaty does not affect the "rights and responsibilities" of the Four Powers. For their part the three Western powers declare in an exchange of Notes that the Treaty "does not affect and cannot affect" the rights and responsibilities of the Four Powers.

Quadripartite Agreement on Berlin, 3 September 1971

The Federal Republic was not directly involved in the agreement of the Four Powers on Berlin. From the beginning, however, a satisfactory Berlin settlement was a precondition for the treaties with the East. Bonn's efforts to pursue its Eastern policy were anchored firmly in the attempts by the West and the Soviet Union, acting on the basis of their rights and responsibilities, and of their wartime and postwar decisions, to achieve practical improvements in the existing situation in the divided former capital of Germany.

The most important requirement for the legal relationship between West Berlin and the Federal Republic is contained in Part II (B) of the Agreement: the three Western powers declare "that the ties between the western sectors of Berlin and the Federal Republic of Germany will be maintained and developed, taking into account that these sectors continue not to be a constituent part of the Federal Republic of Germany and not to be governed by it."

Within the framework of the Quadripartite Agreement the signatories also endorsed agreements in both German States, in particular relating to travel to and from Berlin and the possibility of visits by West Berliners to East Berlin and the GDR.

Treaty on the Bases of Relations between the German Democratic Republic and the Federal Republic of Germany (Basic Treaty), 21 December 1972

The Basic Treaty "notwithstanding the different views" of both sides "on fundamental matters, including the national question" (Preamble), creates conditions for the development of mutual cooperation on a wide range of levels. The two German States agreed to develop "normal good neighbourly relations with each other on the basis of equal rights" (Art.1). They "affirm the inviolability now and in the future of the frontier existing between them, and undertake fully to respect each other's territorial integrity" (Art.3); they "proceed from the consideration that neither of the two States may represent the other in international affairs or act on its behalf" (Art.4) and that "the sovereign power of either State shall be confined to its respective territory" (Art.6).

Treaty on Mutual Relations between the Federal Republic of Germany and the Czechoslovakian Socialist Republic (Prague Treaty), 11 December 1973

The Prague Treaty was concerned chiefly with a matter on which the Federal Republic and Czechoslovakia differed, that is, how to take account of the *de facto* ending of the Munich Agreement of 29 September 1938. Whereas the ČSSR wanted a declaration that the agreement was invalid *ex tunc*, that is, from the beginning, the Federal Republic could not accede to this, given the unacceptable consequences which would result for the Sudetenland Germans.

In the end the two sides agreed to declare "under the present Treaty" the Munich Agreement to be "void with regard to their mutual relations" (Art.1), while the Treaty would "not affect the legal effects on natural or legal persons of the law as applied in the period between 30 September 1938 and 9 May 1945" (Art.2). As with the other Eastern Treaties, the questions by which act in international law territorial sovereignty reverted to the newly constituted Czechoslovak State, or whether the *status quo* confirmed by the Treaty of 11 December 1973 needed any further legitimation in international law, were left open.

In each agreement, all the essentials of Germany's legal position regarding its frontiers of 31 December 1937 were safeguarded through a clause specifying that it "shall not affect" previously concluded international arrangements (Art.4, Moscow and Warsaw Treaties; Art.9 of the Basic Treaty; para.3, Pt. I of the Quadripartite Agreement on Berlin). In the *Letters on German Unity* issued on conclusion of the Moscow Treaty and the Basic Treaty, the Federal Republic stated that the treaties did not contradict the political goal of the Federal Republic "to work for a situation of peace in Europe, in which the German people will regain their unity with freedom of self-determination."

By their twofold character, covering the renunciation of force and the decision to cooperate, the series of agreements reached with the East between 1970 and 1973 were a major contribution to the reduction of tensions in Europe. Following the Eastern agreements, the Soviet Union and its allies could no longer, as formerly, represent the question of European security exclusively as a problem of security against Germany, against a German threat to peace in Europe. A quarter-century after the founding of the Federal Republic, the Berlin political scientist Richard Löwenthal could comment:

The opposition between the political systems in East and West provided the basis of a conflict with the Soviets which was shared by the Western powers and the West Germans, in which priority was given to the pursuit of internal development in freedom and security on this side of the divide. But demands for reunification by free Germans in the West, and for the review of the Eastern frontiers, were the basis of a special conflict which the FRG had with the Soviet Union and the Soviet bloc, in which Bonn could count on Western support only on certain conditions and, as time went on, to a decreasing extent. The history of the gradual change in West Germany's policy towards the East over a quarter of a century is the history of increasing recognition of this difference and of the necessary diminution of Germany's special conflict with the East, which resulted from the growing integration of the Federal Republic into the economic, political and military system of the West, as well as from the growing limitation of more general forms of conflict between East and West as a consequence of détente.[17]

The *Ostpolitik* of the Social Democratic and Liberal coalition in Bonn was only one aspect of Western policy toward Eastern Europe, taking its place within the wider framework of the comprehensive range of relationships between the superpowers and their allies on both sides. In this respect *Ostpolitik* was not only an adaptation to change but also an attempt to explore and, if possible, to extend the range of options for West German foreign policy. The German-born American political scientist Wolfram Hanrieder sees this as follows:

> Willy Brandt's greatest service was, through diplomacy and personal effort, to make a virtue out of the necessity in which the FRG found itself, of having to accept the status quo. In the same way it had been Adenauer's greatest contribution to make a virtue out of the need to find a constructive modus vivendi with the Western powers. Both were faced with the difficult task of directing German diplomacy, in response to unavoidable pressures, towards accepting the situation imposed by international developments, discarding some aspects of the German position, and making compromises. . . .
>
> However dynamic Brandt's Ostpolitik was in many respects, it consisted basically of a policy of resignation, designed less to create change

---

17. Richard Löwenthal, "Vom Kalten Krieg zur Ostpolitik," in Richard Löwenthal and Hans-Peter Schwarz, eds., *Die zweite Republik, 25 Jahre Bundesrepublik Deutschland – eine Bilanz*, (Stuttgart: Seewald Verlag, 1974), 604f.

in the immediate future than to prevent the chances of change in the longer term being removed.[18]

The Building Blocks for a European Germany

This left the way open for the introduction of a process of détente and normalization throughout Europe. By May 1972, almost simultaneously with the Bundestag's ratification of the Eastern treaties, the countries of NATO and the Warsaw Pact decided to arrange a Conference on Security and Cooperation in Europe (CSCE). This Conference was not concerned primarily with solving the key problems arising from Europe's division between East and West; rather, its goal was to facilitate the achievement of greater international security and stronger cooperation in a situation whose characteristic feature was the very fact that these problems were unsolved.

Final Act of the Conference on Security and Cooperation in Europe (CSCE), 1 August 1975 (Helsinki Final Act) (extracts)

The Helsinki Final Act can be seen as the cornerstone, at multilateral level, of West Germany's social-liberal *Ostpolitik*. The list of Principles in the so-called "Basket I" (questions relating to security in Europe) essentially reproduces elements of the Eastern treaties, while not standing in the way of peaceful change in Europe.

Principle I establishes "sovereign equality" and "respect for the rights inherent in sovereignty," and also the recognition of the participant States "that their frontiers can be changed, in accordance with international law, through peaceful means and by agreement." The most important case in which "peaceful change" would occur is with the realization of the right to self-determination of peoples, guaranteed under Principle VIII. According to this, "all peoples always have the right, in full freedom, to determine when and as they wish, their internal and external political status, without external interference, and to pursue as they wish their political, economic and cultural development."

Principle II ("Refraining from the threat or use of force") contains a general prohibition on force, especially emphasizing that the "territorial integrity" and "political independence" of any State should be protected.

Principle III repeats, with minor differences of formulation, the pro-

---

18. Wolfram Hanrieder, *Fragmente der Macht, Die Außenpolitik der Bundesrepublik* (Munich: Piper, 1981), 82.

visions of the Eastern treaties regarding the "inviolability of frontiers": the participating States "regard as inviolable all one another's frontiers as well as the frontiers of all States of Europe and therefore they will refrain now and in the future from assaulting these frontiers."

Finally, Principle X contains a "shall not affect" clause, in the statement of the participants "that the present Declaration does not affect their rights and obligations, nor the corresponding treaties and other agreements and arrangements."

The Final Act, signed in Helsinki at the beginning of August 1975, represents a declaration of common policy intent to create a system of political and moral rules for the future behavior of the thirty-five signatory States (including the United States and Canada). Ten years after Helsinki, the American diplomat John J. Maresca, deputy head of the U.S. delegation at the CSCE negotiations, saw them as a surrogate peace treaty for Germany as well:

> The two most important aspects of the CSCE have generally been overlooked. The first is its historic role as a surrogate World War II peace treaty. A peace treaty of classic form is not possible in the present circumstances, since it would have to be signed with Germany, as one of the principal belligerents. Yet Germany is now divided into two countries, which could not by themselves sign a peace treaty underlining the fact that they really form one nation. By including the two Germanies in a much larger conference, it became possible to address the issues left from the war and to reach a conclusion that, accepted by all the belligerents, formally consigned the war to history.
>
> The second point is the CSCE's role as a continuing European institution, now ten years old and still a dynamic enterprise. This institution is broad in scope and membership, flexible, and resistant to the moods of international relations. It has become a forum for debate and discussion between East and West, neutral and engaged, large countries and small, and has proven itself capable of positive contributions, even during periods of East-West tension. It has not been subverted to Soviet objectives — on the contrary, it has been used to advance many Western views — and its possibilities are far from exhausted. It seems clear that the CSCE has become a permanent part of the European landscape.[19]

The interpenetration between the German question and the European order manifested in the CSCE Final Act can also be

19. John J. Maresca, *To Helsinki. The Conference on Security and Cooperation in Europe, 1973-1975* (Durham, NC: Duke University Press, 1985), XII.

shown in a number of thought patterns thrown in for debate by politicians and experts since the 1960s. Many of the considerations made then became topical again in the preparations for the CSCE special summit conference .held in November 1990, intended to make a major contribution to achieving a European peace order. At the same time, it is becoming clear that the general consensus on tying German-German rapprochement into the overall processes of European unification involves widely varying interpretations and objectives.

Public discussion about the actual shape of a European peace order began in the Federal Republic of Germany more or less simultaneously with talks going on in a NATO context about reshaping East-West relations, which were subsequently incorporated into the Harmel Report. In a July 1967 interview with the *Deutschlandfunk*, Willy Brandt, foreign minister in the Grand Coalition between CDU/CSU and SPD formed in the previous year, for the first time put his ideas on this question somewhat more precisely.

Interview with Federal Minister for Foreign Affairs, Willy Brandt, on the *Deutschlandfunk*, 2 July 1967 (extract)

Firstly, in relation to the Soviet Union and the East European countries, we are in favour of declarations renouncing the use of force. These should be binding in international law. And we are prepared to incorporate in them the questions arising out of the division of Germany. Secondly, we are in favour of renunciation of nuclear weapons. Thirdly, we are in favour of mutual and balanced reductions in troop levels in East and West . . . .

A European peace order should not be seen in other respects either as if it were simply a matter of confirming what the Second World War left behind in Europe. The European peace order ought to level out the barriers and make new forms of cooperation possible. For example, it should include a European law to protect ethnic minorities. It ought not simply to proclaim human rights, but to practice them in essential areas.

A European peace order also means, finally, an economic alliance; that is, over and above bilateral trade relations between East and West, the EEC and Comecon should be brought together in a workable association.

In the mid-1960s, leading politicians of the Western alliance had similarly acted on the assumption that a reunification of

Germany would only be possible at the end of a lengthy process of rapprochement between East and West. The French President, Charles de Gaulle, gave an important impetus to the thinking behind Bonn's *Ostpolitik* at the beginning of 1965, with his ideas of a "Europeanizing of the German Question." The General advanced the view that the German problem could be solved only through the involvement of all neighboring countries after the whole of Europe, "from the Atlantic to the Urals," had rediscovered its unity. As a precondition of this, however, the Soviet Union must cease to be a totalitarian State, and the East European countries would have to be able to act independently. At the same time, de Gaulle left no doubt that he considered necessary the recognition of the Oder-Neisse line and a definite renunciation of atomic weapons on the part of Germany.

Press conference by French President Charles de Gaulle, 4 February 1965 (extract)

The German problem is the European problem *par excellence*. European — just think back — since the emergence of the Roman Empire, that is, since Europe ceased historically to be limited to the shores of the Mediterranean, in order to extend as far as the Rhine; European, because the areas settled by the Teutons in the heart of our continent lay in between the Gauls, the Latins and the Slavs; European, because in the course of a long and difficult history, it was burdened with many upheavals, many fateful consequences which have left behind through the centuries bitter resentment and much prejudice among all neighbouring peoples against this country which was in the throes of an eternal becoming. It is a European problem, because the German people is a great people in the fields of economics and also of the intellect, science, and the arts, as well as in the spheres of military capability, and because Europe sees in it an essential part of itself; European, too, because Germany has always been filled with anxiety and at times with anger — born out of its own insecurity regarding its frontiers, its unity, its political order and international role — and therefore its fate continues to appear to the whole continent as all the more worrying, the longer it remains uncertain. . . .

So the problem is posed anew against the background of history. For France, everything can be summarized in three closely interconnected observations: that we have to act so that Germany becomes a sure factor for progress and peace; to contribute, on this condition, to its reunification; to pursue the path and to choose the framework which will make this possible.

While German unity was still an integral part of de Gaulle's vision of a future Europe, the formula for Europeanizing the German Question employed by CSU Chairman Franz Josef Strauss since 1965 (see his book *The Grand Design*) was an altogether too revolutionary viewpoint for contemporary minds. By describing nation-states as quasi-anachronistic structures, he suggested to the Germans that they should give up their outdated efforts at reunification in favor of creating a great regional system in Europe:

> Since the German people live in the middle of a Europe which is divided politically and ideologically, they ought not to waste their energies in striving for restoration of the nation-state, which even theoretically would only be thinkable with unsatisfactory limitations, but even basically would neither correspond to the general course of developments, nor encourage it. . . .
>
> If they understood that the nation-state represents a survival from the past which can no longer serve the peoples of Europe as a stronghold for their self-determination, their prosperity and their further intellectual development, it would be easy for the Germans to decide to see the chief aim of their national interest in the creation of a great regional system in which, too, it would again be possible for their nation to live together in a natural way.[20]

Klaus Bloemer, at that time Strauss's adviser on foreign policy, was considerably clearer on the practical form that a European peace order would need to have in order both to guarantee that the German potential would be built organically into the whole construction of Europe and, at the same time, to take into account the natural interests of the Germans and their neighbors:

> The "Europeanizing of the German Question" ought not to degenerate into a fashionable political catchphrase. Over-worked slogans, which some people use to conceal their harping on an outdated set of ideas, and with which others seek to escape from uncomfortable and, they fear, unpopular consequences, are quite common enough in national and international politics. Someone who says that A is necessary for overcoming the division of Europe should not shy away from the B of decisions needed at political level in Western Europe, which in turn make changes to the existing structure of the Western alliance unavoidable. But in

---

20. Franz Josef Strauß, "Nation mit neuem Auftrag. Die Einheit der Deutschen im geeinten Europa," in *Die politische Meinung*, 2–3, 1967, 13ff.

reality both A and B belong with the C of personally coming to terms with the fact of two German States; this should be understood as a conscious and active first step towards a solution based on an all-European community, a Community of Greater Europe. The other way round produces no solution which other Europeans would accept. In other words, we would simply be accused of wanting to Germanize the European question instead of Europeanizing the German one.[21]

The electoral decision by Germans in the GDR for freedom and unity has made the debate about the contradiction between German and European unification obsolete, but not the search for a European framework within which Germans can find a way toward one another. The Helsinki Final Act in the mid-1970s gave participant States a code of conduct for their peaceful coexistence. In a speech in Potsdam in early February 1990, Federal Foreign Minister Hans-Dietrich Genscher sketched the outlines of a European peace order in light of the German autumn revolution.

Speech of Federal Minister for Foreign Affairs Hans-Dietrich Genscher on the occasion of the SIPRI-IPW Conference in Potsdam, 9 February 1990 (extracts) .

The breathtaking tempo of developments everywhere in Europe, but particularly in the GDR, is bringing many to ask what the basis and framework for the developments in Europe are. The answer is the Helsinki Final Act. The CSCE process must now develop its full effect. Part of this is that the signatories to the Final Act should come together into a partnership in stability for the whole of Europe, politically, economically and in security aspects. This partnership in stability too is embodied in the Helsinki Final Act and in the CSCE process. The CSCE process must become the Magna Carta of a stability order for Europe being built up on the basis of human rights and fundamental freedoms.

The Helsinki Final Act gave the participant States a binding code of conduct for their peaceful co-existence. It made the West-East conflict controllable and alleviated its consequences for people. Today the CSCE is taking on a new dimension. It must become the bearing along which

---

21. Klaus Bloemer, "Die Europäisierung der Deutschen Frage im Geiste kooperativer Koexistenz. Gastvorlesung am Otto-Suhr-Institut der Freien Universität Berlin," 5 February 1968, in *Die politische Information*, March 1968, special issue, 8.

the overcoming of our continent's unnatural division is steered. After antagonism, and then regulated coexistence and even cooperation, the stage now beginning is the third one, in which Europe is to find its unity. . . .

The CSCE summit conference can also make its contribution to the partnership in stability between West and East and to the creation of a European peace order by deepening the CSCE process and taking steps in the direction of institutionalizing it. Part of this is the development of all-European institutions in the CSCE framework. Among these might be:

1. An institution to coordinate economic West-East cooperation. The European Development Bank should also be seen in this context.
2. An all-European institution to guarantee human rights. Application of the Council of Europe's Convention on Human Rights to the whole of Europe would suggest itself.
3. A center for the creation of a European legal area, with the object of legal harmonization.
4. A European environment agency.
5. Extension of EUREKA cooperation to the whole of Europe.
6. Cooperation between ESA and corresponding institutions of the East.
7. A center for the development of a European telecommunications structure.
8. A center for the development of a European transport infrastructure and transport policy.
9. A European·verification center.
10. A European culture center.

Consolidation of the CSCE process could further be assisted by setting up a Council of Foreign Ministers of CSCE States, meeting at regular intervals.

A few weeks after the first free elections to the Volkskammer in·the GDR and the triumphant victory of the conservative parties combined in the "Alliance for Germany," the Federal Minister for Intra-German Relations, Dorothee Wilms, was able to participate, at the historic Wartburg near Eisenach in the GDR, in the European Congress of the Circle of Catholic German Students' Associations (RKDB). The Wartburg was where Luther in 1521 translated the New Testament from Greek to German in ten months, thus laying the foundations for the German written language. On the fourth anniversary of the Battle of Leipzig, on 18 October 1817, students held a demonstration here against oppression and petty-statehood and called for a struggle for national unity and a free constitution. In her speech, Dorothee Wilms recalled these traditions and located them in the context of freedom and unity in the Europe of the 1990s.

Speech by Federal Minister for Intra-German Relations, Dr. Dorothee Wilms, 28 April 1990 (extracts)

Wartburg and students' associations are, as it were, a synonym for the black, red and gold colours, for the freedom and unity of the Germans.

We may all appeal with justified pride to that tradition of German history — without forgetting that it too has not remained unthreatened by narrow-minded nationalism and German great-power ambitions.

It is a welcome event for German students to be able to meet here again in 1990, again united under the black, red and gold colours, under the sign of freedom and unity in Germany. To many of us this may seem a miracle, for so many in the Federal Republic of Germany had already given up the hope and the endeavour for the goal of German unity in freedom as a vestige of allegedly backward-looking tendencies to be banned from consciousness.

I find it still more welcome that this Congress of Catholic student associations is taking place under the banner of Europe, thereby showing that national unity at the end of this century can be seen only within European unity. . . .

Today we know better than ever that the German question is a European question; its core is freedom. The individual human being, in inviolable dignity, is the core of the spiritual, political and cultural heritage of our continent. . . .

Today we have the unique opportunity of creating, on the basis of our European traditions, a European peace order that we hope may make war unthinkable in any form. The overcoming of the division of our nation is an active contribution to removing tensions in the heart of Europe and thereby securing peace on our continent.

That is why united Germany is a threat to no one, but quite to the contrary an opportunity. A source of constant tensions in Europe has been dried up through the restoration of our unity.

Only a quarter-century after General de Gaulle aroused controversy with his slogan of a "Europe from the Atlantic to the Urals," the face of the continent has changed in such a way that that vision is now within the range of actual possibility. President Mitterrand's suggestion of a "European Confederation" on the basis of the CSCE Final Act picks up from that idea; his main concern, however, is the danger that Europe, "again coming back into its history and its geography," might fall back into a state of fragmentation like that of 1919. In his New Year's address for 1990, he formulated his thoughts on the reshaping of Europe.

New Year's message by French President François Mitterrand, 31 December 1989 (extracts)

It is plain that Europe will never again be as we have known it for half a century. Yesterday, it was still dependent on the two superpowers, but tomorrow it will already be finding its way back to its history and its geography, like anyone coming back home. Now new questions are arising, to which there are no immediate answers, but they are hanging in the air: what is to become of the alliances, the Atlantic Alliance and the Warsaw Pact? How quickly is disarmament to be pushed forward? In what form and on what terms will the German people reunite? How will cooperation between East and West take shape? Are existing frontiers untouchable or not? How far should the rebirth of nationalities go? . . .

Either the tendencies to dissolution and fragmentation will increase and we shall find ourselves back in the Europe of 1919 — and we know what happened after that — or Europe will grow together. This can come about in two stages, firstly through our Community of Twelve, which absolutely must strengthen its structures, as was recently decided in Strasbourg.

I am convinced that the Community has through its mere existence made a major contribution to the rise of the peoples of Eastern Europe by serving them as a lodestone and an anchor.

The second stage is what we must create now. I expect that on the basis of the Helsinki agreements, a European confederation in the true sense of the word will come about in the 1990s, in which all the States of our continent will be linked in a common, lasting organization of trade, peace and security. That will be possible only after the introduction in the Eastern countries of party pluralism, free elections, a representative system and freedom of information. At the rate things are going, we are perhaps not so far off that.

This confederation for the 1990s would contain not only the existing twelve member countries of the European Community, but also the six Member States of the European Free Trade Area (EFTA). The Eastern and Central European countries that have become democratic would likewise find a place in the European confederation. The basis and precondition for this Confederation of States must, however, be the Community of Twelve, whose economic and political unification must be pushed forward.

The Revolution in the East and the Vision of Europe of 1992

President Mitterrand's plan for confederation was an attempt to respond conceptually to changes in the whole of Europe and to bring France into this process as an actor contributing to the determination of events. It is certainly no coincidence that the French President publicly formulated this idea at a time when reflection on the forms and content of a political reshaping of Europe was in full swing among his neighbors on the other side of the Rhine. Apart from that German policy objective, François Mitterrand, like his predecessor in the mid-1960s, was also concerned with expanding the European horizon of French foreign policy by reactivating France's traditional political interaction with Eastern and Central Europe.

The Soviet Union's new course at home and abroad, the reform movements in the East, and the impending impetus of integration in the European Community are now posing a great test of constancy for each of the twelve Member States. On the one hand, there is fear that creation of the internal market could lead to an exclusion of all those who do not belong to that structure, thereby widening the gap that separates Europe into West and East. The argument that the Community should instead slow down the dynamics of its integration in order not to increase its distance from the Eastern and Central Europeans is opposed by the demand to strengthen the Community so as to be able to promote the reform processes in that region effectively as an efficient partner in the modernization of Eastern Europe. Finally, the question also arises of how far the EC market of 1992 can already be counted on as a foundation that could support other members as well. In an analysis in the spring of 1989, Bonn political scientist Hans-Peter Schwarz embarked on the attempt to describe the great changes in the continent:

Three objective developments in Europe would seem to be the most important ones at present.

Europe is experiencing the internal collapse of communism as an idea and as a practice in the organization of large societies. This is a world-historical process of the first rank, the medium- and long-term effects of which can only be discerned in outline. What will emerge from the collapse cannot yet be foreseen; but the forty years of decoupling of Eastern and Central Europe from modernity are coming to an end. In one form or another, a reunification of Europe will come about.

The process of European integration in the European Community framework has attained a quality in which the States involved can no longer autonomously determine their economic and social policy — the central elements of modern sovereignty. Western Europe is caught up in a development process out of which a new type of political and economic unit must come — be it called federation, union or confederation.

In parallel with this, the American century is coming to an end. While the United States will continue to be the strongest power in the community of North Atlantic democracies, the days when it could be seen as the hegemonic power and sole protector of Western Europe are numbered.

The three developmental trends just described act dialectically upon one another.[22]

The political recommendation that emerged from this analysis was that the Community adopt a long-term policy to create a tie from Eastern and Central Europe to the dynamics and pluralism of Western Europe; that is, a reunification of Europe in the Community's gravitational field, albeit not yet in full integration with it. A few months later, now under the impression of the revolutionary change in the GDR and in Czechoslovakia, the Dutchman Max Kohnstamm, General Secretary for the Action Committee for Europe and, as a former collaborator of Jean Monnet, well acquainted with the beginnings of Western European integration, drew three lessons for the future from the operations of the founding fathers of European unification:

Firstly, that peace does not simply break out but must be created.

Secondly, that Europe has so far experienced only armistices thanks to the so-called balance of forces.

22. Hans-Peter Schwarz, "Auf dem Weg zum post-kommunistischen Europa," in *Europa-Archiv*, 11, 1989, 319.

Thirdly, that the European Community is not an end in itself, but a transitional stage on the road to tomorrow's world that still has to be constructed. That is why the Community must remain open to all democratic States of Europe prepared to join the core of no longer autonomous States.[23]

In the early 1950s the impending end of the Marshall Plan had made the question of the future shape of economic relations ever more pressing for the European States. In 1950 to 1952, private European organizations and personalities of political and economic life therefore put forward a number of proposals for the advancement of economic and political integration. At the government level it was France that, with the path-breaking government declaration on 9 May 1950 of then Foreign Minister Robert Schuman (inspired by Jean Monnet), took the initiative for the next step. It was directed primarily at overcoming the Franco-German antagonism, and aimed for a "*de facto* solidarity" in the area of the coal and steel industry, one that would rule out future wars in Europe.

Declaration by French Foreign Minister Robert Schuman, 9 May 1950 (extract)

World peace cannot be guaranteed without creative efforts proportionate to the dangers threatening it. The contribution that an organized, vital Europe can make to civilization is indispensable for the maintenance of peaceful relationships . . . . Europe will not come about at a stroke, nor as a joint construction. It will come into being if practical achievements have first created *de facto* solidarity. The coming together of the European nations requires the elimination of the centuries-old antagonism of France and Germany. The steps to be taken must in the first place concern France and Germany.

The task of the near future is to extend our solidarity to the emergent East European democracies. On 17 November 1989, a few days after the opening of the German internal frontier,

23. Max Kohnstamm, "Wie der Friede gewonnen gewonnen wird. Die Europäische Gemeinschaft: eine Ordnung für ganz Europa," in *Die Zeit*, 29 December 1989.

Ex-Chancellor Helmut Schmidt together with *Die Zeit* editor Countess Marion Dönhoff, presented the European Council with a proposal for an economic aid program in favor of the East European States that were taking the path of economic reform and political pluralism. Six months later, the two authors of this initiative drew up a balance sheet:

> The West has won the Cold War. Not taking advantage of this victory now but instead stopping a hundred yards before the finish line and folding one's arms as if one had arrived would be not only inconsistent, but almost a crime. For it would throw the people in the countries of Eastern Europe, who have waited forty years for freedom, back into hopelessness and misery again in a short time, perhaps even force them under a new authoritarian yoke again. Democracy can survive there only if the governments in office are assisted.
>
> The initiative should come from Bonn. We Germans have a pressing interest in the consolidation of democracy and in the economic rise of our immediate neighbours in Eastern Europe. We must feel a shared responsibility, even in our own interest, for the well-being of our neighbours. If a neighbour's house catches fire, then one's own may catch it too — and that too is a reason for helping the neighbour to put it out.[24]

In their committed plea for powerful "pump-priming finance" they recall the precedent of the Marshall Plan, which helped sixteen European States (Stalin forbade the communist States to take part), lasted more than four years (1948 to 1951) and cost the United States, on an average for the whole period, $3 billion per year, a total of $12 billion dollars; at today's prices that would be around $16 billion per year, or a total of $64 billion. But this time the number of States and of people to be helped is far smaller — as long as the Soviet Union is not to be included.

According to the authors' calculations, an annual $16 billion over four years for a West European Marshall Plan to benefit Eastern Europe would take some 0.3 percent of the European Community's gross social product annually; if the United States and Japan were to be involved, then for all participants it would amount to a bare 0.1 percent of gross social product. If one averages its

---

24. Countess Marion Dönhoff and Helmut Schmidt, "Der Osten braucht unsere Solidarität. Ohne westliche Unterstützung können die osteuropäischen Demokratien nicht überleben," *in Die Zeit*, 25 May 1990.

four years, the first Marshall Plan cost the United States ten times as much; namely, 1 percent of its gross social product. The new European Bank for Reconstruction and Development (EBRD) could play a major role here, particularly if a timely, radical debt settlement on the model of the London Agreement on debts concluded in the 1950s with the Federal Republic of Germany could be set as a goal.

Since the winter of 1989 to 1990 the European Community did manage to arrive at some efforts. First, a large aid package was prepared in Brussels, amounting essentially to credits through the European Investment Bank (EIB), which had existed for decades, and to an expansion of the Community budget. Second, the European Bank for Reconstruction and Development was founded, with the United States, Japan, the Soviet Union, and the States of Eastern Europe all involved. The regular session of the European Council in Strasbourg in early December 1989 dealt exhaustively with the question of how the countries of Eastern and Central Europe could be brought to the model of the European Community, in the same way as it was done for the former GDR.

Declaration of the European Council in Strasbourg on Central and Eastern Europe, 8/9 December 1989 (extracts)

Expressing the feelings of the people of the whole Community, we are deeply gladdened by the changes taking place. These are historic events and no doubt the most important since the Second World War. The success of a strong and dynamic European Community, the vitality of the CSCE process and stability in the area of security, in which the United States and Canada participate, have contributed greatly to them.

These changes give reason to hope that the division in Europe can be overcome in accordance with the aims of the Helsinki Final Act, which seeks, through a global and balanced approach and on the basis of a set of principles which retain their full value, to establish new relations between European countries whether in the area of security, economic and technical cooperation, or the human dimension.

We seek the strengthening of the state of peace in Europe in which the German people will regain its unity through free self-determination. This process should take place peacefully and democratically, in full respect of the relevant agreements and treaties and of all the principles defined by the Helsinki Final Act, in a context of dialogue and East-West cooperation. It also has to be placed in the perspective of European integration. . . .

At this time of profound and rapid change, the Community is and must remain a point of reference and influence. It remains the cornerstone of a new European architecture and, in its will to openness, a mooring for a future European equilibrium. This equilibrium will be still better ensured by a parallel development of the role of the Council of Europe, EFTA and the CSCE process.

Construction of the Community must therefore go forward: the building of European union will permit the further development of a range of effective and harmonious relationships with the other countries of Europe.

In a lecture to the Congress of the PEN club of the Federal Republic of Germany on 12 May 1990, Berlin journalist Peter Bender also called for assistance from Germany's neighbors to the East. With arguments deriving from political ethics and from a consideration of the burden of the German past, he pleaded energetically for simultaneous advancement of both German unification and European integration, and for involvement of Eastern and Central Europeans in these dynamics as well:

> For forty years the Federal Republic drew its strength and its respect from the support and trust of Western Europe and America. A united Germany can draw life only from the same source.
>
> But a united Germany cannot tolerate the position that the European Community ends at the Oder. The Poles, Czechs, Slovaks and Hungarians, and later the Romanians and Bulgarians too, are all striving towards Brussels. Yet they have to stand in line and wait to see if they can be let in. The Germans in the GDR got an entrance ticket right away, because they have a relative in the Brussels management. So those who are waiting remember that it is because of the Germans that they have to stand in line. For it was only Hitler's war that brought communism to the Elbe.
>
> . Why does the Federal government not make itself the advocate of our Eastern neighbours who want to enter the European Community? In less than ten years full membership is quite impossible, but the nations there need a sign of hope. All the suffering we now know from the GDR is prevalent there too, but much worse. To help only one's own people is first of all shabby and second shortsighted. If nationalisms clash to our east and southeast, if powerful men bid the still weak democracies farewell, if poverty bursts out in social explosion, then the ruins will be crashing about our ears too, and most of all about us Germans as the neighbors.[25]

Bender's warning was directed primarily at the Federal Republic, but concern that the Germans in Europe were too preoccupied with themselves was expressed by GDR intellectuals too. For more than four decades, all thought and feeling, in both the leadership and the population, had been determined by the two poles of Moscow and Bonn; yet, the GDR, in contrast with, say, Poland, Czechoslovakia, and Hungary, never saw itself primarily as a European country. Except among a few churchmen and members of peace groups, in the past there had been scarcely any impetus to reflection about the structural European framework for the German position. This shortcoming, in the view of East Berlin writer Lutz Rathenow, not only existed as to the as yet scarcely realized European Community perspective, but also concerned relations with the neighboring countries in Eastern Europe:

> A people is awakening from its sleeping-beauty slumber of a real social-ism that is wasting away. Barely has it tasted the verve of political demonstrations when by government decision general freedom to travel breaks over the people. The West as the opium of the people; the powerful pulled the last emergency brake. . . .
>
> All the cards are being reshuffled. Yet the GDR's problems are by no means problems of the GDR alone. The crisis of the whole real socialist world is expressed in them. And we are still an occupied country. The narrow GDR perspective — particularly among the opposition — is fatal. A stubborn child wants to build its tower on its own. On the one hand the most active opposition people deny the classification of their movement in a context of Eastern European dissidence; on the other they dispute any German-German special road. There remains the fanatical dream of the GDR as the first truly socialist State in the world. The SED is slowly letting the economic facts out of the secrets bag — and in just a couple of weeks we, like Poland and Hungary, are facing economic collapse.[26]

On the other hand, there were also skeptical voices to be heard, which asked whether the European Community ought to help the Eastern European reform movements to their feet at all, with a comprehensive aid concept, and thus degenerate into a kind of "Good Samaritans" association for waylaid socialist regimes. In

---

25. Peter Bender, "Die grosse Chance für den alten Kontinent. Das Interesse aller-und gerade der Deutschen–verlangt die Einigung Europas," in *Die Zeit*, 1 June 1990.

26. Lutz Rathenow, "Nachdenken uber Deütschland," in Hubertus Knabe, ed., *Aufbruch in eine andere DDR*, 285ff. *op. cit.*

a report from Brussels, with the significant title "Eastern upsurge infects the West," *Times* correspondent Michael Binyon portrayed the mood in February 1990:

> Can 1992 survive the revolutions in Eastern Europe? Have the sudden changes and prospects of imminent German unification thrown into disarray the Single Market programme and halted the momentum of West European integration?
>
> These questions are now being asked with increasing urgency here as EC leaders grapple with ways to react to the unpredictable surge of events. There is a very real fear that all the old certainties no longer hold true; that the assumptions on which the Community was founded have become outdated; that public attention has shifted east, and so have political priorities. Rarely have West European leaders been so uncertain.
>
> All plans now have to be revised to take account of Eastern Europe, but everything has to be left open: few dare predict the outcome of the spring elections, the implosion of economies and political structures.[27]

Collapse in the East, reunification fever in the center, stability fears in the West — this is indeed an accurate description of the situation of European affairs in the spring of 1990. To be sure, there was more or less agreement among political élites of Europe that the growing together of the European States into a new ordered structure called for a process in which the front lines drawn in the ideological age would have to be overcome. Yet, at a stroke, the expectation that any European order would for the foreseeable future be based on the continued division of Germany became obsolete. To this was added uncertainty as to how one might estimate any possible threat from the East when one could no longer rely on a sharply defined image of the enemy. After all, not least in importance was the Soviet leadership under Gorbachev in the freeing of the peoples of Eastern Europe from the straitjacket of communist ideology and domination.

A few months before the Seventeenth of June — the "Day of German Unity" — was given a whole new meaning by the autumn revolution in the GDR, Erhard Eppler, a member of the SPD executive, set forth in the Bundestag a few reasons why the rapid

27. Michael Binyon, "Eastern upheaval infects the West," in *The Times*, 10 February 1990.

decay of the European stability structure in the late 1980s would develop a special dynamic at the point at which it began to include Germany.

Speech by Dr. Erhard Eppler in the German Bundestag on 17 June 1989 (extracts)

There is a difference between what is today fermenting in the Baltic or in Yugoslavia and what might happen in Germany. Whether Slovenes, Serbs and Croats want to live in a single State is their concern alone. The walls that they might put up among themselves do not affect the statics of the European house. The ugly wall of steel and concrete that was put up across Germany has more to do with the statics of this European house than we like to feel. Whoever wants to tear it down must recalculate the statics of the whole house, indeed perhaps rebuild it entirely. What will become of Germany interests all Europeans. . . .

We should not wonder if now, when national waves are passing over Europe, our neighbours are again querying what we Germans want. We have not yet been able to say sufficiently exactly and in what detail what is to happen in Germany if the Iron Curtain rusts through faster than expected. Perhaps we shall never be able to say it so exactly as to tranquillize them all.

But one thing we can say right now: among all the political forces of this House there is more consensus than controversy on German policy, even if this consensus is necessarily quieter and less striking than conflict. At any rate it seems to me that the points I shall now list can be taken as a consensus of an overwhelming majority of democratic forces:

Firstly: the Germans, like all peoples, have a right to self-determination. It has not been done away with, even by what Germans did to Europe.

Secondly: we subordinate this right to the requirements of peace. These always have priority. What is to bring Germans together again must serve and promote peace in Europe; it must not endanger it.

Thirdly: we pursue our policy on Germany as Europeans, in European responsibility. We wish together with our neighbours to build a Europe in which Germans can come together again.

Fourthly: this excludes any special German road. Freedom from alliances and neutrality was a topic of the early 1950s. It has been eliminated by the normative force of facts.

Fifthly: where we think in terms of potential, whether economic, political or even military, we think European. The times of national power-policy in Europe are for us irrevocably over.

Sixthly: freedom comes before unity. This has always meant for all parties in this House that unity in unfreedom is not in question. But this means today too that we welcome more free development and a right to a say by the people in the GDR even if they strengthen their loyalty to the other German State and thereby stabilize that State. The construction workers in the Stalinallee too wanted first of all more freedom and more human living and working conditions.

Seventhly: we have become a Western country through and through. Our political culture has and continues to have a Western stamp. Even those among us who are convinced that our democracy is far from achieving all its possibilities rely firmly on the Western catalogue of values. Where new movements demonstrate against the destruction of nature or arms madness, they do so in the forms of Western civil rights movements.

Eighthly: History has not conferred any special mission on us Germans, but geography faces us with special tasks. We are not wandering between two worlds, but the two blocs, while they may have the attraction for the superpowers of being easily perceptible zones of influence, are for us Central Europeans only a temporarily necessary evil.

Ninthly: NATO was founded above all so that Western Europeans could live the way they want to. An overcoming of the blocs that guarantees just this and if possible gives the other Europeans at long last the opportunity for that is not a spectre for us, but a return to European normality.

Tenthly: if the two parts of Europe grow together, the two parts of Germany must also grow together, but in such a way that the growing together of Europe is not thereby disturbed or blocked.

New Dimensions of Security Relations in Europe

The question raised by Eppler, that of the statics of the European house if the walls and frontiers between the two German States are to be torn down, indeed calls for new answers. Political change in Eastern and Central Europe, and particularly in the ex-GDR, is opening up the possibility that countries belonging formerly to the Warsaw Pact, and hitherto committed to the Soviet communist system, may make their security-policy links available. For the Soviet leadership the greatest challenge lies in the fact that with the departure of the GDR and the dissolution of the Eastern alliance not only is the basis of the Soviet military presence endangered, but the whole influence of the USSR on Eastern and Central Europe shaken. In the contribution to the international symposium organized by *Die Zeit* in early December 1989 on the "Causes and Consequences of the Eastern European Revolution of '89," Polish historian and Chairman of the Solidarnošč parliamentary group in the Sejm Bronislaw Geremek stated the following:

> We are at present living through a time where we must not think in categories linked exclusively with the old conceptual world of earlier organizational forms. We must make reference to value concepts. I wish by this to make clear that the disappearance of communism we are at present experiencing in Central Europe is not simply a victory for capitalism. It cannot be understood as a conflict between the two systems. It is the return to freedom in Central Europe, the victory of freedom over totalitarian phenomena. It is certainly not a matter of the balance of power between the two superpowers, the USSR and the USA, either. Anyone thinking only in these categories is deceiving himself. Considerations made in the West about Central Europe, have very often attempted to respect and consider imperial sensibilities, instead of keeping international security in the forefront. Perhaps attention has been paid rather more to taking account of the pride of the Empires than to thinking about the security of the whole world or of Europe. But we cannot find the way beyond Yalta if the spheres of domination are left untouched.[28]

In the spring there had already been reflection on the Western side as to the function of the alliances in this changed international environment. In a keynote speech on 31 May 1989 in Mainz, U.S. President Bush spoke of an era "beyond containment" and of the fact that we are at the threshold of a new age. The Cold War, said President Bush, has come to an end, with a victory for the West along a broad front. That will also affect the East-West conflict in Europe. It is not disappearing, but shifting from exclusive concentration on the military level to the level of politics and economics.

In an analysis of Europe's situation "beyond containment" announced by President Bush, Frankfurt political scientist Ernst-Otto Czempiel, author of a book on the United States and the Soviet Union in the 1980s, retrospectively described the stabilizing role of the alliances as follows:

---

28. Bronislaw Geremek, "'Ende des Kommunismus – und was nun?' Contribution to the debate for the symposium organized by *Die Zeit* in early December 1989 on 'Causes and Consequences of the East European Revolution of '89'," in *Die Zeit*, December 29, 1989.

Over the past forty years they ensured stability in a divided Europe, arranged the functionally outdated European medium and small States into viable larger units, quieted the German question, froze the Berlin problem and forced on the East European States their political position at the side of the Soviet Union. Not least, NATO constituted a guarantor of the Federal Republic's link with the West and of continuing cooperation of the West European States among themselves and with the United States. This order was provisional and unsatisfactory, but it was stable. Through armament and the accompanying strategy, not only was the Soviet Union deterred and the situation of non-war in Europe consolidated; political linkages and alliances were also created.[29]

The stormy acceleration of political change in Eastern and Central Europe has ensured that previous alliances have indeed lost a major part of their political structure and function. On 12 December 1989, a few days after the U.S.-Soviet summit meeting in Malta, which was completely devoted to European issues, U.S. Secretary of State James A. Baker, in a speech to the Berlin Press Club, undertook to design "a new architecture for a new age."

Speech by U.S. Secretary of State James A. Baker to the Berlin Press Club on 12 December 1989 (extracts)

This new architecture must have a place for old foundations and structures that remain very valuable — like NATO — while recognizing that they can also serve new collective purposes. The new architecture must continue the construction of institutions — like the European Community — that can help draw together the West while also serving as an open door to the East. And the new architecture must build up frameworks — like the CSCE process — that can overcome the division of Europe and that at the same time can bridge the Atlantic Ocean.

This new structure must also accomplish two specific purposes. First, as a part of overcoming the division of Europe there must be an opportunity to overcome, through peace and freedom, the division of Berlin and of Germany. The United States and NATO have stood for unification for forty years, and we will not waiver from that goal.

Second, the architecture should reflect that America's security — politically, militarily and economically — remains linked to Europe's security. The United States and Canada share Europe's neighborhood....

29. Ernst-Otto Czempiel, "Europa nach der 'Überwindung des Containment'," in *Europa-Archiv*, 12, 1989, 373.

As we construct a new security architecture that maintains the common defense, the non-military component of European security will grow. Arms control agreements, confidence-building measures and other political consultative arrangements are going to become more important. It is in such a world that the role of NATO is going to evolve. NATO will become the forum where the Western nations cooperate to negotiate, to implement, to verify and to extend agreements between East and West . . . .

Third, NATO should also begin considering further initiatives the West might take, through the CSCE process in particular, to build economic and political ties with the East, to promote respect for human rights, to help build democratic institutions, and to fashion, consistent with Western security interests, a more open environment for East-West trade and investment.

And finally, NATO may have its greatest and most lasting effect on the pattern of change by demonstrating to the nations of the East a fundamentally different approach to security. NATO's four decades offer a vision of cooperation, not coercion; of open borders, not iron curtains. The reconciliation of ancient enemies, which has come about under the umbrella of NATO's collective security, offers the nations of Eastern Europe an appealing model of international relations.

Their Soviet Foreign Minister Shevardnadze was very willing to take up the slogan of the political function of the Western alliance; a few days later he spoke to the Political Affairs Committee of the European Parliament in Brussels and used this slogan in an attempt to give the Warsaw Pact too a new legitimation. In a first estimate of change in the "socialist community of States," he put forward the view that the Eastern alliance ought to become a political alliance of sovereign treaty partners on an equal footing.

Speech by Soviet Foreign Minister Eduard Shevardnadze to the Political Affairs Committee of the European Parliament in Brussels, 19 December 1989 (extracts)

As those [eastern European] countries are changing, everyone has had a chance to see that people there are completely free to choose their own path and their own methods for building a new society. Our respect for their choice means respect for full sovereignty of the countries of Eastern Europe, unconstrained by any ideology; respect for their independence without precluding possible transformations in their socioeconomic and political institutions.

It is notable that all of those countries have reaffirmed their alliance obligations under the Warsaw Treaty. We regard this as an important prerequisite for preserving stability in the current situation. Of course, our time calls for adjustments in the system of relations within our alliance. Modernizing its structure can only benefit our common interests. It is our view that its nature must change, with political aspects prevailing over its military substance....

In this context we welcome recent remarks by the US Secretary of State Mr. James Baker about the first new task of NATO, in which the military component should be reduced and the political component reinforced.

Officially, the Warsaw Pact was established in 1955 as a response to West German rearmament and the Federal Republic's entry into NATO. In reality, it had already existed since Stalin's time in the form of pacts of friendship and assistance among the East bloc States. Agreements on the stationing of troops in the GDR, Poland, Hungary, and, following the defeat of the "Prague Spring," in Czechoslovakia as well, allowed the Soviet Union effective control of Eastern Europe. The Pact was originally limited to thirty years but was extended in 1985 by a further twenty.

While the onetime East bloc States drifted westward, the Soviet Union was seeking to maintain its influence over the destinies of Europe in new ways. Its defensive glacis — the securing of which had been the real objective of the Warsaw Pact — had already been lost. It is well-nigh fantastic that the last summit conference of the Pact, held in Moscow in early June 1990, was attended by three declared anti-communists: de Maizière for the GDR, Mazowiecki for Poland, and Antall for Hungary. The USSR nevertheless succeeded, through proposals for transforming the military alliance into a kind of "disarmament pact" and for creating a review commission, in fending off dissolution until July 1991. The temporary committee called into being in Moscow, which was to work out routes toward a total functional shift for the Warsaw Pact, had also, however, been assigned a bloc-bridging role. The point was to deprive NATO of former threat scenarios and offer itself to it as a model for adaptation of the alliances to the new overall international conditions.

In history, traditional alliances have as a rule disappeared, along with the threat they were set up against. The North Atlantic Pact, by contrast, is for its members not primarily a means of defense against a specific threat but above all an expression of membership in the Western community, as well as a way of anchoring the United States in Europe. The decision of the London NATO meeting of July 1990 to change the strategy of "flexible response," to replace forward defense by a mobilization concept and henceforth to grade nuclear weapons only as a "last resort" for the extreme case of danger to existence, testifies to the willingness of the Western alliance to reform. But the summit was also a response to the challenges of the German question.

The unification of the two German States compels a rethinking of Europe's security structures, since it inescapably poses the question of what larger whole Germany is to be fitted into. Moscow's agreement to a free and sovereign decision by the Germans as to their alliance membership has opened the way to a NATO solution to the problem of European security, but it is combined on the Soviet side with the hope and expectation that the Soviet Union will not be pushed to the margins in Europe.

The discussion has only begun as to how, given the upheavals in Eastern and Central Europe, the stability that can prevent wars is to be maintained or restored in a new form in the whole of Europe. The shift from containment of Soviet power aspirations to cooperation between West and East in Europe can be accomplished only if all existing organizations are called on to collaborate, before thoughts of replacing, or at least overlaying, the existing alliances with a collective all-European security system can begin. The decisive test for the much-vaunted "end of the postwar period" will come when the consensus arrived at in the negotiations on the framework conditions for the security status of united Germany is to be converted into reality.

It was on this very question that only close harmonization among the various levels of talks and the various negotiating parties can promise prospects of success. The Two-Plus-Four Talks at which the two German States met with the Four Powers responsible for Berlin and for Germany as a whole; the disarmament talks in Vienna; and the CSCE structures were three complementary forums for discussing these issues. It would certainly be overstraining the CSCE process to treat it as already being a new European security system; still, it can play an important part as a stable framework for the dramatic developments in the whole of Europe. In a committed contribution to the objectives of Helsinki II, Count Luigi Vittorio Ferraris, the former Italian ambassador in Bonn, gave vent to reservations about putting exaggerated hopes on all-European structures:

A conference about Germany for Germany and around Germany would be a means of taking official cognizance of the predominant position of the 80 million Germans, who additionally have a direct influence on a further 100 million Europeans in the East. Such a position of predominance can be expressed positively in an Atlantic or a European context, but certainly not in connection with an overall framework in which the interests are much more diffuse and therefore less controllable and less able to be balanced. At the Helsinki I conference there was a refusal to accept the concept of a pan-Europa. The basis of this idea was a Soviet concept seeking to have the differences in political and social systems forgotten and at the same time aiming at the ambivalent concept of the "common house." Do these differences no longer have any importance? We would do better to wait before starting to sing paeans of victory.[30]

A bare year earlier, in a talk to the Royal Institute of International Affairs in London, British historian Sir Michael Howard had attempted to give an answer to the question: Does 1989 mean "a new turning-point in the times"? In connection with the development of East-West relations in Europe, he made the following predictions:

> The military framework of East-West relations in Europe may therefore not change very much before the end of the century. But it will become increasingly inappropriate to the political structure of the continent, as the states of Eastern Europe come in closer contact with those of the European Community and Germany returns to its natural role as a link, rather than a barrier, between East and West. This political evolution is being shaped by events east of the Rhine, and British, American and even French political leaders can do very little about it. They may watch with consternation as the familar pattern disintegrates and the traditional formulae no longer work, but they appear sadly incapable of devising new ones.[31]

Howard linked his statements with an allusion to the disarmament and arms control talks underway in Vienna and Geneva, calling for "fewer Genevas and more Locarnos," thus expressing his conviction that the political shaping of Europe's future was more important than

---

30. Luigi Vittorio Ferraris, "Kurzer Einhalt vor dem Siegesgeheul. Eine KSZE-Konferenz über Deutschland würde dieses in einen goldenen Käfig zwingen." *Süddeutsche Zeitung*, 13 March 1990.
31. Michael Howard, "1989 – A farewell to arms?" in *International Affairs*, Summer 1989, 407.

"splitting hairs over technicalities of the military relationship of forces." The historic challenges of the 1989 revolutions in Eastern and Central Europe lend this appeal additional weight, but the question of the balance of forces is posed anew, particularly in the context of German unification.

3

The External Aspects of German Unification

For more than four decades the German question has lingered on in an odd state of suspension, in which not only the division of Germany, but also the rights of the victorious Allies were perpetuated. The Federal Republic and the GDR were the only States within a European system that for the other States had disappeared long ago: the system of the wartime alliance against Hitler's Germany. The genesis of the two German States had, moreover, been inseparable from the East-West confrontation of the immediate postwar period and the formation of political blocs that in the mid-1950s led to military alliance integration on either side.

The simultaneous persistence of elements of the unstable system of cooperation of 1944 to 1945 alongside structures of confrontation that became dominant slightly later was of decisive importance for the international position of the Federal Republic of Germany and the German Democratic Republic. The clash of two politically and ideologically opposed systems on German soil, which led in 1949 to the plurality of two Germanies, accelerated the diverging development of political forces in the Eastern and Western sub-States.

Once the underlying geopolitical structure of postwar Europe began to shift in 1989, the question of the relationship between the four-power responsibility for Germany as a whole and for Berlin and the alliance membership of the two German States was posed in an entirely new way. On the one hand, with the end of the European postwar system, the time had also come to transfer the special rights of the Allies back to the Germans. On the other hand, a glance at the regional integration of the Federal Republic and the GDR, particularly in the security-policy area, shows that the process of German unification in its external aspects raised a range of problems that had to be solved jointly by both the Germans and the four Allies, with an eye to the international environment as a whole.

Allied Responsibility for Germany

German expansion between 1939 and 1945 shattered the old European system of States, so that in 1944 to 1945, in the course of its military advance, the Soviet Union was able to extend its own claim to political and ideological hegemony as far as the River Elbe.

From the start, the great powers that created the coalition against Hitler agreed on what they were fighting against and what their goals should be. The first priority was to defeat and to occupy Germany and, at the same time, to liberate the territories Germany had taken over. A second aim was to root out National Socialism and to create conditions that would, as far as possible, prevent German expansionist policies from ever reemerging again. Discussions of the peace aims of the Western democracies and of Soviet communism in Germany and in Europe demonstrated less agreement. The wartime alliance between Great Britain, the United States, and the Soviet Union began to fall apart as soon as military victory was won, and the factors that divided the Allies again became starkly apparent.

In 1944, the European Advisory Commission, a Three Power body with its headquarters in London, worked out the first proposals for the procedure on the capitulation of Germany and for the zones to be occupied by the Allies. The so-called London Protocol of 12 September 1944 also introduced the concept of "Germany in its frontiers of 31 December 1937," in accordance with the view of the victors that the territorial gains of the Third Reich after 1 January 1938 — including the Austrian *Anschluss* and the annexation of Sudetenland — had no validity.

Protocol on the zones of occupation in Germany and the administration of Greater Berlin, 12 September 1944 (extract)

1. Germany, within her frontiers as they were on the 31st December, 1937, will, for the purposes of occupation, be divided into three zones, one of which will be allotted to each of the three Powers, and a special Berlin area, which will be under joint occupation by the three Powers.

The second London Agreement of 14 November 1944, which created the Allied Control Council, laid down the organization of the control machinery for the administration of Germany. For the period immediately following the unconditional surrender, Germany was to be governed by the Allied Control Council, consisting of the three (later four, with the entry of France) military commanders-in-chief, who were to exercise supreme authority jointly "in matters affecting Germany as a whole."

Agreement on the Control Machinery in Germany of 14 November 1944 (extract)

Supreme authority in Germany will be exercised, on instructions from their respective governments, by the Commanders-in-Chief of the armed forces of the United States of America, the United Kingdom and the Union of Soviet Socialist Republics, each in his own zone of occupation, and also jointly, in matters affecting Germany as a whole, in their capacity as members of the supreme organ of control constituted under the present Agreement.

In contrast to these agreements over the occupation zones, plans for the political division of Germany at the end of the war were far from clear. At the conferences of the Big Three in Tehran (28 November – 1 December 1943) and at Yalta (4–11 February 1945), Churchill, Roosevelt, and Stalin all called for the "dismemberment" of Germany; but by the time of Germany's surrender on 7 and 8 May 1945 (in Rheims and Berlin), there was still no binding agreement between the Allies on how Germany was to be divided and on how its borders were to be drawn.

At Yalta, the German problem was assigned a minor place in the wide range of political issues discussed. The conference ratified the agreement on occupation zones that had been worked out in 1944, which in effect fixed the political division of Germany, as well as the status of Berlin. The agreement was extended by the creation of another zone for France. No consensus could be reached, however, on the final position of Poland's western border. The Western powers had been unable to persuade Stalin to give up the gains made in 1939 by his treaty with Hitler about Poland. Already at Tehran they had approved, in principle, a westward shift of the Polish border, but at Yalta the fixing of a new German-Polish border was deliberately postponed to a later Peace Conference. The two English-speaking powers made their agreement to major additions to Polish territory "in the north and west" conditional upon the reestablishment of an independent and democratic Poland.

Declaration at Yalta, 11 February 1945 (extract)

II. It is our inflexible purpose to destroy German militarism and Nazism and to ensure that Germany will never again be able to disturb the peace of the world. . . . It is not our purpose to destroy the people of Germany, but only when Nazism and militarism have been extirpated will there be hope for a decent life for Germans, and a place for them in the comity of nations. . . .

VI. [The three Heads of Government] recognize that Poland must receive substantial accessions of territory in the north and west. They feel that the opinion of the new Polish Provisional Government of National Unity should be sought in due course on the extent of these accessions and that the final delimitation of the western frontier of Poland should thereafter await the Peace Conference.

On the day of victory — by Soviet reckoning, 9 May 1945 — Stalin declared publicly that the Soviet Union did not intend to dismember or destroy Germany. Yet, by his decision on 1 March 1945 to place under Polish rule the German territories east of the rivers Oder and Neisse that had been conquered by the Red Army and to incorporate northern East Prussia, including the city of Königsberg, into the Soviet Union, division was a *fait accompli* even before the end of the war. In this way he signaled that, contrary to the London Agreements, he considered Germany no longer to be defined by its December 1937 frontiers, but rather to consist only of territory west of the Oder and the Western Neisse rivers.

The unconditional surrender of German forces on 7 and 8 May loosened the constraint of political and military necessities among the powers in the anti-Hitler coalition. Decisive for the future legal position of Germany was the "Berlin Declaration," of 5 June 1945, which transferred supreme administrative authority to the four main victors. This declaration, incorporating the substance of the London Agreements of September and November 1944, stated specifically that the assumption of government powers and the division into zones for occupation purposes did not "effect the annexation of Germany."

Berlin Declaration regarding the defeat of Germany and the assumption of supreme authority with respect to Germany, 5 June 1945 (extract)

The Governments of the United Kingdom, the United States of America and the Union of Socialist Soviet Republics, and the Provisional Government of the French Republic, hereby assume supreme authority with respect to Germany, including all the powers possessed by the German government, the High Command and any state, municipal, or local government or authority. The assumption, for the purpose stated above, of the said authority and powers does not effect the annexation of Germany. The Governments of the United Kingdom, the United States of America and the Union of Soviet Socialist Republics, and the Provisional Government of the French Republic, will hereafter determine the boundaries of Germany or any part thereof and the status of Germany or of any area at present being part of German territory.

The already growing conflicts among the former Allies cast a cloud over the Potsdam Conference (17 July – 2 August 1945), where major arguments arose over the future internal order of Poland and Stalin's unilateral action regarding the Oder-Neisse line. Allied statesmen were loath to admit to their own people, so soon after the end of the war, their inability to reach agreement. In the Potsdam Agreement, which consisted of a Communiqué and a detailed Protocol of decisions at the Three Power Conference in Potsdam on 2 August 1945, all the issues on which no agreement could be reached were accordingly resolved by a series of compromise formulas.

There was no longer any mention of Germany's political frontiers of December 1937, but only of the treatment of Germany as an "economic unit" during the period of the occupation. The decision, however, to allow each occupying power the right to take reparations chiefly from its own zone, made it difficult to maintain the principle of economic unity, at the same time it put a question mark over the return of Germany to political unity. Even though the Potsdam Agreement did not finally assign Germany's eastern territories to Soviet or Polish "administration," the resolution to defer those issues to a future peace settlement was made considerably harder to implement by the decision, made without any stable definition of Poland's borders, to expel Germans from Poland, Czechoslovakia, and Hungary.

The expulsion of Germans, who still numbered in the millions, from the eastern parts of Central Europe, the former Reich territories east of the Oder and Neisse, and the Sudetenland and Hungary, and the reduction of the territory covered by the Reich in 1937 to the area west of the Oder-Neisse line, created, as early as 1945, a situation in which the highly complex German problem was confined *de facto* to the area of the four Zones of Occupation and Greater Berlin.

This German migration, the largest migration of people in modern history, involved a total of 11.7 million Germans. Of the 16.5 million Germans living in the Eastern Territories (including East Prussia) and in Eastern and Southeastern Europe at the end of the war, 2.1 million either died or disappeared without trace. The Western Powers were unable to affect this mass exodus, let alone stop it once it had started; the Soviet Union and the new Communist governments of the countries where these Germans had lived tried between 1945 and 1947 to eliminate the problem of minority populations that in the past had formed an obstacle to the development of their own national identity. It was only with the expulsion of the Germans — described in the Potsdam Agreement as the "orderly transfer of German populations" — that victory, and the countries conquered by the Third Reich, were made secure, while the social burden of this unprecedented population transfer was for the most part put on the West.

Communiqué on the Three Power Conference in Berlin (Potsdam Agreement) of 2 August 1945 (extracts)

VI. *City of Königsberg and the Adjacent Area*

. . .

The Conference has agreed in principle to the proposal of the Soviet Government concerning the ultimate transfer to the Soviet Union of the city of Königsberg and the area adjacent to it . . . subject to expert examination of the actual frontier.

The President of the United States and the British Prime Minister have declared that they will support the proposal of the Conference at the forthcoming peace settlement.

. . .

IX. *Poland*

. . .

The three Heads of Government agree that, pending the final determination of Poland's western frontier, the former German territories east of a line running from the Baltic Sea immediately west of Swinemunde, and thence along the Oder River to the confluence of the western Neisse River and along the western Neisse to the Czechoslovak frontier, including that portion of East Prussia not placed under the administration of the Union of Soviet Socialist Republics in accordance with the understanding reached at this Conference and including the area of the former free city of Danzig, shall be under the administration of the Polish State and for such purposes should not be considered as part of the Soviet Zone of occupation in Germany.

XIII. *Orderly Transfer of German Populations*

The conference reached the following agreement on the removal of Germans from Poland, Czechoslovakia and Hungary:

The three Governments, having considered the question in all its aspects, recognize that the transfer to Germany of German populations or elements thereof, remaining in Poland, Czechoslovakia and Hungary, will have to be undertaken. They agree than any transfers that take place should be effected in an orderly and humane manner.

At Potsdam, any question of dividing Germany into separate States was supposed to have been disposed of formally. Yet, as

Germany's future was caught up in the struggle for the domination of Europe, joint Four Power control, as promulgated on 5 June 1945 in the Berlin Declaration, could not survive the collapse of cooperation between the wartime Allies. As the East-West conflict intensified, the differences in development between the occupied zones created deeper and deeper rifts in Germany, despite the fact that no formal decision to divide Germany for the foreseeable future had been made.

The last directive of the Four Powers that mentioned reunification of Germany as a joint goal dates back to the Geneva summit conference in July 1955. For the first time since Potsdam, and this time with the participation of France, the Heads of State and of Government of the former victorious powers came together to discuss the German question, European security, disarmament, and East-West relations. The Four Power conference had only a few tangible results, and brought no agreement as to positions on the German question.

It would be another thirty-five years before the Four Powers would again make a joint statement on Germany as a whole, as the Potsdam Agreement had bound them to. Four-power responsibility had admittedly turned into a Two-plus-Four mechanism: the two German States were holding joint talks with the four victor and occupying States of 1945 about the "external aspects" of German unification and about the security of Germany's European neighbors. The procedure had been agreed upon by ministers from NATO and Warsaw Pact countries at a conference in Ottawa on 13 February 1990, the actual object of which was aerial verification in connection with future disarmament measures. In a certain sense the wheel was coming round full circle here too, since the "open skies" concept, which had been U.S. President Eisenhower's idea, had first been discussed at the Geneva summit conference in 1955.

The restoration of German unity presupposed agreement in Europe as to where Germany would belong politically. As long as that was lacking, joint responsibility by the victorious powers continued its shadowy existence. The issue came to life again at the point when the objectives mentioned in the Yalta "Declaration on Liberated Europe" — peace, free elections, and democratic structures —were finally having a chance to be defined and achieved by all Europeans in agreement. Thus, the debate on replacement of reserved Allied rights over "Germany as a whole" also has direct effects on the fate of Europe "as a whole." This connection between European security and the German question was described by Eberhard Schulz, then deputy director of the Bonn Foreign Policy Research Institute, in the following terms, a few months before the opening of the Berlin Wall:

> That four great powers should be attacked by a fifth one, then come to an agreement to occupy its capital jointly in order in future to be able reliably to control the aggressor, then fall out but continue unfailingly to hold to their joint rights as victors — this is no doubt a unique case in history. Such a special case of course arises only when there are inexorable reasons for it. It is needful to recall this background, because most people in Germany itself, but also in the victor countries of 1945, are no longer even aware that the German question does not concern only the relationship of the two States in Germany to each other.... On only one point are the Four Powers to date agreed: the self-determination of the Germans must not be allowed to lead to restoration of the former situation, namely to an all-German State with its sovereignty not restrained by any ties, whose superior potential would allow it a hegemonic position in Central Europe, if not indeed the oppression of its neighbours.[32]

How little preparation there really was for the repercussion of upheaval in Europe on the German question is shown by George F. Kennan's reaction to the breaching of the Wall. Under the immediate impression of the events of 9 November, this U.S. diplomat, who in 1947 had provided the theoretical underpinning for the Western policy of Soviet containment and later, as professor at Princeton, had repeatedly written on Germany within Europe, firmly stated that the *status quo* of division should be retained, at least in relation to Germany:

> The principle by which most of us were guided when we found ourselves faced, 40 years ago, with the problem of Germany's future was this: that there must not again be a united Germany, and particularly a militarized one, standing alone in Europe and not firmly embraced in some wider international structure — some structure that would absorb its energies and, by doing so, give reassurance to Germany's neighbors.... Even if the liberalization of political conditions in Eastern Europe were to progress in the near future to a point where they were little different from the conditions prevailing in the German Federal

---

32. Eberhard Schulz, "Europäische Sicherheit als ein Aspekt der deutschen Frage," in *Deutschland Archiv*, 5, 1989, 523.

Republic, this would of itself be no reason for an immediate German unification; and this is, therefore, not the time to raise the subject.[33]

This position seems to confirm the correctness of Paul Valéry's assertion that the only agreements that count are agreements between *arrières-pensées*. Kennan's opinion, however, is not to be regarded as the official position of the United States, which in contrast to the many other allies of the Federal Republic unambiguously supported the much-vaunted unification of Germany when it finally appeared on the agenda. Admittedly, alongside U.S. support in principle for a peaceful, democratic process of unification, concern for stability and consideration for Soviet reservations initially played a part in the U.S. attitude; yet German-American cooperation in removing the obstacles on the road to unity worked quite smoothly. As early as 4 December 1989, a day after the summit meeting with Soviet head of Party and State Gorbachev in Malta, President Bush set forth four principles for overcoming the division of Europe and Germany in freedom that were decisively to influence the outcome of negotiations in the Two-plus-Four talks.

Speech by U.S. President George Bush to the NATO council, 4 December 1989 (extract)

Of course, we have all supported German reunification for four decades. And in our view, this goal of German unification should be based on the following principles.

First, self-determination must be pursued without prejudice to its outcome. We should not at this time endorse nor exclude any particular vision of unity. Second, unfication should occur in the context of Germany's continued commitment to NATO and an increasingly integrated European Community, and with due regard for the legal role and responsibilities of the allied powers. Third, in the interests of general European stability, moves toward unification must be peaceful, gradual, and part of a step-by-step process. Lastly, on the question of borders, we should reiterate our support for the principles of the Helsinki Final Act.

An end to the unnatural division of Europe and of Germany must proceed in accordance with and be based upon the values that are becoming

---

33. George F. Kennan, "Europe is the Issue, Not German Unity," in *International Herald Tribune*, 15 November 1989.

universal ideals, as all the countries of Europe become part of a commonwealth of free nations.

The attempt to harmonize the need for a partnership on an equal footing with the prerogatives of being a one-time victorious power was certainly easier for the United States than for France or Britain. While all three Western Allies agree that the whole of Germany should belong to the West, the idea of a sovereign, economically powerful State in the center of Europe arouses concern that new imbalances may arise. This duality was articulated in a particularly clear way by French President Mitterrand during his State visit to the GDR in December 1989.

Press conference by French President Mitterrand at the conclusion of his State visit to the GDR, 22 December 1989 (extracts)

I have no intention at all of dictating to Germany what its future status is to be. And how its alliances and the nature of its alliances are to be decided concerns Germany. France has taken measures for itself. It does not make them into a gospel . . . .

We are also the guarantors of peace in Europe. We are ourselves guarantors of the status of Germany. But 45 years have gone past, and I do not want to give Germans any lessons; I do not arrogate that right to myself. I have no intention to speak for them, to say to Germany we will act towards you as if we have just got over the conflict in which we were adversaries. There are new generations now, this is a new page in history; I personally therefore refuse to take it that the Germans can be treated as if they were under tutelage. But as soon as the issue is one of the status of Europe, that does concern us; and we must ensure that no imbalance emerges that would ultimately lead to a restoration of the Europe of wars.

The great resistance to the termination of Allied rights came naturally from the USSR, for which much more was at stake than for the three Western powers. The division of Germany and the stationing of Soviet troops in its eastern half were for decades spoken of in propaganda terms as the masterstroke of Soviet security policy. In postwar history, all Soviet scenarios for overcoming the division had been linked to the demand for neutrality, and a unification of Germany on Western terms had always been treated as an unacceptable option.

Even after Gorbachev had assured Chancellor Kohl in February 1990 that the Germans could determine the time and process of unification themselves, the question of alliance membership remained open, and the Soviets repeatedly sought to impose their views of what military neutrality would mean for a united Germany. Among the most remarkable documents of the first half of 1990 is undoubtedly the interview in the *Spiegel* with long-time ambassador in the Federal Republic and expert on Germany Valentin Falin, who sought to give emphasis to his advocacy of German freedom from alliances with unconcealed and highly undiplomatic references to the Soviet Union's special rights:

> SPIEGEL: Mr. Falin, what is to happen, then, if in a few weeks a newly elected Volkskammer decides on accession to the Federal Republic and NATO has no intention of letting this Federal Republic out of the Western military alliance?
>
> FALIN: I am no lover of speculation. I would only ask you to take the following fact into account: there is no legal vacuum in Germany. Either the GDR — irrespective of what government will be in power there — fulfills its mandates and its agreements, the commitments that the Republic has undertaken to the Warsaw Treaty and to us, or the latent rights of the Soviet Union will become patent.
>
> SPIEGEL: Do you believe that emergency measures under right of conquest, even acts of force, can still uphold something?
>
> FALIN: No. The Germans are intelligent enough to understand that it cannot be in their interests to provoke a confrontation. We are not threatening anyone; but we do not want to be threatened either. That would be the worst development of all when after all the solid, long-term solution, and the gentlest one for the German people, lies within reach — is not only possible, but is even knocking at the door.[34]

Falin's statements were, moreover, not only rather undiplomatic, but also incorrect. For by signing the Warsaw Treaty in 1955, then GDR Prime Minister Otto Grotewohl had inserted a reservation whereby the GDR asserted, vis-à-vis its alliance partners,

---

34. Valentin Falin, "Für militärische Neutralität," in *Der Spiegel*, 8, 1990, 172.

its right to international freedom of action in the event of German reunification.

Report of GDR Prime Minister Otto Grotewohl to the GDR Volkskammer, 20 May 1955 (extract)

The GDR continues as previously to regard reunification of Germany on a peaceful and democratic basis as the main task for it and for the whole German people, and will do everything to speed reunification of Germany. In signing the present treaty on friendship, cooperation and mutual assistance, the government of the GDR takes the position that reunified Germany will be free of the commitments that one part of Germany has entered into in military treaties and agreements concluded before reunification.

The GDR's Legacy in Terms of Alliance Policy

By the time of the electoral defeat of the GDR's Communist Party at the very latest, however, it must have been clear even to Moscow that the "latent rights" of the Soviet Union could offer only limited room for maneuvering. Even in August 1989, when the Honecker government was getting into serious difficulties as a consequence of the rapid expansion of the refugee movement, the then Rector of the Academy for Social Sciences under the Central Committee of the SED, Otto Reinhold, had warned Moscow against incautiously risking the existence of the GDR by pressing for reforms. Earlier than many others, the SED's chief ideologue had understood that a GDR without a "socialist identity" had little chance for survival:

> As for no other socialist country in Europe ... the dialectical link between cooperation and confrontation is an unavoidable essential feature of the conception of society. The core question here is particularly what one might call the GDR's socialist identity. On this question there is quite clearly a difference in principle between the GDR and other socialist countries. They all existed, before their socialist transformation, as States with a capitalist or semi-feudal system. Their existence as States did not therefore primarily depend on the socio-political system.
>
> It is different for the GDR. It is conceivable only as an anti-fascist, a socialist State, as a socialist alternative to the FRG. What entitlement

to existence would a capitalist GDR have alongside a capitalist Federal Republic? None, of course. Only if we always keep that fact in the forefront of our minds will it become clearly recognizable how important for us is a social strategy oriented uncompromisingly towards consolidation of the socialist system. There is no place here for carefree playing with socialism, with socialist State power.[35]

In many respects, the diagnosis drawn up by a team of German authors in spring 1989 with an eye to the Federal Republic, applies to developments in the GDR as well. Gorbachev's reform policy, and the fact that, for the first time since the GDR came into existence, a Soviet politician was being regarded by the population as a bearer of hope and an agent for change had, in view of the strategic position of the "frontline State" in the eastern alliance, to have particularly far-reaching consequences:

> Under the influence of glasnost and perestroika, both certainties and enemy images are collapsing. This new unclarity that has come out of a world of upheaval includes hopes as well as doubts and uncertainties. Everything is coming to be seen in a new light, and it is hard to say whether, in this illumination from afar, it is hope or irritation that has the upper hand.[36]

Conversely, it is true for the Soviet Union that the shape of relationships with the GDR belongs among the issues that were controversial well before the SED regime lost its hold on the GDR. A memorandum by social scientist Vyacheslav Dashichev, head of the foreign policy section of the Moscow Institute for the Economy of the World Socialist System, available to the Soviet leadership previous to Gorbachev's visit to the Federal Republic in the spring of 1989, gave an extremely sharp critique of the SED leadership along with a recommendation not to turn the maintenance of socialism in the GDR into dogma:

> The regime that has come into being in the GDR could and can exist, politically and economically, only if isolated from the FRG, and supported on violence against its own population. Among the pillars of its existence were the cultivation of outdated dogmas and the maintenance of an enemy image in the form of West German imperialism.

35. Otto Reinhold, "Überlegungen in einem Beitrag für Radio DDR am 19. August 1989," in *Blätter für deutsche und internationale Politik*, 10, 1989, 1175.
36. *Fernaufklärung, Glasnost und die bundesdeutsche Linke*, (Cologne: Verlag Kiepenheuer & Witsch), 1989, 9.

The ideas of the common European house, openness to the outside world, glasnost, the rights to freedom of the individual, are alien to the power structure of the GDR that has come into being, and dangerous for it. For it, certain tensions in East-West relationships are advantageous, since they allow justification of the course toward isolation and demarcation from the FRG . . . .

The new Europe can come about only in a broad consensus of all its States and peoples. It is completely clear that unity, peace and stability will prevail in it only once a dividing line between East and West no longer runs through the heart of the continent, through Germany and through Berlin, and the German people secures the possibility of determining its fate itself in peace and in mutual understanding with all the neighbouring peoples.[37]

Barely a year later, many of the objectives set out in this concept have become reality. The Soviet Union, in renouncing its victor rights over Germany, has abandoned the last remaining token of its dominance in Eastern Europe and has made its peace with Germany. However, what Federal Chancellor Brandt stated precisely twenty years earlier, at the signing of the Moscow Treaty, applies to the Kohl-Gorbachev agreement of 16 July 1990 as well: "Nothing is being lost through this treaty that had not been played away long ago anyway."

Declaration by Federal Chancellor Helmut Kohl on the outcome of the talks with President Gorbachev of 16 July 1990 (extract)

Firstly:
The unification of Germany covers the Federal Republic of Germany, the GDR and the whole of Berlin.

Secondly:
With restoration of Germany's unity, the four-power rights and responsibilities in relation to Germany as a whole and to Berlin come to an end. United Germany will at the time of unification secure complete, unrestricted sovereignty.

Thirdly:
United Germany can, in exercise of its full and unrestricted sovereignty,

---

37. Vyacheslav Dashichev, "Das gemeinsame Europäische Haus und die deutsche Frage," in *Der Spiegel*, 6, 1990, 150ff.

itself decide freely whether and to which alliances it will belong. This is in accordance with the spirit and the letter of the CSCE Final Act . . . .

Fourthly:

United Germany concludes a bilateral treaty with the Soviet Union on accomplishment of the withdrawal of troops from the GDR which, as the Soviet leadership has stated, should be completed within three to four years . . . .

For that period, a transition agreement on the effects of the introduction of the Deutschmark shall also be concluded.

Fifthly:

For the duration of the presence of Soviet troops on the territory of the present GDR, no NATO structures will be extended into that territory. Articles 5 and 6 of the NATO Treaty shall on unification immediately apply to the whole territory of united Germany.

Sixthly:

Non-integrated units of the Bundeswehr, that is, territorial defense units, can immediately upon unification of Germany be stationed in the territory of the present GDR and in Berlin.

Seventhly:

For the duration of the presence of Soviet troops on the territory of the present GDR, according to our conceptions the troops of the three Western powers should remain in Berlin. The Federal Government will ask the three Western powers for that and propose an agreement to that effect to them. For the continued presence of the Western armed forces, a legal basis must be created through an agreement between the government of united Germany and the three powers. We assume as a matter of course that the numbers and equipment of these troops will not be more than at present.

Eighthly:

Following withdrawal of Soviet troops from the territory of the present GDR and Berlin, NATO integrated troops may also be stationed in that part of Germany, though without nuclear-capable delivery systems. Foreign troops and nuclear weapons shall not be moved there.

Ninthly:

The Federal Government declares its willingness to give a declaration of commitment, in the current Vienna negotiations, to reduce the armed forces of the united Germany to a personnel strength of 370,000 within three to four years. This reduction shall start with the entry into force of the first Vienna Agreement. This means that if the existing nominal strength of the Bundeswehr and the National People's Army are combined, the armed forces of the future united Germany will be reduced by 45 percent.

Tenthly:
United Germany will renounce the manufacture, possession and availability of atomic, biological and chemical weapons and remain a member of the non-proliferation treaty.

In this settlement, the Soviet Union abandoned its ideas of a German hybrid position: that of neutrality, the "French solution" of leaving the NATO military structure or a dual membership in the two systems of pacts that would have been contradictory from a security-policy viewpoint. Extending the link with the West to united Germany was also the best guarantee against Germany becoming, like a loose cannon on deck, a rogue political quantity in central Europe. It expands the Federal Republic of Germany's key position at the center of Europe — until now as a frontline State in the event of war, but in the future also as a bridge to Eastern Europe — to the former GDR as well, assigning to the whole of Germany the role of a major pillar of European security.

The Soviet Union's legal titles vis-à-vis the GDR, in particular its right to station troops there, thus became obsolete. While the USSR's treaties with Hungary and Czechoslovakia provided an actual legal basis for the stationing of troops, the presence of Soviet troops in the GDR and the former German territories of Poland was based solely on the victor's right, under the international law of war, to occupy the territory of the vanquished people. The stationing agreements with these two countries, regulated only specific questions, such as that of civil or criminal liability, and with respect to the GDR applied only to the separate contingents — including Soviet ones — of the United Command of the Warsaw Pact States.

The Soviet Union had explicitly retained original victor's rights in the so-called Sovereignty Treaty with the GDR of 20 September 1955. Even in June 1989, when the "Group of Soviet Armed Forces in Germany" was renamed the "Group of Soviet Armed Forces in the West" (and not "in the GDR"), this measure was accompanied by a statement that neither the 1955 Treaty nor the rights and responsibilities of the four powers would be affected thereby.

Treaty on Relations Between the German Democratic Republic and the Union of Soviet Socialist Republics of 20 September 1955

Article 4: The Soviet troops at present stationed on the territory of the German Democratic Republic in accordance with existing international agreements shall for the present remain in the German Democratic Republic on terms to be set in an additional agreement between the government of the German Democratic Republic and the government of the Soviet Union.

The Soviet troops temporarily stationed on the territory of the German Democratic Republic shall not interfere in the internal affairs of the German Democratic Republic nor in the country's social and political life.

By contrast, the "sovereignty declaration" of 25 March 1954 appears in quite a new light today. In it the Soviet government stated that it would be guided "unfailingly by the endeavor to contribute to the settlement of the German problem in accord with the interests of peace and of the securing of Germany's national reunification on a democratic basis." Certainly, what has now become a reality — practical measures "for the rapprochement of East and West Germany" and the holding of "free all-German elections" — was then determined by the tactical motive of Moscow presenting itself as the proponent of the Germans' national aspirations; nevertheless, it remained a document valid in international law. The GDR since then possessed a legal title that became relevant in 1990: according to the sovereignty declaration it would "possess the freedom to decide at its own discretion on its internal and external affairs, including relations with West Germany."

Declaration by the Government of the USSR on the granting of sovereignty to the German Democratic Republic, 25 March 1954 (extract)

The Government of the Soviet Union will be guided unfailingly by the endeavour to contribute to the settlement of the German problem in accord with the interests of the consolidation of peace and the securing of Germany's national reunification on a democratic basis.

These goals shall be served by practical measures for the rapprochement of East and West Germany, the holding of free all-German elections and the conclusion of a peace treaty with Germany . . . .

1. The Soviet Union shall maintain the same relations with the German Democratic Republic as with other sovereign States.

The German Democratic Republic shall possess the freedom to decide at its own discretion on its internal and external affairs, including relations with West Germany.

2.   The Soviet Union shall in the German Democratic Republic retain the functions connected with the guaranteeing of security and resulting from the commitments arising for the Soviet Union from the Four-Power Agreement . . . .

In the past, the Soviet Union's reserved rights had been brought to bear via the inclusion of the GDR in the Eastern military alliance as well. The Warsaw Pact of 14 May 1955 constituted, not merely *de facto* but also *de iure*, an unequal treaty for the GDR, because at that time it was not fully sovereign in the question of deciding its security policy. By contrast with other member States it had, to all appearances, been subjected to decisions of other members even as far as fulfillment of its assistance obligations was concerned. Whereas all non-German versions of the Warsaw Pact treaty of 14 May 1955 stipulated that each participant State has to afford its allies the assistance that "it" considers necessary, in the German version it is assistance that "they" consider necessary that is required. The USSR *de facto* claimed for its troops on East German territory a quasi-sovereign immunity, with no limitations on their ability to intervene in East German internal affairs.

Warsaw Pact Treaty of 14 May 1955 (translation of extract from the German version)

Article 4: In the event of an armed attack in Europe on one or more of the States Party to the Treaty by any State or group of States, each State of the Treaty shall, in the exercise of the right of individual or collective self-defense, in accordance with Article 51 of the United Nations Charter, afford the State or States so attacked immediate assistance, individually and in agreement with the other States Party to the Treaty, by all means they consider necessary, including the use of armed force.

The peculiar position of the GDR within the Eastern bloc was even stipulated in constitutional law. East Germany was the only country in the world that in its very constitution had allied itself "irrevocably" with the Soviet Union and had declared itself an inseparable component part of the socialist community of states.

At the same time, it was also the only State within its alliance that lacked an independent national identity within the confines of its own frontiers.

Constitution of the German Democratic Republic of 9 April 1968, amended 7 October 1974 (extract)

Article 6(2): The German Democratic Republic is allied forever and irrevocably with the Union of Socialist Soviet Republics. The close and brotherly alliance with it guarantees the people of the German Democratic Republic further progress on the path of socialism and peace.

The German Democratic Republic is an inseparable component part of the socialist community of states. True to the principles of socialist internationalism, it contributes to its strengthening, fosters and develops friendship, mutual collaboration, and mutual aid with all states of the socialist community.

The Soviet Union's rights and responsibilities for Berlin and for Germany as a whole eventually became — having been a taboo subject for decades — a topic for debate in the GDR as well. In the journal of the East Berlin Institute for International Politics and Economics (IPW), two security-policy experts set forth in early 1990 "Considerations on the GDR's Foreign Policy Interests;" these throw light on many frustrations of the past:

> The further shaping of the relationship between the GDR and the USSR as a political alliance within the framework of European security and European State relationships presupposes a higher level of political coordination on a basis of equality of rights. The Soviet forces in the GDR must be drastically cut to the level that is actually militarily necessary and defined unambiguously in nature as allied forces. At the same time, the GDR could bear a part of the stationing expenses. A move should be made toward genuine military integration between the remaining Soviet forces and those of the GDR (and as far as possible with integration with those from Poland and Czechoslovakia too). That would make defense functions more effective and mean far lower costs as well as greater leeway for disarmament maneuvers. At the same time, the mutual military and political obligations and reliances and mutual trust would be strengthened, not least as one of the bases for the activation of German-German relationships.

In view of the difference in interests that naturally exists between the USSR and the GDR for geostrategic, economic and political reasons, it is in view of the existential importance of this relationship for our government absolutely necessary to create an effective permanent mechanism to overcome these differences.[38]

The International Context of the Federal Republic

In contrast to the communist-governed GDR of the Honecker era, the Federal Republic saw Allied responsibility for Germany as a whole as the last bracket holding the German nation together, the last link in international law spanning both parts of Germany. The basic decision in favor of the West, expressed in the set of treaties in the 1950s, was taken on the assumption that the Western powers would promote reunification. Restoration of Germany's national unity was not excluded in any of the treaties then signed, although initially, in view of the East-West confrontation, freedom for at least one part of the German nation took precedence over unity.

What had to be decided at that time was whether the Federal Republic was prepared to be involved in the military defense of Western Europe and willing to accept an alliance-type link with the West. Bound up with this was the prospect of ending the occupation regime and securing sovereignty, burdened with a few remaining reserved rights. The process in the course of which these decisions were taken began in the spring of 1951 and ended four years later. Until 1990, the treaties of Bonn and Paris determined the Federal Republic's position in the Western community of States and in the community of international law.

On 26 May 1952 the "Convention on Relations Between the Three Powers and the Federal Republic of Germany" was signed in Bonn. Federal Chancellor Adenauer immediately, and unofficially, gave it the punchier name of "The Germany Treaty." It was coupled with the "Treaty establishing a European Defense Community" (EDC) signed a few days later in Paris. Ratification of this second treaty failed after a prolonged debate in the French National Assembly in August 1954.

---

38. André Brie and Wolfram Wallraf, "Überlegungen zur auBenpolitischen Interessenlage der DDR," in *IPW-Bericht*, 1, 1990, 28.

Only a hastily improvised substitute solution in the autumn of 1954, providing for the Federal Republic's direct accession to NATO and doing without the EDC, made it possible for the "Germany Treaty" to be signed once again on 23 October 1954, in an abbreviated and — from the German viewpoint — improved version, as part of the "Paris Treaties." In May 1955 it was ratified by all the treaty partners and came into force. Only then, after long years of occupation, did the Federal Republic gain the sovereignty it had striven for, although its international freedom of action continued to be restricted by the reserved rights of the Allies in relation to Berlin and Germany as a whole.

Convention on Relations Between the Three Powers and the Federal Republic of Germany (Germany Treaty), as amended on 23 October 1954 (extract)

Article 1(2): The Federal Republic shall have accordingly the full authority of a sovereign State over its internal and external affairs.

Article 2: In view of the international situation, which has so far prevented the reunification of Germany and the conclusion of a peace settlement, the Three Powers retain the rights and responsibilities, heretofore exercised or held by them, relating to Berlin and to Germany as a whole, including the reunification of Germany and a peace settlement.

Article 7(1): The Signatory States are agreed that an essential aim of their common policy is a peace settlement for the whole of Germany, freely negotiated between Germany and her former enemies, which should lay the foundation for a lasting peace. They further agree that the final determination of the boundaries of Germany must await such a settlement.

(2): Pending the peace settlement, the Signatory States will cooperate to achieve, by peaceful means, their common aim of a reunified Germany enjoying a liberal-democratic constitution, like that of the Federal Republic, and integrated within the European Community.

(3): (deleted)

(4): The Three Powers will consult with the Federal Republic on all matters involving the exercise of their rights relating to Germany as a whole.

The Three Powers' reservation concerning "Germany as a whole" did not establish any exclusive powers for the Allies, and was moreover subject to restrictions in content. The common goal of the four signatory States, indicated in Article 7(2), was a "re-unified Germany enjoying a liberal-democratic constitution, like that of the Federal Republic, and integrated within the European Community." This statement took on an unsuspected topicality as German unification drew nearer. In the view of diplomat and international lawyer Wilhelm Grewe, then prominently involved in the negotiations concerning the end of the Occupation Statute, it could not be deduced from this in any binding way that Germany as a whole would also have to remain in NATO:

> What was meant was the general linkage with the West of the Federal Republic, which was not equated with NATO membership. This was also reasonable because no one believed that the Soviet Union would ever tolerate a shift in NATO's military frontier up to the Oder-Neisse line.
> Membership of a united Germany too in the Atlantic Alliance — perhaps a NATO altered by the changes now under way — is certainly the best solution and the one that most promotes European security. Were it however to be made a binding *conditio sine qua non* of uni-fication, the notion would be strengthened among Germans that the Western partners are concerned primarily with a control system direct-ed against them — not exactly favourable to the cohesion and solidari-ty of an alliance community.[39]

NATO membership not only brought the Federal Republic the termination of occupation rights, but also guaranteed it a voice in the Western system. "Defense contribution," as a circumlocution for the fact that the Federal Republic would again have soldiers, characterized two aspects that were important in the 1950s and are still important today. On the one hand, the phrase made clear the limits to the kind of military power being conceded to the Germans, and, on the other, it indicated that the Federal Republic could not defend itself on its own, but would need the contributions of others to its — to the common — defense. In reflections on the connec-tions between the link with the West and the postwar system, just before the Twenty-Seventh Strategy Conference of February 1990, Josef Joffe, the security expert of the *Süddeutsche Zeitung*, published in Munich, came to the following conclusions:

39. Wilhelm Grewe, "Konföderation, Grenzfrage und Friedensregelung. Die Grundbegriffe der Deutschlandpolitik im Lichte des Wandels im Osten. Neue Perspektiven für altbekannte Probleme," in *Die Welt*, 21 December 1990.

The postwar order that has been collapsing since 9 November served, after all, not only to contain the Soviet power but also to restrain Germany, the heavyweight in the center of the continent, which in view of its power and its position can shift things for the better (as after 1945) or the worse (as before 1945). When the Soviets complete their withdrawal, a power vacuum will arise in Central Europe, which the Germans will fill — whether they want to or not.

For such a country there can be no neutrality. Left to its own devices (which is the essence of neutrality) it will have to try to control the circumstances around it, or else others will try to control this country. This role was spared the Federal Republic, by contrast to the Reich under Bismarck or under Hitler — to the profit of the Germans and the relief of their neighbours. The brilliant aspect of the postwar order was that it did not surround the Germans but fitted them in. It offered the Germans a refuge and a community that took away from them the fear of encirclement and from their neighbours the fear of an onslaught.

The postwar order took the sting out of the "curse of geography": the fact that it is now falling apart is one reason the more for saving the best structures of the old system into the new times in such a way that Europe and Germany can really grow together.[40]

The Federal Republic's freedom of action is limited in the context of the NATO Treaty above all by the fact that all armed forces of the Member States stationed in the area controlled by Supreme Allied Command in Europe (SACEUR) come under the command of SACEUR or another competent NATO command authority. By agreeing to this procedure before accession to the NATO Treaty, the Federal Republic from the outset renounced national command over the use of the Bundeswehr in the event of war. With the NATO membership of Germany as a whole, as accepted by Moscow, the question of the units of the Territorial Army under national command also gained in importance, since they — by contrast with the Bundeswehr units integrated in NATO — could, immediately upon unification, be stationed in the territory of the former GDR and in Berlin.

Resolution of the NATO Council on the outcome of the Four and Nine Power Conferences, 22 October 1954 (extract)

40. Josef Joffe, "Welche Nach-Nachkriegsordnung?" in *Süddeutsche Zeitung*, 5 February 1990.

IV a) All forces of NATO countries stationed on the Continent of Europe
        shall be placed under the authority of SACEUR, with the excep-
        tion of those which NATO has recognised or will recognise as
        suitable to remain under a national command.
     c) The location of such forces shall be determined by SACEUR after
        consultation and agreement with the national authorities concerned.
     d) Such forces shall not be redeployed on the continent nor used
        operationally on the Continent without his consent, subject to
        appropriate political guidance from the North Atlantic Council.
     g) The forces ... shall be inspected by SACEUR.

The simultaneous accession of the Federal Republic to the North
Atlantic Treaty and to the West European Union (WEU) set the
seal on the basic direction of Bonn's foreign policy, which within
a few years received full support from all the major parties in
the Bundestag, and from the SPD opposition in 1960. The West
European Union, which developed out of the Brussels Treaty of
1948, was modified and completed by protocol in 1954; it is
significant primarily because it commits the seven member States
(Great Britain, France, the three Benelux countries, West Germany,
and Italy) to giving each other automatic assistance, thus going
further than the NATO treaty. This advantage is nevertheless
restricted by the fact that the WEU as an organization has no
military planning organization and thus would not be in a position
either to plan or to carry out joint action by the forces of its
member States.

The North Atlantic Treaty itself was suitable neither in overall
conception, nor given its signatory States, for incorporating arms
limitation and control arrangements that did not discriminate
against the Federal Republic; on the contrary, Article 3 of the
Treaty bound the signatory States to increased armament. The
arms restrictions on the Federal Republic, desired particularly by
France, were worded in protocol no. III and annexed to the WEU
Treaty as a voluntary self-limitation, although in a way that does
exclude unilateral withdrawal.

The Federal Republic's self-restraint covered in particular the
unconditional renunciation of the manufacture of atomic, biological, or chemical weapons (so-called ABC weapons) on its territory,
which was later confirmed in the Nuclear Non-Proliferation Treaty
of 1968 and in the Convention banning biological weapons of
1972, and extended to possession of such weapons. Conventional-

arms limitations on manufacture of guided missiles, warships, and strategic bombers were agreed conditionally, that is, subject to possible amendment by WEU Council decision, in 1954, but have since been removed as a discrimination against Germany that is now anachronistic.

The NATO Forces Convention of 19 June 1951 and the additional agreement thereto regulate the legal conditions for the accommodation of Allied forces in the Federal Republic, but does not regulate how many and what kind of troops may be stationed there. The only published legal basis for such a stationing of troops is the Presence Convention of 23 October 1954, which was initially concluded with the United States, Britain, and France; Belgium, Denmark, Canada, Luxembourg, and the Netherlands acceded later.

Convention on the Presence of Foreign Forces in the Federal Republic of Germany, 23 October 1954 (extract)

Art. 1(1) From the entry into force of arrangements for the German Defense Contribution, forces of the same nationality and effective strength as at that time may be stationed in the Federal Republic.

(2) The effective strength of the forces stationed in the Federal Republic pursuant to paragraph 1 of this Article may at any time be increased with the consent of the Government of the Federal Republic of Germany.

(3) Additional forces of the States party to the present Convention may enter and remain in the Federal territory with the consent of the Government of the Federal Republic of Germany for training purposes in accordance with the procedures applicable to forces assigned to the Supreme Allied Commander, Europe, provided that such forces do not remain there for more than thirty days at any one time.

Art. 3(1) The present Convention shall expire with the conclusion of a German peace settlement or if at an earlier time the Signatory States agree that the development of the international situation justifies new arrangements.

The exchange of notes accompanying the Franco-German Government Agreement on stationing rights and the status of French troops in Germany of 21 November 1966 — a consequence of France's withdrawal from the integrated NATO structure — again made it clear that the Alliance was not the sole legal basis for the presence of Allied troops on the territory of the Federal Republic. Alongside the stationing agreed to by treaty, there was stationing on the basis of the Allied reserved right, confirmed in the Germany Treaty of 1954; thus, restrictions tied to German agreement existed only as regards the exercise of the right to a presence. In a detailed study of the German defense contribution in the context of the rearmament debate of the early 1980s, Heidelberg international lawyer Torsten Stein stated:

> While, thus, the Three Powers wished to tie exercise of the stationing right, which continued to be based on reservations as to occupation rights, to agreement with the Federal Republic, this was not intended to go so far that a refusal of German agreement could render this stationing right illusory; for here the alternative consists not in simply withdrawing the units but instead, without further query, there would be armament or rearmament. . . . This perception may have contributed to the formulation on the German side that the extent to which the stationing of particular weapons was dependent on assent by the host country concerned was ultimately a matter for political decision. The political decision may also lie in not putting the question of the assent requirement in so decisive a way as to provoke answers that would not be congenial to the political climate.[41]

Indeed, the Federal Republic had a special position in the political sphere in the Western Alliance. In a Three-Power declaration of 3 October 1954, which all NATO States confirmed, initially on 22 October 1954, the Federal Republic's partners included Berlin (West) in the area protected by the Alliance, and committed themselves to reunification.

Since then, the position of the German question in resolutions of the Western Alliance has changed several times; nevertheless, those commitments can be seen as the tradeoff for the Federal Republic's accession to the Western Alliance system. If the passages on Germany in North Atlantic Council resolutions initially dealt with the problem of disarmament and European security, after the Harmel report of December 1967 the connection between the German question and the European peace order came to the fore. Since the conclusion of the Eastern Treaties in the

---

41. Torsten Stein, "Die Verträge über den deutschen Verteidigungsbeitrag," in: *Deutschlandvertrag, westliches Bündnis und Wiedervereinigung*, (Berlin: Duncker & Humblot), 1985, 99f.

early 1970s the Alliance has, at irregular intervals, spoken on the question, using formulations from that set of treaties and contained in the notes on German unity. In the 1980s, the twenty-fifth anniversary of the Paris Treaties, and five years later the fortieth anniversary of the foundation of the Alliance, offered the occasion to highlight the German question.

On 31 May 1989, in a speech in Mainz one day after the NATO jubilee summit, U.S. President Bush conceded to the West Germans that they were not only "friends and allies" but, along with the Americans, "partners in leadership." The viability of this new role has been substantiated in the negotiations on the international legal framework and the general political conditions for Germany's national unification.

For the United States, the priority was to remove a situation of political vacillation in the heart of Europe as quickly as possible, and at the same time to guarantee an American troop presence in the Old World. Both goals were secured when the Soviet Union assented to NATO membership for the whole of Germany. This also explains the overwhelmingly positive response to the German-Soviet Agreement of 16 July 1990. Moreover, President Bush did important preparatory work preliminary to this round of negotiations.

At the Washington superpower summit, the Americans presented a polished, coherent concept aimed at harmonizing the Western solution to the alliance question with Soviet security interests. Bush's "Nine Points" of 4 June already contained the essential assurances of German and Western self-limitation that then opened up the road to the NATO solution: the fixing of upper national limits for troops in the central region of Europe, including Germany, at the Vienna negotiations on Conventional Armed Forces in Europe; no stationing of NATO troops or arms on the territory of the then GDR; a transitional solution for a continued presence of Soviet troops in the GDR; economic agreements between Germany and the Soviet Union; takeover of costs for a Soviet troop presence and assistance with their resettlement.

An additional impetus to Soviet agreement came from the NATO summit in early July. The "London declaration on a changed North Atlantic Alliance" of 6 July, providing both for a downgrading of the importance of nuclear weapons and a restructuring of NATO troops and a nonaggression pact with the East, while it mainly just offered options, was enough for the Kremlin to save face. Barely two months later, at long last, the conditions had been created for solving a problem regarded for forty years as insoluble: to end the division of Germany in agreement between West and East.

Certainly, the negotiators in the Two-plus-Four talks on the "external aspects" of German unity were pressed by the events in Germany, which continually nullified all ideas about the timing of the stages of unification. But it took not only a perception of historical necessities but also the good will of all those involved for the "Treaty on the Final Settlement with respect to Germany," celebrated by the media as a "diplomatic world record," to be signed on 12 September 1990 in Moscow — only seven months after the Ottawa conference.

Treaty on the Final Settlement with respect to Germany, 12 September 1990 (analysis and text extracts)

The Two-plus-Four Treaty consists of ten articles and an agreed minute. The preamble gives an assurance that the security interests of each of the parties will be taken into account. Germany, "as a State with definitive borders" will contribute to peace and stability in Europe. In recognition of the fact that "thereby, and with the unification of Germany as a democratic and peaceful State, the rights and responsibilities of the Four Powers relating to Berlin and to Germany as a whole lose their function," Germany was to become a sovereign power.

The Treaty calls the existing "borders of the German Democratic Republic and the Federal Republic of Germany" the definitive external frontiers of Germany. Germany and Poland will "confirm the existing border between them in a treaty that is binding under international law" (Article 1). It reaffirms the renunciation by united Germany of "the manufacture and possession of and control over nuclear, biological and chemical weapons" and embodies the assurance that German armed forces will be reduced to 370,000 over four years (Article 3); it announces that Germany and the Soviet Union wish to regulate the terms and duration of the presence of Soviet forces and their withdrawal by treaty. Withdrawal is to be completed by the end of 1994 (Article 4).

Until Soviet withdrawal, "only German territorial defense units not integrated into the alliance structures" will be stationed on the territory of the ex-GDR; at German request, until then French, British and American forces will "remain stationed in Berlin by agreement to this effect." After Soviet withdrawal, German forces integrated into the alliance may also be stationed in the ex-GDR, "but without nuclear weapon carriers." Foreign forces and nuclear weapons and their delivery vehicles will not be "stationed in that part of Germany or deployed there" (Article 5).

The Treaty assures united Germany of the right to "belong to alliances, with all the rights and duties arising" (Article 6). It provides that the four powers hereby terminate "their rights and responsibilities" in Germany; accordingly, united Germany has "full sovereignty over its internal and external affairs" (Article 7). The Treaty enters into force with deposition of the instruments of ratification (Article 9).

Thus, a coincidence in time between national unity and the final abolition of the rights of the Four Powers was not totally achieved; but it was agreed in Moscow that the foreign ministers would, on 1 October 1990, before the start of the CSCE meeting in New York, sign a document laying down that the reserved rights and responsibilities of the four victorious powers of the Second World War would be set aside at the time of completion of Germany's national unification on 3 October 1990. The "sovereignty treaty" signed in Moscow and entered into force on 15 March 1991 is not conceived as a peace treaty settlement, yet with its definitive frontier arrangements and political provisions it incorporated elements of a classical peace treaty.

An Alliance without full membership for the Germans would no longer be the linchpin holding the United States and Europe together. And the CSCE alone, which Bonn's Foreign Minister Genscher has at times suggested as a substitute for the Alliance, would not, in the long term, have been able to have transatlantic linking effect. There were, however, also warning voices from the United States saying that the Alliance has paid too high a price for the membership of the whole of Germany. Henry Kissinger, who spoke unambiguously in favor of German unification at a time when many American experts still saw it as endangering Gorbachev's political chances of survival, justified this concern as follows:

> Despite the general euphoria at the Kohl-Gorbachev agreement regarding NATO membership for a united Germany, I cannot help being concerned about the fundamental cohesion of the West. Against a widespread opinion, and at the risk of paining good friends, I must confess that I have reluctantly come to the conclusion that there has been quicker progress with German unification than with solving the new problems the West is confronted with . . . . There is now the danger that German membership in NATO may have been purchased through renunciation of the military substance of the Alliance; that it will henceforth play a political role only within the Conference on Security and Cooperation.

If present trends continue, NATO will at best be the framework for a unilateral American nuclear guarantee, allowing the various European nations, and particularly Germany, to pursue national goals on their own.[42]

Just twenty years earlier President Nixon's then security adviser had given expression in a memorandum to his concern that *Ostpolitik* by a divided Germany might in the hands of unscrupulous people become a new form of classical German nationalism; so here, in reference to the whole of Germany, there reappears one of the suspicions that has confronted the Federal Republic at regular intervals, and still does: ties to the West are interpreted as a provisional feature and not as a fundamental decision of German policy after the Second World War.

Germany According to the 1990 Frontiers

Mistrust of the long-term intentions of Germans was also the reason for the stubbornness with which the Poles, until the decisive Paris Round of the Two-plus-Four Talks on 17 July 1990, pressed for ever-new guarantees on the border question. Forty-five years to the day after the start of the Potsdam Conference among Churchill, Truman, and Stalin — which had Germany as its object, with no influence, and a Polish delegation under CP leader Bierut — Poland's first noncommunist postwar foreign minister sat with representatives of the Federal Republic and the GDR; and, as in 1945, the Oder-Neisse border question was again on the negotiating table. The disagreement as to Germany and its borders that had arisen at the Potsdam Conference, riddled as it was with serious conflicts among the Big Three, could not be dispelled until that moment under the Two-plus-Four umbrella. Only now could there be unanimity as to the other "external aspects" of German unification.

The code word for the preparation of the Potsdam Conference was "Terminal," and in its own way, the Paris Conference has now become the "terminus" of the development that had emerged in outline in the course of serious intermediate talks. The path

42. Henry Kissinger, "L'OTAN risque de devenir une coquille vide," in *Paris-Match*, 2 August 1990.

toward that point was by no means straight; but the agreement reached in Paris on Germany's future frontiers removed one of the last obstacles to the conclusion of the Two-plus-Four talks in Moscow.

Resolution of the Two-plus-Four Conference in Paris on the "definitive nature of Germany's frontiers," 17 July 1990

1. United Germany will include the territories of the Federal Republic of Germany, the German Democratic Republic and the whole of Berlin. Its external frontiers will definitively be the frontiers of the Federal Republic of Germany on the day of entry into force of the final settlement. Confirmation of the definitive nature of Germany's frontiers is an essential contribution to the peace order in Europe.
2. United Germany and the Polish Republic shall confirm the existing border between them in a treaty binding in international law.
3. United Germany has no territorial claims on other States, nor will it raise any in future.
4. The governments of the Federal Republic of Germany and of the German Democratic Republic will ensure that the constitution of united Germany will contain no provisions incompatible with these principles. This applies *mutatis mutandis* to the provisions laid down in the preamble and Article 23(2) and 146 of the Basic Law for the Federal Republic of Germany.
5. The governments of the USSR, the USA, the United Kingdom and France have formally received the relevant commitments and declarations by the government of the Federal Republic of Germany and of the German Democratic Republic, and find that their implementation will confirm the definitive nature of the frontiers of Germany.

But 1990 was also the anniversary of two further events, each of them milestones of German-Polish reconciliation after World War II. The Federal Republic could look back on forty years of the Charter of Germans Expelled from the Homeland and on twenty years of the Warsaw Treaty; the GDR on forty years of its own border settlement as enshrined in the Görlitz Treaty.

The Charter, adopted on 5 August 1950 in Stuttgart, was scarcely noticed abroad at the time; worry and concern over the Korean war, which had broken out a few months earlier, occupied people's minds far more. But the content of the document, in which thirty elected

representatives of expellee associations and East German homeland associations declared their renunciation of vengeance for the
suffering that had come upon them, affected a sixth of the West
German population. They also spoke for their fellows in the GDR,
who numbered over 4 million in 1950, even if these people were
not allowed to call themselves either expellees or refugees, but
were instead known as "resettlers."

At the FRG's first census in September 1950, out of the 47.7
million inhabitants of Federal Territory (then without the Saar),
7.9 million were listed as expellees who on 1 September 1939 (the
day war began) had been living in the Prussian east provinces or
outside the 1937 Reich frontiers. The expellees were not only
distributed in variable proportions over the Federal Länder (33
percent of the inhabitants of Schleswig-Holstein, only 5.1 percent
in the Rhineland Palatinate), they also differed very strongly from
the indigenous population as to occupation. Against 46 percent
of locals, 75 percent were workers — clear downward mobility
by comparison with the prewar period, quite apart from the loss
of possessions as a result of expulsion.

The economic integration of expellees is undoubtedly one of the
most outstanding achievements of German postwar history. One
need think only of the worldwide flows of expellees and refugees
today, or of the Palestine refugees, in order to see and to evaluate
how such problems can become fuel for social discord. But it
should also be recalled that concern for the feelings of the expellees
and their decades spent demanding recognition of the fundamental
right to a homeland (not only freedom of movement) has till very
recently played a considerable part in the tug-of-war over the
definitive character of the German-Polish border.

Charter of Germans expelled from their homelands, 5 August 1950
(extracts)

1. We, the expellees, renounce vengeance and retaliation. For us, this is
a solemn and sacred resolve in memory of the endless suffering which has
been brought to mankind especially in the last decade.

2. We will support with all our power every initiative directed towards
the creation of a united Europe, in which its peoples can live without
fear or compulsion.

3. We will through hard and unremitting labour play our part in
rebuilding Germany and Europe.

We have lost our homeland. Displaced persons are strangers on this earth. God placed people in their own lands. To separate people by force from the land of their birth is to kill them in spirit.

We have suffered such a fate and survived it. Therefore we feel ourselves called upon to demand the right to one's homeland be recognized and acted upon as a God-given basic right of humanity.

The border question was controversial for forty-five years not only in internal German policy. The "1937 frontiers" drawn at Versailles, which the Germans had never been able to accept, became a weapon already in 1945 and increasingly thereafter in the Cold War between East and West, between the victorious powers that now were at loggerheads. The contradiction, given solid embodiment in the Potsdam Agreement between the declared temporary nature of Polish administration until final determination in a peace settlement and the merciless definitiveness of the mass expulsion of the German population of those territories, for decades nourished false hopes on this side and unjustified fears on the other side of the Oder and Neisse.

In spring 1947, after Western hopes of averting the Sovietization of Poland had been smashed, U.S. Foreign Minister Marshall and his British colleague Bevin called in Moscow for revision of the provisional borders in favor of Germany, while Stalin's Soviet Union was able to increasingly play the part of sole guarantor even vis-à-vis the noncommunist Poles. The Note from the United States to the People's Republic of Poland of 11 August 1960, that clarified the U.S. position, also made satisfaction of the Polish desire for definitive settlement of the border question dependent on the "reunification of Germany in peace and freedom," which then seemed unacceptable to the East.

When the GDR, in a Treaty with the People's Republic of Poland on 6 July 1950 in Zgorzelec, the part of Görlitz that had become Polish, gave quasi-recognition to the "untouchable frontier of peace and friendship" along the Oder and the Lusatian Neisse (according to its wording, the agreement had only declaratory significance) it was done under Soviet pressure. In September 1946, later GDR Justice Minister Max Fechner was still stating as top Berlin candidate of the SED that his party would "oppose any reduction of German territory" and that the eastern frontier was only provisional. Six years after the Görlitz Treaty, in which the GDR felt itself thoroughly entitled to take a position on territorial questions affecting the whole of Germany, East Berlin stressed, on the occasion of the Franco-West German Saar negotiations, that the fate of the Saar was an all-German matter and that unilateral settlement without participation by the GDR was contrary to international law!

Agreement between the Republic of Poland and the German Democratic Republic on the demarcation of the established and existing Polish-German national frontier (Görlitz Treaty), 6 July 1950 (extracts)

The President of the Republic of Poland and the President of the German Democratic Republic

guided by the desire to give expression to the wish for consolidation of general peace and with the intention of making a contribution to the great work of harmonious cooperation among peace-loving peoples...

guided by the desire to stabilize and consolidate their mutual relationships on the basis of the Potsdam Agreement establishing the frontier along the Oder and the Lusatian Neisse...

recognizing that the established and existing frontier is an untouchable border of peace and friendship that does not separate the two peoples but unites them —

have decided to conclude the following agreement...

Article I. The High Contracting Parties state their agreement that the established and existing frontier running along the line west of the town of Swinoujscie and from there along the river Oder to the confluence of the Lusatian Neisse and along the Lusatian Neisse to the Czechoslovak frontier constitutes the national frontier between Poland and Germany.

The Warsaw Treaty concluded between the Federal Republic of Germany and the People's Republic of Poland on 7 December 1970 (cf. Chapter II, p. 42f.) could in turn, twenty years later, become a bone of contention between the Federal German parties because, in contrast to the Görlitz Treaty, the Warsaw Treaty fully respected the rights and responsibilities of the Four Powers relating to "Germany as a whole." After all, it was only when the right of the Allies to determine the external modalities of unification and definitively to lay down the frontiers ended that unrestricted confirmation of the Polish western frontier became possible at all.

This follows clearly from the exchange of notes with the three Western powers on the occasion of initialing of the Treaty.

Note from the Federal Government to the Three Western Powers, 19 November 1970

In the course of the negotiations carried on between the government of the Federal Republic of Germany and the government of the People's Republic of Poland about this Treaty, it has been made clear by the Federal government that the Treaty between the Federal Republic of Germany and the People's Republic of Poland does not affect the rights and responsibilities of the French Republic, the United Kingdom of Great Britain and Northern Ireland, the Union of Soviet Socialist Republics and the United States of America as reflected in the well-known treaties and agreements, nor can it affect them. The Federal government has further pointed out that it can act only in the name of the Federal Republic of Germany.

Yet the Warsaw Treaty would have thoroughly met its objective of clarifying frontier questions for the Federal Republic — not for sovereign Germany as a whole — if in recent debate the form of restriction, rather than the confirmation of the frontier, had not all too often been treated as the real content of the Treaty. This is also the deeper reason for the reserved response that Kohl's November 1989 Ten-Point Plan for Germany encountered, particularly abroad. It lacked a "Point Eleven" on the Polish western frontier, as a journalist of the Bonn daily *Die Welt* accurately pointed out:

> In both home and foreign policy terms, pressure is growing on Federal Chancellor Helmut Kohl to extend his ten-point plan for Germany by an eleventh point — recognition of the Oder-Neisse frontier. In both West and East, this recognition is increasingly being regarded as one of the decisive preconditions for achievement of Germany's right to self-determination. This line is agreed to by such varied politicians as François Mitterrand, Mikhail Gorbachev, Margaret Thatcher, Lech Walesa, Giulio Andreotti and GDR dissident Wolfgang Schnur.
>
> In order to remove the stumbling block of the frontier on the path to German unity, a clear distinction has nevertheless to be drawn between political intent and the legal position. It is indubitable that a

great majority of Germans in the Federal Republic, as in the GDR, does not question the present Polish western frontier, still less wishes to endanger restoration of unity on its account. Bonn's task is to cast this in political form without detriment to German legal positions.[43]

In the ensuing months there was fierce German-Polish controversy on the border question, in which influential voices from other countries could be heard taking positions for or against this hesitation by the Federal Chancellor. Here the question was again the old one of who, in international law, had the right to state the definitive renunciation of the former eastern territories of the German Reich called for by Poland: the old Federal Republic, which had no border with Poland, or an all-German State formation that could as successor to the Reich or as a subject legally identical with it dispose of the former Reich frontiers and territories? In a lecture to the German Foreign Policy Association in Bonn in early February 1990, Polish Foreign Minister Krzysztof Skubiszewski, who as a professor of international law was well acquainted with the material, presented his country's position.

Talk by the Minister for Foreign Affairs of the Republic of Poland, Prof. Dr. Krzysztof Skubiszewski, on 7 February 1990 in Bonn (extract)

The cause of the whole debate in the Federal Republic and in Europe, in particular among the Western as well as the Eastern neighbours of the Federal Republic, including Poland, lay in the fact that the Federal Chancellor's Ten Point Programme did not in a single word mention the frontiers of the confederation or federation. An important comment in Point 6 of the programme on the — I quote — unrestricted respect for the integrity and security of every State would remove this shortcoming if it referred to the existing frontiers, which was not the case. . . . In the Europe that is growing into unity, this frontier belonged among the important factors of stability. Agreement is possible only in established frontiers and without territorial disputes. Poland has no such territorial disputes with anyone. We have been hearing for years that in the future united Europe, which will be a Europe of freedom, frontiers will lose importance. We do not dispute the correctness of that prophecy. Before then, however, there must be clarity about the frontiers. Their importance

---

43. Bernt Conrad, "Der Grenz-Stein und 'Punkt elf' des Deutschlandplans," in *Die Welt*, 14 December 1989.

will otherwise not become less, and reconciliation with neighbours will not come about.

The Poles' disappointment was particularly great also because representatives of the first noncommunist government, which had existed since September 1989, explicitly favored implementation of the right to self-determination of the German people, even before the German question broke in its utterly unexpected way onto the agenda of world politics on 9 November. For emerging democratic Poland, the end of the Stalinist GDR meant the long-desired political relief on its West, yet sympathy and joy at the fall of the Wall was soon overshadowed by the new uncertainty as to German willingness to recognize Poland's territorial integrity definitively. This split in feelings was expressed on 1 February 1990 by Mieczyslaw Pszon, adviser on German policy to the then Prime Minister Mazowiecki, at the first Berlin meeting of the newly founded "Forum for Germany":

> It cannot be denied that it is the same German people that live on both sides of the Elbe, and they cannot be denied the right to a common life. But we ought not to forget either that Germany has twice in this century set Europe ablaze, and that a Germany that became a power always developed imperial urges. . . . If, then, there is to be reunification, let it be only in the framework of general European political structures with a clear confirmation of the inviolability of the present frontiers. And if the countries that at Helsinki confirmed the territorial structure of Europe are to give their agreement to the reunification of Germany, then a solemn recognition of the permanency of the Oder-Neisse frontier is a precondition for that unification — otherwise removal of the German internal frontier could become the detonator for a general revisionism. . . .
>
> The overcoming of the division is of course an opportunity for Germany, a political, economic and civilizing opportunity. The question is how that opportunity will be used, whether it will become a prospect for Europe.[44]

Despite the reassuring political signals from Bonn, after the GDR elections of March 1990 it became additionally clear from East

---

44. Mieczystaw Pszon, "Die Sicht der europäischen Nachbarn," in Forum für Deutschland, ed., *Die Überwindung der Teilung Europas – eine Perspektive für Deutschland?"* (Bonn: Dokumentation der Tageszeitung *Die Welt*, 1990), 94f.

Berlin that it was not only the frontier question that was worrying the Poles, but also that broad sections of the population had very fundamental fears and apprehensions regarding an economically and politically powerful Germany. On the one hand, many Poles, from their own historical experience, perceived the division of Germany as unnatural. On the other, there was a traumatic fear of the possibly fatal repercussions of unity on Polish national interests, expressed also in opinion surveys in 1990. Of all the European neighbors of the Germans, the Poles felt most threatened by the unification endeavors of their German neighbor, and rejection of it — between 68 and 80 percent — was just as high as was agreement to it among the others.

In view of the danger that in connection with the dynamics of German reunification relations between Bonn and Warsaw could be lastingly impaired, both sides have since made efforts to oppose these tendencies. The fundamental restructuring of the German-Soviet relationship will very soon be followed on the German side by a German-Polish counterpart. The border treaty signed in Warsaw on 14 November 1990 is to be followed by an agreement on broadly-based cooperation that should also take into account the economic disadvantages accruing to Poland from loss of its COMECON partner, the GDR.

The unstable economic, social, and political position of Poland, as it implements the peaceful change in system from real socialism and a State-planned economy to parliamentary democracy and a market economy has certainly played an important part in the revival of national fears against the Germans. Similar considerations apply to the mood in Czechoslovakia, whose Foreign Minister and former spokesman for the civil rights movement Charter 77, Dienstbier, described them in a speech at Harvard University in the spring of 1990.

Speech by Foreign Minister of Czechoslovakia, Jiři Dienstbier, on 16 May 1990 at Harvard (extracts)

Politically, and to a certain extent in the defense sphere too and assuredly in the sphere of the economy, there is an uncertain area, a vacuum it is often called, opening up eastward of Germany. It will perhaps be filled soon economically by a strong united Germany, and in view of the glaring inequality to the detriment of the East European countries in economic respects, that filling could display undeniably neo-colonial traits. But in a situation of economic failure, social disharmony and continued lack of success for the new political structures, Soviet pressure could again appear in this area, should Gorbachev's policy suffer a defeat....

As the Americans filled a power-vacuum in 1947 on the basis of the Marshall Plan, so today they should support the setting up of an all-European security system. It would fill the defense vacuum left by the disintegration of the existing defense system in Central and Eastern Europe. This old system had the military power of the Soviet Union as its basis, but was at the same time subject to the former hegemonistic claims of that great power, now abandoned by the present Soviet leadership. Support for creation of an all-European security system additionally offers the possibility of settling the fears of the neighbours of a future greater Germany, the fears they may nourish of the possibility of a catastrophic development by that State.

Here the connection between European security and the German question becomes clear again, in the completely changed international environment of the early 1990s. The value of an all-European security system lies mainly in the fact that it would tie the two world powers into Europe so that they would not feel themselves excluded or repelled by a Europe that is growing together. Neighbors' concern at a too-powerful Germany in the center of Europe can, however, be resolved only through Germany's closer cooperation within the European Community.

Even without German internal developments, the European Community would today be facing the question of which systematic goal merits priority: further development of the Community in the direction of political union, or gradual expansion into an all-European institution. With the accomplishment of German unity, integration of the Western Europeans also gains in urgency. And because the resolution of the German question advanced faster than could be expected even in autumn 1989, Western European integration, too, must also take place faster than planned.

4

Right and Wrong Routes to German Unity

In Germany's more recent history, the German question has invariably had a dual nature. While always a question of the existence of Germany as a State and of its position in Europe, the "question" at issue also involved the problem of the development of democracy in Germany and how deep-rooted such democracy was. In Europe's recent experience, the combination of a unified German State with nondemocratic rule has twice threatened Germany's neighbors and all States associated with Europe.

The unconditional surrender and occupation brought an end for a while to the period in which Germans could choose for themselves the framework of their life together. For the time being, the question of German unity was decided through the organization of the Germans into two States. The German collapse meant at the same time an end to two centuries of policies intended to maintain the balance of power in Europe. For more than forty years, debates over the reestablishment of a power balance were carried on by the two new world powers — the United States and the Soviet Union — in the middle of Europe. The partitioning of what was once the most powerful Central European nation had an additional consequence, however, in that each German State saw itself as the representative of one of the two opposing systems. The question of democracy in Germany had been resolved with a bourgeois-liberal democracy in the West confronting a communist counter model in the East.

At the same time, the East-West conflict was for Germans not simply a question of foreign and security policy or of belonging to different alliance systems. Both States became the leading economic unit after the top country in their respective alliances, and both, thanks to their geographical and strategic position, carried great military weight. Beyond this, each German State claimed that since its foundation, partly in response to internal and social changes in the other State, it had been able to make the basic values of its own social order binding. However different, even diametrically opposed, the motivations and goals of the Federal Republic and the GDR, their policies were in all respects intended to act as models vis-à-vis the competing system.

Ties with the West as a Commitment to Values

Of all German postwar politicians who have projected the restoration of German unity, Kurt Schumacher came closest to the reality of the autumn of 1989. From the outset, the SPD chairman had advocated that Germany should commit itself to the social form of Western democracy and orient itself in the context of Western European ideas. He saw the Germans' turn away from the great West European ideas of freedom, parliamentarianism, and internationalism as the most important intellectual cause of the catastrophe of recent German history.

In the spring of 1947, when all problems of the continent — reconstruction, European integration, the German question — were becoming bogged down in the East-West conflict, Schumacher developed what later came to be called the magnet theory. To the leading political bodies of his party he described, on the occasion of the Clay-Robertson agreement setting up the Economic Council of Bizonia, the policy hopes for Germany that Social Democrats associated with the political and economic shaping of the Western occupation zones.

Speech by Kurt Schumacher to leading representatives of the SPD, 31 May 1947 (extract)

Democracy for the whole of Germany cannot be implemented with a programme of mere words. Social and economic facts must be created that testify to the superiority of the three Western zones to the Eastern zone, that prove life in the West to be more beneficial, more rational, more pleasant. The prosperity of the Western zones that can be achieved on the basis of the concentration of the bizonal economic policy can make the West into an economic magnet. In terms of *realpolitik* there is no other way from the German viewpoint to secure German unity than through this economic magnet-effect of the West, which must exercise its attractive powers so strongly upon the East that in the long term the mere holding of the power apparatus will be no safe means against it.

That is certainly a difficult and no doubt a long road. But we must go down it, for the sake not only of the West but also of the East and above all of Berlin. The separateness of Berlin, battered on all sides by communist waves, can be maintained only if the economic foundation of that great, brave city comes about, through the economy of the West.... With a Berlin supported in that way, we shall have a powerful bastion to the outside and a centre of political influence for the Eastern zone. That Berlin would protect the West, but in that way the West would protect Berliners and protect freedom.

Although Schumacher wished no doubts to arise as to Germany's adherence to Western patterns of life, he wished to enter into security-policy ties only after the regaining of German sovereignty. The debates that started soon after the setting up of the Federal Republic of Germany in 1949 between Federal Chancellor Konrad Adenauer and opposition leader Kurt Schumacher on Bonn's foreign policy concentrated on the details of Western policy, primarily on the methods in principle to reincorporate Germany into the European community of States.

The granting of equal rights and freedom of action was for Schumacher the essential precondition for Germany's commitment to a "Western bloc" under the aegis of capitalism. He rejected a military contribution by the Federal Republic because he feared the negative consequences of rearmament policy for the endeavor toward reunification. Adenauer and the CDU/CSU by contrast rated the inclusion of the Federal Republic in the Western alliance system as an unavoidable contribution to the creation of military security for the Germans, one that did not reduce the chances of reunification.

These basic differences of opinion between government and opposition remained in existence until the end of the 1950s. Only in 1960 did the SPD accomplish a reorientation in security policy: in a Bundestag foreign policy debate its deputy chairman, Herbert Wehner, for the first time unreservedly supported the ties to the West and the Federal Republic's national defense.

Speech by SPD Deputy Chairman Herbert Wehner to the German Bundestag on 30 June 1960 (extract)

The Social Democratic Party of Germany starts from the position that the European and Atlantic treaty system to which the Federal Republic belongs is the basis and framework for all efforts of German foreign and reunification policy.

The Social Democratic Party of Germany has neither called for nor intends to bring about the withdrawal of the Federal Republic from its treaty and alliance obligations. It takes the view that a European security system would be the proper way to make reunited Germany's contribution to security in Europe and in the world.

The Social Democratic Party of Germany supports by word and deed the free and democratic basic rights and the constitutional order, and supports the country's defense....

Why should we not, on the basis of a recognition of the moral and national integrity of our domestic policy opponent, seek to arrive at results that could help us all tomorrow or the day after? There are still enough individual questions left over to clear up. Among them I see such important ones as what can be done with German policy, and what must be done to prevent the nuclear arms race swallowing up all prospects of military détente. It depends whether the attempt is to be made or not. I feel it is really clear that the attempt must be made because the very point is not to let the Federal Republic fail in its real task: to fulfill its commitment to Germany as a whole.

The SPD's change in foreign-policy position no doubt marks the most important turning point in the party's postwar history. Along with the November 1959 Godesberg program, which had been directed at far-reaching review of the party's domestic policy concepts, Wehner's speech created the precondition for admitting the SPD to government responsibility and operated against the fear, then widespread at home and abroad, that any electoral victory for the SPD might introduce a phase of foreign-policy uncertainty for the Federal Republic. Support for the ties to the West was also embodied in renunciation of the extraparliamentary peace movement of the 1950s with which the Social Democrats had allied themselves in order to secure additional forces for the fight against rearmament. Finally, the SPD in this speech also distanced itself from its "Germany plan" conceived in March 1959,

which linked creation of a European security system with concepts
of confederation that had previously been suggested by the Soviet
Union and the GDR as well.

The new consensus on foreign policy also created favorable conditions for the smooth implementation of the desired European
integration process; with the signing of the Rome Treaties in March
1957 this had been extended beyond the coal and steel sector to
the whole economy of Western Europe.

Not only as an economic community but also as a political
factor and as a community of democratic values, the European
Community has a decisive role in making the hope for a "magnetic"
democratic, prosperous Germany and Europe eventually a reality. A
bare six months before Honecker's fall, the parliamentary State
Secretary to the Federal Minister for Intra-German Relations,
Ottfried Hennig, in a speech on ideas for policy on Germany, put
this connection very clearly and gave an interim stocktaking of it.

**Speech by Parliamentary State Secretary to the Federal Minister for Intra-
German Relations, Ottfried Hennig, to the Evangelical Working Group,
Cologne, 27 April 1989** (extract)

The importance of European integration for postwar developments in
Europe can scarcely be overrated. . . . It has also and especially given us
Germans, dependent as we are on international cooperation, the possi-
bility of a rapid recovery after the catastrophe of Hitler's dictatorship.

Also — and this should not be underestimated — it constitutes an
important operative factor for developments in East and Central Europe
too. Here the memory of basic national and European traditions is again
emerging, and ways are being sought to link up with the developments
coming about in the West of the continent. This is a consequence of the
weakening of the political creative capacity of the hegemonic power, the
Soviet Union, but at the same time a consequence of the attractive power
of the European integration process. The old magnet theory proclaimed
after the war in relation to the Western zones of Germany has been confirmed and validated in the larger European framework.

The day before the opening of the Wall, French expert on
Germany Alfred Grosser had urged his countrymen to rejoice at
the recent events in Eastern and Central Europe, despite their

concern at the new uncertainties of the international situation:

> It is really paradoxical. At the very moment when the countries of the Soviet sphere of influence are one after the other making a surprising turn towards Western values, those who in France always feared that West Germany might drift eastward are becoming more fearful and pessimistic than ever . . . .
>
> Before being afraid again, ought one not to celebrate the massive victory of the Western world? It is to its values that the peoples of Eastern Europe are appealing, thereby exposing the non-representativity of the systems once called "people's democracies." Of course, backsliding and repression cannot be ruled out. And, of course, the "German question" is being posed again.
>
> In 1949 West Germans made a choice whose urgency concealed its tragic nature: they chose freedom over the nation. For forty years they have been enjoying this freedom, but they should not be overproud of it. Like the French and the other Western Europeans, they let the price of freedom be paid by the Europeans under Soviet rule. In the case of our German counterparts, the price was paid by members of the same nation. It rightly offers special satisfaction to see them in particular arriving at more freedom and even coming close to self-determination.[45]

In the radically changed situation of autumn 1989, alongside the magnet theory, other Germany-policy strategies of earlier decades were also verified for their content and validity. While the "policy of humanitarian alleviation" that had since the 1960s decisively contributed to the mitigation of the consequences of division and to the permeability of the borders was supported by all parties, the Social Democratic concept of "change through rapprochement" came increasingly under the crossfire of criticism.

The reason lay largely in the fact that Egon Bahr himself, who had advocated this policy in 1963 as the sole feasible route to reunification, was twenty-five years later revising this objective in favor of an accommodation with the division of Germany. In a policy "for European peace" conceived as an "answer to Gorbachev" he gave priority, in contrast to his conceptual approach of the 1960s, to European security and the status quo over a solution to the German question, putting the position that what

---

45. Alfred Grosser, "Quelles Allemagnes pour quelle Europe?," in *Le Monde*, 10 November 1989.

the two German States had in common should be brought forward to replace the sterile search for unity:

> It must be understood that until a peace treaty there is no longer an active need for a structural change in our relationship with the victors and with the GDR, not even an important negotiating need. European security has primacy. For this period, the duration of which cannot be foreseen, there is no need to amend our Constitution either. Politically, German self-determination is being exercised in these set limits by the two German States. The real question is how much that will be happening against each other, alongside each other or with each other; sterile repetition of a claim to a German right to self-determination that is neither renounceable nor enforceable helps no one. . . .
>
> But the very unaltered continuing existence of the Federal Republic of Germany and the German Democratic Republic allows both States to act in favour of change by coming together in the European interest, without vacillating in their respective camps or becoming unreliable. The logical position underlying this is that European peace is more important than German unity. It is not unity but togetherness that is the key to German opportunities. What the two States have together, the interest in promoting reliable security, can become an important force in the service of Europe.[46]

In the light of the increasing discontent of people in the GDR at the closure of the SED regime against reform forces in its own country and in the Soviet Union, Bahr's formula was changed in various ways: SPD politician Norbert Gansel spoke in September 1989 of the need to secure "change through distance" from the East Berlin leadership, while CDU General Secretary Volker Rühe reproached the SPD with having, as an opposition party, practiced "change through toadying." This accusation was directed above all against the paper on the "culture of conflict" adopted jointly by the SPD and SED in late August 1987, a few days before Honecker's State visit to the Federal Republic of Germany.

Critics of this initiative had at the time already raised the reproach that this was the first time the SED was being treated as a legitimate negotiating partner for Western Social Democrats, even on fundamental questions for the societies. The SPD's reply was that this paper brought the SED into a debate on the

---

46. Egon Bahr, *Zum europäischen Frieden. Eine Antwort auf Gorbatschow* (Berlin: Corso bei Siedler, 1988), 44ff.

Western catalogue of values, and could no longer escape questions about political pluralism, human rights, and freedom. At any rate, publication of the paper in the SED organ *Neues Deutschland* — like the printing of the CSCE Final Act in August 1975 — sparked off passionate debate inside and outside the then ruling party, even though the Politburo in East Berlin had pulled the ideological emergency brake in the autumn of 1987 with a selective treatment of the content.

The close connection between ties to the West and ties to values is quite certainly a very decisive reason why the Federal Republic's allies were in the main relaxed about the prospect for a united Germany that for many came unexpectedly closer in the autumn of 1989. Admittedly, in October 1989 hardly anybody was still expecting a speedy end to dual statehood, but no one was willing to rule out the possibility completely. In an interview on the occasion of the fortieth anniversary of foundation of the GDR, Rupert Pennant-Rea, editor in chief of *The Economist*, justified his basically positive attitude as follows:

> Assuming that a reunited Germany would again take up the old nationalist expansionist ambitions of the first 45 years of this century, it would quite definitely threaten peace. But is a revival of such tendencies likely? Only to those who judge the development of the European Community since 1958 as pessimistically as they do the nature of the reforms introduced by Gorbachev.
>
> In the West, the European Community has truly developed a deep-rooted sense of democracy and a market economy. These factors have helped the Federal Republic to unprecedented prosperity and stability. I can simply not conceive of the Germans giving up these blessings. In the East, we are seeing not only the collapse of communism but also the last feeble throes of totalitarianism as a government system. The young people leaving the GDR are certainly not prepared to subject themselves to a new edition of German fascism.
>
> That is why the trend in both East and West is the same: towards the victory of pluralism. In these circumstances it is normal to welcome any growing together of the two Germanies. But I suspect that German reunification will come about neither suddenly nor soon.[47]

Against the background of the resumed debate on the meaning of the military alliances when the once sharply outlined lines of

47. Rupert Pennant-Rea, "Wiedervereinigung: Der Traum wird wahr. Aber die Träumer müssen noch lange warten," in *Die Bunte*, 12 October 1989, 24.

confrontation are starting to blur and the overcoming of Europe's division seems possible, the question of the security-policy aspect of German ties to the West also presents itself in new terms. With the dissolution of the bloc structures of the Cold War, the two States in Germany lose an important constraint on their positions, exchanging it for the certainty that the community of values hitherto termed Western would now include all those Eastern and Central European States that support individual freedom, democracy, and the rule of law.

In a critical settlement of accounts with intellectuals and politicians in the two German States who had thought that the division had to be recognized so that feelings of identity in the Federal Republic and the GDR could grow, long-time editor-in-chief of the *Süddeutsche Zeitung* (and actual President of the FRG'S Goethe-Institute) Hans Heigert felt strongly that Germans must recognize themselves:

> Among the (West) Germans the pressure for "Europe" always contained an aspect of flight. Many thought they could thereby escape the old, unpleasant question of "Germany." To our (Western) neighbours this was fine and dandy, since they could rely on the fact that the Germans tied in and allied with them no longer wished to try any national experiments.
>
> The same was true for forty years in the GDR. Their State doctrine was called "socialism" and that always meant complete integration into the power system of the USSR. The rest of the world perhaps found it hard to accept, but it was nevertheless a fact that could reasonably be lived with — including mutual deterrence. The Germans too grew accustomed to it for four decades. But their historical image got lost in the process. . . .
>
> The history of the other European States too will have to be rewritten. Germany in the middle no longer as a disruptor or a danger, but as a genuine member of the Western community of values . . . .The Germany that is coming no longer has much in common with Bismarck's Reich or with the Weimar Republic. Its roots lie deeper in the federal history of those to whom self-determination was always the highest value.[48]

With the breaking down of the Wall, a new state of the nation came about particularly for the people of the GDR. The development toward a common statehood in Germany came about in

---

48. Hans Heigert, "Des Deutschen Vaterland," in *Süddeutsche Zeitung*, 31 March 1990.

steps that sometimes raced ahead of the consciousness of East Germans themselves. Many saw simple "accession" to the Federal Republic of Germany as not the ultimate fulfillment of their political vision. In the common State that would be different because they had joined it, they wanted to bring in their own values, the prime motivations of the autumn of 1989: empathy and solidarity with the peoples of Eastern and Central Europe who were also struggling for democracy and prosperity. In the months after the opening of German internal frontiers members of the civil rights movements in particular pleaded that, for all the understandable fascination with the West, solidarity with former companions in suffering in the East bloc ought not to be forgotten. In the words of Ludwig Mehlhorn, of the opposition group "Democracy Now":

> In all other East and Central European countries, the idea of the "great fatherland, Europe" plays an important part. In the GDR by contrast there is instead considerable under development of the awareness of living in international contexts that reach further than West Berlin, Cologne or Munich.
>
> The reunification debate being emotionally carried on in the German-German context is letting the East European context of the democracy movement be almost forgotten. Without the West nothing can happen any more, yet it is nevertheless the case that the vacuum in relations among the former bloc countries that has come about since the collapse of the old regimes had to be filled.[49]

In the commemoration of the day of German unity, held jointly on 17 June 1990 for the first time by the politicians of the two German States, in the East Berlin Schauspielhaus Manfred Stolpe ventured to call for patience in adapting to Western ways of life. Before being nominated by the SPD as the first Minister President of the new East German Land of Brandenburg, Stolpe had been, from 1982 to 1990, Consistory President, chief manager and political head of the Evangelical Church of Berlin-Brandenburg. Thanks to his good contacts even with the old SED regime, he was able to provide civil-rights people and peace groups with hideouts and with the room for maneuver, thus contributing to the success of the peaceful revolution in the GDR.

---

49. Ludwig Mehlhorn, "Furcht vor einem neuen Graben mitten durch Europa," in *Süddeutsche Zeitung*, 18 January 1990.

After forty years of division, said Stolpe, the GDR was facing a cultural shift that was endangering people's sense of their own value; this called for comprehension. GDR citizens, faced with total, radical social change, still had to learn to live with freedom and its dangers. The highest priority was the question of the credibility of the social market economy. People in the GDR would measure acceptance of the new order by whether it gave them a chance at a decent way of life. Conversely, the coming unification would also be a challenge to FRG citizens and to their identity, because each society had, after all, defined itself for forty years in relation to the other, as a counter-identity.

The memorial ceremony on 17 June 1990 was unique in two respects, for it was also to be the last time that the rising of 17 June 1953 would be honored by a holiday. The unification treaty signed in East Berlin on 31 August 1990, which defined the terms by which the GDR would accede to the Federal Republic pursuant to Article 23 of the Basic Law, also regulates the future significance of accession day. Already in 1990, the 3rd of October was a statutory holiday as Day of German Unity, replacing the 17th of June. With the accession of the five ex-GDR Länder, there are now sixteen Bundesländer with a total of around 78.7 million inhabitants. While the number of inhabitants increases by about a quarter, the area of German territory increases by almost half, to 357,000 km².

Address by Consistory President Manfred Stolpe at the joint German commemoration in East Berlin, 17 June 1990 (extracts)

The West is now coming into the GDR, but the GDR is also coming into the West!

Intra-German intercourse has to be learned. After four decades of separation, a broad social consensus has to be found for the forthcoming joint Germany. A fundamental consensus on the foundation of the Basic Law can largely be presumed. But the common constitution must not be allowed to remain an abstract quantity, unknown to many . . . .

The coming German unity is the will of the people and the result of European détente. Without the European peace process, the 17th of June 1953 could have been repeated in October 1989. In the meantime, the process of German unification is engaged in overtaking the European peace process. Great diplomatic skill will be needed to ensure that German unification promotes peace instead of disrupting it.

It is with thanks and respect that we see the willingness of the four victorious powers and our neighbouring States to approve German unification. This is trust in advance, which we were not entitled to expect after everything that Germans have done to other peoples, and which we shall justify. For future Germany remains firmly tied into the European Community. This is not endangered by the GDR's accession. Even today, European consciousness is widespread here.

The GDR was for long the model pupil in the Eastern Alliance, and is now the favoured candidate for Western Europe. We are bringing along into joint Germany the moral obligation to stand by the States of Eastern Europe and the Soviet Union too on the road to better quality of life including human environmental conditions.

Germany, the Heart of Europe

With the approach of unification, the question of the symbols for the new Germany also arose. "What name? What anthem? What national day?" In the summer of 1990 these three questions were put by the Hamburg weekly *Die Zeit* to a range of prominent figures from Germany and abroad, sparking off a range of readers' letters that displayed intense reflection about Germans and their future role in Europe. From the GDR came a proposal for a new, joint German anthem (printed in the July 6 issue), to be understood as a synthesis not only of the two previous national anthems but also of the two forcibly separated partial identities. With its strong supranational component and the underlying liberal tenor of links among peoples, this text is encouraging testimony to the growing European consciousness in the former GDR mentioned by Manfred Stolpe in his speech commemorating the 17th of June.

Germany, the Heart of Europe

Re-arising out of ruins
with to Europe faces turned
let us all in freedom serve thee
Germany, one Fatherland!
Unity and right and freedom
are for peace the pledging-band;
flourish in the heart of Europe –
flourish German Fatherland!

Flourish in the heart of Europe –
flourish German Fatherland!

To our peoples, every one our friends
let us reach a clasping hand.
Homeland be the whole of Europe
Germany our Fatherland.
People's friendship, love of country
joy and peace both far and wide,
let us strive that this our Germany
live forever and abide!
Let us strive that this our Germany
live forever and abide!

The metaphor of Germany as the "heart of Europe" stands for a geographical location that since Madame de Staël's famous book on Germany of 1810 has repeatedly cropped up in journalism and in the speeches of politicians. Its central position in Europe is indeed the great constant of German history and belongs among the scarcely changeable structures of the "long time" that French historian Fernand Braudel, in his theory of time strata, distinguished from the short time of the history of events and the medium one of social and economic circumstances.

German geography professor Karl Ernst Haushofer endeavored to make geopolitics into the "geographical conscience of the State," and since his conception of "living space" for the "heartland" of Europe was adopted, with all its expansionist connotations, into the ideological mishmash of National Socialist conceptions and thought patterns, the political geography of Ratzel, Kjellen, and Mackinder, with its terminology, had been radically discredited.

It is only with the first indications of détente between East and West that reference to the Germans' geographical position in the center of Europe is again coming to belong among the categories of political self-perception, although without the primacy of geography being deduced from it. On the contrary: the geographical position is portrayed not as an unavoidably fixed datum but as a framework that leaves room for the creative capacity of political leaders, parties, and interest groups.

After 1945, politicians and journalists thought initially in terms of hostile ideological blocs and of a system of world powers defined in bipolar terms, of the opposition between the free West and the totalitarian East.

In view of the power-policy confrontation of the great powers in Central Europe, the powerlessness of the conquered, disarmed Germans, and the practical unfeasibility of a third way between the blocs at the center of the world political confrontation, at the time any relinking with Bismarck's conceptions of a balancing function for Germany in the European system of States was condemned to failure from the outset. The option in favor of Western democracy became the basis of the security and the *raison d'état* of the Federal Republic of Germany, at home and abroad.

The German question in Europe has always been also the question of where the Germans belong: looking westward or wandering between East and West; recognizing their geographical central position or breaking out of it? Despite the discontinuities in German history in the last hundred years, the same questions were and are continually posed anew and require answers from responsible statesmen, always keeping in view the continually changing patterns of international relations.

The answers found by German foreign-policy makers, from the founding of the Reich in 1871 until Brandt's *Ostpolitik* a century later, lead Berlin historian Arnulf Baring to distinguish three basic patterns, three different attempts to find a solution:

1. A kind of balance achieved through a complex set of relationships on all sides, represented by Bismarck, Stresemann and Brandt;
2. a breaking out of the central position by grasping for hegemony over the territory of Europe and Western Asia, embodied by Hitler;
3. dissolution of the German nation State, for the good of the Germans and the general good of Europe, in the supra-national empire of medieval Christendom, uniting the traditions of Western, Southern and Central Europe; to this Adenauer felt he belonged.[50]

The transitions between these various schools of thought are, however, more fluid in practice than this categorization would suggest. Thus, Konrad Adenauer had already criticized the uncertainty and vacillation of Gustav Stresemann's foreign policy of the 1920s, and after 1945 resolutely supported the Federal Republic's integration with the West; for him the basis for a lasting democracy in Germany was inseparably bound up with the unreserved integration into the Western community of States. That

---

50. Arnulf Baring, "Die Wurzeln der Bonner Ostpolitik," in *Europäische Rundschau*, 4, 1990, 59ff.

the Germans in their exposed position needed, with ties with the West, a settlement with the East as well, is an insight that can be found in speeches by the first Federal Chancellor as early as the mid-1950s. In many respects, the declaration of principle made by Adenauer in September 1955 on the occasion of his first (and only) journey to Moscow already contains important features of the détente concept of the 1970s and late 1980s.

Declaration of Principle by Federal Chancellor Konrad Adenauer in Moscow, 9 September 1955 (extract)

The supreme good that all Germans should uphold is peace. We know all too well how much in particular the Soviet and the German people suffered from the last war, and I therefore also believe that I shall meet with understanding in saying that horror at the destructiveness of modern war, at the millions of human victims, at the destruction of homes and workplaces, at the desolation of cities and countryside, has made a deep impression on everyone. In Germany too we also know that scientific and technical progress made since the last war in the field of nuclear fission and related areas have given man possibilities of destruction that we can think of only with a shudder. Ultimately everyone in Germany knows that our country's geographical position would particularly endanger us in the event of armed conflict . . . .

Were the Soviet Union to regard an impairment to security as a likely consequence of the reunification of Germany, then we are thoroughly prepared to do what we can to collaborate on a security system that would remove these concerns too. It seems to me right to consider the security system for Europe at the same time as the discussions on how Germany's unity is to be restored.

It is insight into these necessities that must guide us when we set about jointly dealing with questions of the restoration of diplomatic, economic and cultural relations. The Federal Government shares the view that restoration of those relations can be of great benefit to both countries and to their mutual relationship. Direct contact between the two governments will certainly contribute towards arriving at more exact judgements that recognize and evaluate the realities on each side. The economic circumstances of each country undoubtedly contain possibilities for mutual complementarity. Resumption of exchange of cultural values and scientific work is another desirable goal.

But this approach did not come into being until the policy of Eastern treaties in the Brandt era released Bonn from the self-restraint in dealings with the countries of Eastern Europe that had been imposed in the 1950s, and until changing European and international framework conditions gave Germans back part of their traditional room for maneuver. In a contribution to the spring 1969 conference of the London Royal Institute of International Affairs, at which British and West German scholars analyzed the foreign policy of both countries in this new context, Waldemar Besson, a political scientist from Konstanz — who died in 1971 — made the following forecast:

> After twenty years' history of the Federal Republic, we see that the Germans are unable to escape from their past role in Europe, and so today the fundamental question is posed as to how far the tradition of a primary option for the West, which Adenauer initiated, can be brought into harmony with the constant factors of the earlier experience. At all events it is evident that Bonn's foreign policy has lost the certainty of attitudes and objectives which characterized the 1950s in the face of new challenges. A bridge needs to be built to join post-1945 Germany with the basic geographical and historical factors of the German situation, factors which the rigid dualism of two hostile blocs at the beginning of the 1950s seemed to have obliterated.
>
> It is therefore by no means argued that the Adenauer tradition is in the course of being replaced by another, as if the Germans could turn back the clock. Historical events are not accomplished so simply. It is rather the case that a kind of synthesis of both traditions is in the making, Adenauer meeting Bismarck, and thus the experience of security meeting the desire for a more active shaping of national history.[51]

Unification under a Western aegis creates a completely new situation: for the first time in their history Germans are offered the chance, as an integral component of the Western community of values, to be a bridge to the East as well. The European solution of the national question determined with its neighbors and with the powers involved with Germany also removes the conflict of objectives between German unity and European unification, which

51. Waldemar Besson, "The Conflict of Traditions: the Historical Basis of West German Foreign Policy," in Karl Kaiser and Roger Morgan, eds., *Britain and West Germany, Changing Societies and the Future of Foreign Policy*, (London, 1971), 62.

had, in the days of dual statehood, been a burden to Bonn's foreign policy. The need to keep several balls in the air and the impossibility of choosing between the Atlantic, Western European, and Central European options is now reduced to the task of seriously applying the formula Bonn politicians like to use: that the German question was never in history the exclusive property of Germans. In a reflective consideration of the election result in the GDR, the editor-in-chief of *Die Zeit* described this connection as follows:

> The Germans are in the situation of a man beaming with joy because he has managed to struggle through to the building of his own house. But it is only now that the harder part begins: financing of the project has to be secured; details of the building plan have to be determined with the family and the architect; agreement must be secured from the neighbours and the authorities. That takes time, strains the nerves, causes bother. Persistence has to be accompanied by insight if there is soon to be a topping-out ceremony.[52]

The removal of the division of Germany at a point in time when Moscow has stopped being the navel of the world for its East and East-Central European neighbors, changes not only Germany's weight in Europe but also the East-West relationship as a whole. If the postwar system in Europe was suitable for bringing about containment of the Soviet Union by the same token as it did the suspension of the German question, the point is now to cope with the risks of instability posed by change in Eastern Europe, in particular change in the Soviet Union. Here the task that devolves on a united Germany is both to support the processes of peaceful change in all of Europe as a power irreversibly tied into the West and to underpin them on an economic level. R. Gerald Livingston, Director of the Washington Institute for Contemporary German Studies, thus describes this new German foreign-policy option:

> Germany's "Mittellage," its central location in Europe, has always determined its foreign and much of its domestic policy. It becomes a huge economic and political advantage in a Europe that is no longer divided. . . .
> Hitler tried to make Europe a bulwark against the Russian Bolsheviks. His disastrous war brought them into the heart of the continent instead. Today's German leaders see their mission as keeping the Soviets

52. Theo Sommer, "Vor der Einheit: Einigkeit bei uns, Einigung mit anderen," in *Die Zeit*, 23 March 1990.

in Europe — not militarily, but politically, economically and cultur-
ally. . . .

Sharing Western liberal democratic values, irrevocably incorporated
into Western institutions and possessing a dynamic economy, Germany
is best equipped to win and keep Eastern Europe and Russia for the
West.[53]

While Livingston expressed lingering unease at the possible risks
of such a vision of the future, Michel Debré, French President de
Gaulle's long time prime minister, was already predicting a "replacement of Yalta by Rapallo" a few days after the Wall was opened.
The name of that north Italian coastal resort where, on Easter Sunday
1922, Russians and Germans surprisingly concluded an agreement
on the sidelines of the Genoa Economic Conference, has for almost
seventy years now been a symbol of German political seesawing
between East and West — and has reappeared at every actual or
feared rapprochement of Germans with Moscow's positions — in
the collective memory of Germany's neighbors. In the context of
9 November 1989, this was how Debré saw the situation:

> Let us consider the past. When it has felt threatened by German policy,
> Russia has sometimes looked in the direction of France. But when
> Germany has seemed favourably disposed, then Russia tends to turn
> in its direction. Before the German-Russian alliance took shape as an
> agreement between the two barbarians Hitler and Stalin, it bore the
> countenance of peace. Let us recall Rapallo on 16 April 1922. At
> present the economic activities of the two German States are linked
> together, and contact between the societies restored. Tomorrow the
> question of political reunification will arise, and in a further future un-
> doubtedly that of the choice of Berlin as sole capital. The Soviet Union
> can help Germany in this development in exchange for financial support,
> which the German Republic can better offer than any other country
> — particularly us. Against the background of current events and
> particularly the end of the Berlin Wall, we have to see the epoch that
> can be discerned for the future as that of a new Rapallo.[54]

This assessment cannot simply be dismissed as the nightmare
of a single conservative politician with a highly developed historical awareness, even if this viewpoint ascribes far greater binding

---

53. Robert Gerald Livingston, "New Germany: Not just a Bigger Federal
Republic," in *International Herald Tribune*, 16 July 1990.
54. Michel Debré, "Quand Rapallo peut remplacer Yalta," in *Le Monde*, 14
November 1989.

effect to Napoleonic geography as the "destiny of peoples" than to the "geography of values" that West German politicians like to invoke. How strongly marked by historical reminiscence is political thinking, even in parts of the French government circles, is shown by a 21 May 1990 speech by left-wing socialist Jean-Pierre Chevènement, at that time Mitterand's Defense Minister. This speech deserves attention also because the audience chosen, the respected Institute for Defense Questions, is traditionally used to set forth France's basic security-policy ideas.

Speech by French Defense Minister Jean-Pierre Chevènement to graduates of the Institut des Hautes Etudes de Défense Nationale, 21 May 1990 (extracts)

It is henceforth certain that the Soviet Union will in future play a less important role in Central Europe than has been the case in the previous half century, while Germany's role will, in one of the seesaw movements familiar to Germans and Slavs for centuries, grow strongly. As could often be seen in the past, the balance between these two powers, which act expansionistically against each other when their intrinsic weights are too different, may in the next phase lead to a kind of agreement. There is an ancient understanding between the two peoples that has taken on various forms, from Catherine II to Bismarck. In our century there have been new examples of it: everyone will recall Rapallo or the Hitler-Stalin pact. Nor should we forget that the Federal Republic in a sense gave the starting signal for détente, through the visit by its Chancellor to Moscow in 1955 — the first visit by a Western statesman. . . .

Whatever way one looks, the future is obscure. One thing is certain: whether Slavs and Germans come to an understanding or once again clash, France must not lose its military capacity, which is a factor of stability and of peace for the whole continent.

When Chancellor Kohl actually did negotiate full sovereignty plus NATO membership for the coming Germany at his meeting with Gorbachev in July 1990, the specter of Rapallo reappeared to many foreign observers. It was asked in many quarters, with skepticism or with concern, whether Germans could meet the high economic expectations of the Soviet Union at all, and whether symbiosis with the socialist ruins of the Soviet Union in disarray would be digestible to Germany with its market-economy orientation.

It was rather abruptly that the Germans got everything at once in July 1990: the end of their country's division and a reconciliation, that had never before worked, with the great power in the east of Europe, which for forty-five years had held the East German pledge in its power sphere. It was not surprising then that the Bonn correspondent of the London *Economist* would give his commentary on the meeting in the Caucasus, in the region of Stavropol where Gorbachev had ruled in the 1970s as First Party Secretary, the catchy headline "Encounter at Stavrapallo." The analysis it contained was, however, aimed rather at refuting the thesis of a repetition of the special relationship of Rapallo:

> When Germany and Russia warm to each other, other states start to shiver. . . .
>
> So far, however, there is little in German foreign policy to raise the spectre of Rapallo. Although the German-Russian talks produced a political breakthrough, they yielded little on the economic cooperation Mr. Gorbachev so badly wants. . . .
>
> There is talk of a German-Soviet pact on economic and political cooperation next year, maybe including bigger Soviet deliveries of natural gas to Eastern Germany. But Mr. Kohl's aides say the chancellor was not trying to be modest when he said that Germany could not hope to meet the Soviet Union's economic needs alone. For that, other western countries' cooperation was essential, and America, Japan and Britain were for various reasons still reluctant.[55]

This hesitation is all too easy to understand if one bears in mind the Soviet Union's desperate economic plight. The explosiveness of the situation lies in the fact that the USSR is politically and militarily a world power, but at the level of the third world in economic terms. In the past, Western progress reached Russia mainly through the way station of Germany, and this law of history seems to have been confirmed again under the aegis of *perestroika*. The Soviet Union needs Western technology, Western know-how, Western money, and all very quickly. In view of the crisis peaking in the Soviet domestic-policy situation, however, skepticism tends to prevail — and its economic partner, the Federal

---

55. "Encounter at Stavrapallo," in *The Economist*, 21 July 1990.

Republic, is no exception — as to the feasibility of rapid conversion from a planned economy to a market economy.

The supply links with the Soviet Union that were guaranteed in the German State Treaty, and the economically moribund COMECON area, create risks that have been hard to assess; risks that could involve the Federal Republic as well. In a study on German unification and the Soviet Union's economic interests done before the July 1990 German-Soviet agreement, economic expert Heinrich Vogel, Director of the Cologne Federal Institute for Eastern and International Studies, comes to the conclusion that, in view of the Soviet Union's immense problems, the importance of trade with the East, even for a united Germany, ought not to be overrated:

> A united Germany with a gross social product of some 30% of the GSP of the European Community enlarged by the GDR represents an economic challenge to all its European neighbours, but at the same time an opportunity for accelerating the growing together of Europe. Peaceful revolutions in the East European States and in the GDR have brought "the East" back into Europe. Unification of the two German States is now opening up for Western Europe a road to the East. Here economic cooperation takes on central importance, for domestic-policy stabilization too. Anyone fearing, because of Germany's new role, a fall back into Rapallo-type structures is underestimating how rooted Germany policy is in the West. The sense of reality and the profit motive of German businessmen are oriented to the world market. In this perspective it is clear that the future of the German economy does not lie in the East. Its share in German foreign trade cannot for the foreseeable future exceed 10%. But it is time to draw practical conclusions from the perception that the world market has now long included Eastern Europe too. The image of a world divided into East and West has been outdated by that alone.[56]

The New State of the Nation

The image of a world divided into East and West is outdated and not only from the viewpoint of economists. It is outdated as well with regard to the new political web of relationships in Central Europe, to which the old positional definitions can be only conditionally

---

56. Heinrich Vogel, "Die Vereinigung Deutschlands und die Wirtschaftsinteressen der Sowjetunion," in *Europa-Archiv*, 13–14, 1990, 414.

applied. These changes, which were and are not without their effects on united Germany's search for its place, can be seen for instance in reactions to the concept of "Germany, one Fatherland" presented by then GDR Prime Minister Hans Modrow in February 1990.

Considered superficially, the communist stop-gap politician's plan, agreed to by Gorbachev, connects seamlessly with the neutrality plans from the Cold War period, and particularly recalls Stalin's famous spring 1952 note offering the Germans reunification on condition of armed neutrality. Looked at more closely, however, the inappropriateness of this sort of proposal against the background of the developing postcommunist Europe was evident, as journalist Brigitte Seebacher-Brandt, the former Federal Chancellor's wife, accurately stated:

> Geography and history, economic power and population figures, do not allow Germany any neutrality, and in a period of European integration still less than ever before. It was the good luck of those Germans who lived in the Federal Republic to be anchored as regards system and security to the Western community. The fact that the 17 million in the Soviet sphere of domination did not so benefit is the German postwar tragedy. They, who constantly had to lose the war yet again, could not be helped by renunciation on the part of those who had drawn the better lot. For in the West everything was to be lost, while in the East there was nothing to be won.
>
> German neutrality in the times of Stalin and of two firmly established military blocs could be defined. But German neutrality in Gorbachev's time? Being neutral against a Warsaw Pact that is barely a shadow of its former self? Neutral against countries that have just embarked on a search for their own road to freedom? A senseless intellectual game, to which no meaning could be attributed even in Moscow.[57]

For Germans, the doubtfulness of the old line separating East and West had become actual historical experience and emotional reality in the early autumn of 1989 when the Hungarians unexpectedly met the wish constantly expressed by Bonn politicians to "make the borders more permeable." On 2 May 1989 Hungary, which six weeks before had joined the U.N. Convention on refugees, began taking down the Iron Curtain along its border with

---

57. Brigitte Seebacher-Brandt, "Moskaus Spiel mit kleiner Münze," in *Rheinischer Merkur/Christ und Welt*, 9 February 1990.

Austria. For then GDR Head of State Honecker, who only shortly before had spoken of the need to keep the Berlin Wall up for another hundred years, this border opening must have been like the writing on the wall. Finally, at midnight on 10 September, the Hungarian government, without prior agreement with East Berlin, allowed all those wanting to flee the GDR to travel freely out to the Federal Republic, via Austria.

For the first time, a communist-ruled State was placing the obligations it had undertaken in international law above ties within the bloc and bilateral agreements, and refusing to allow the GDR's claims to rights of disposal over its citizens apply on its territory. János Hajdú, then Hungarian Ambassador to Switzerland and previously long familiar, as a journalist, with German issues, commented on his country's decision at a platform debate at the Berlin colloquium held from 8 to 10 November 1989 by the Society for Research on Germany together with the Federal Minister for Intra-German Relations. The colloquium was dominated by excitement generated by the revolution taking place in East Germany, which was experienced to the marrow by all participants.

Contribution to debate by Ambassador of the Republic of Hungary to Switzerland, János Hajdú, in the Berlin Reichstag, 10 November 1989 (extract)

Undoubtedly, through that government decision we intervened massively in the internal affairs of the German nation. But it would not, I feel, be in line with the facts to assert here that the Hungarian government had then in early September taken the decision to open our frontier towards Austria for citizens of the German Democratic Republic too with *that* intent. The step we took was simply following a consistently intended domestic policy; and we certainly did intend something. The intention was — I happened to be a witness to the genesis of the decision — formulated in foreign-policy terms more or less to the effect that we could perhaps at the last moment make the GDR government and party leadership aware that things could not go on like that. The intention was not to show 50 or 60 thousand people the road via Hungary to Bavaria.

In further statements, Hajdú stated that it was hard to believe that a united Germany would not "swing between Rapallo and Locarno" and, by "acting as a mediator and doing business between East and West," play an important role in Europe. It was as a "link" between the European Community and the "other Europe" that Daniel Vernet, editor in chief of *Le Monde*, saw Germans' new role, without linking a policy of swings between the liberal West and the East-Central Europeans with it:

> Geography brings certain requirements with it: Germany is so located in the middle of the continent that it is quite naturally destined to be a mediator between the Community of Twelve and the "other Europe" that was for over forty years artificially cut off from its preferred partners. . . .
>
> By its geographical position, its economic potential, its traditional cultural and linguistic influence, Germany has a vocation to play a decisive part in the shaping of the new Europe. Many of the German decision-makers understand that it can do so more effectively if it sets about things not on its own but in close association with its partners in the Community and in particular with France.[58]

Similarly concerned with a balance, in the sense of the new role described by Vernet, was then GDR Prime Minister Lothar de Maizière, when he visited Paris for the first time in June 1990. His formula, that the Soviet Union should not be given the impression that "Gorbachev was now losing the war Stalin had won," aroused the interest of the French President. In his talks with representatives of business and trade, this descendant of Huguenots from Lorraine showed a subtle understanding of the problems the integration of the GDR into the European Community would carry with it, and at the same time praised his country as a bridge to the countries of Eastern and Southeastern Europe. In a speech made at a dinner in the Quai d'Orsay, he made clear why a one-sided orientation to the West would not be desirable for united Germany.

After-dinner speech by GDR Prime Minister Lothar de Maizière in the Quai d'Orsay, 19 June 1990 (extract)

In the changes in Eastern Europe, the Soviet Union has played a decisive part. It recognized the right to self-determination of the peoples in the

58. Daniel Vernet, "Quel nouveau rôle pour l'Allemagne?" in *Le Monde*, 16 June 1990.

Warsaw Pact and thus respected the will of the citizens. It was no longer concerned with maintaining old power structures, but with allowing room for new developments. It was a sensational change.

This should on the other hand have the consequence that changes in Europe should not take place with a one-sided orientation towards the West. The Soviet Union and the East European countries are parts of Europe. Their interests must be upheld in the process of change just as much as the interests of all others.

To a certain extent, the new style in East Berlin's foreign policy after the March 1990 elections, as displayed in Prime Minister de Maizière's intensive visiting diplomacy among neighbors in East and West in the summer of 1990, was a confirmation of the observation Bonn political scientist Hans-Peter Schwarz made in relation to the Federal Republic forty years after World War II. After the traumatic experience with the German "power obsession" in the first half-century, according to Schwarz, the endeavor to settle international differences and secure reconciliation with neighbors and the associated role as harmonizer and creator of peace could now be seen as typical of Bonn policy.

This attitude could remain binding for the new state of the nation and, particularly for the ex-GDR, be founded upon the community of solidarity with the democracies developing in the Eastern and Central Europe, a solidarity rooted both in a past suffered together and in liberation from this past. Winfried Wolk, painter and graphic artist from Schwerin and member of the GDR's CDU executive during the decisive months of 1989, sees the situation thus:

> We have lived for forty years in a community of suffering with the peoples of Eastern Europe, with the Czechs, the Poles, the Slovaks, the Russians, the Romanians, the Bulgarians. Certainly those fraternal links were forced upon us. But we have jointly suffered through the failed experiment of socialism, and that binds us together. That would make a united Germany a bridge between East and West. This is an opportunity that there has never been in Europe before.
>
> The position we are now in Germany, in Europe, would never have come about without the "Prague Spring," which we shall never forget, without the Polish Solidarność movement that displaced the Brezhnev doctrine, without Gorbachev, without the Hungarians who opened up the border for us, without the Romanians. And all the time there were the people from the GDR leaving their country because they could not

live their ideas of happiness there. That is suffering. For even though they really were welcomed in the Federal Republic with open arms, losing one's friends and one's homeland is no joke.[59]

With the unification of Germany under the aegis of the West, and with the abrupt change from a "policy of small steps" to one of "seven-league boots," the prophecies of Stefan Heym, the Nestor of socialist literature in the GDR, were fulfilled: the GDR will remain only a footnote in world history. But the statement by Manfred Stolpe, that the identity as Germany of the people in the Federal Republic would be affected by the fact that through accession by the GDR they were all at once wedded to Eastern Europe, applies as well. At least for a transitional period, the result is a special bond of united Germany to the former COMECON countries, a link that arises as well from the "protection of trust" in the State Treaty of 18 May 1990, the agreement to set up a monetary, economic, and social union between the Federal Republic and the GDR, whereby supply commitments from its socialist past are, under certain conditions, taken over.

Treaty on the creation of a monetary, economic, and social union between the Federal Republic of Germany and the German Democratic Republic, 18 May 1990 (extract)

Article 13

External Economy

1) In patterning its free external economic transactions, the German Democratic Republic shall take account of the principles of free world trade as expressed particularly in the General Agreement on Tariffs and Trade (GATT). The Federal Republic of Germany will make its experience comprehensively available in order further to integrate the economy of the German Democratic Republic into the world economy.

2) The external economic relationships of the German Democratic Republic that have grown up, in particular existing treaty commitments to the countries of the Council for Mutual Economic Assistance, shall enjoy protection of trust. They will be further developed taking the facts of the monetary and economic union and the interests of all involved into

59. Winfried Wolk, "Die Sicht der Deutschen," in *Forum für Deutschland, op. cit.*, 81f. (note 44).

account, and extended in compliance with market-economy principles. Insofar as necessary, existing treaty commitments of the German Democratic Republic shall in accord with its treaty partners be adjusted to these facts.

3) In representing external economic interests, the Contracting Parties shall, taking account of the competences of the European Communities, cooperate closely.

Over the past forty years the GDR carried on 65 to 75 percent of its total foreign trade with communist countries, among them the USSR and the other COMECON countries in particular. In order to secure the 2.3 million or so jobs dependent on trade with the East — over a million on Soviet trade alone — and to maintain the raw materials basis, these traditional trade flows are vitally important for the ex-GDR in the immediate future too, even if, in the opinion of foreign trade expert Maria Haendcke-Hoppe, manager of the Research Center for German Economic and Social Questions in Berlin, they are likely, after the actualization of economic and monetary union, to be both "a walking stick and a leg iron":

> For four decades the eastern trade resulting from the political and economic separation of Germany was the guaranteed economic basis for the German sub-state relatively poor in raw materials, and because of the strict bilaterality of the trade, was the crutch of the GDR's export economy. But under the protective umbrella of sales and price guarantees under the long-term trade agreement and the qualitatively undemanding Soviet market, it was also a major cause of the immense slowness in innovation and increasing international uncompetitivity of the GDR's industry. Yet the maintenance of this trade, so far laid down bindingly in five-year trade agreements with annual specifications in protocols at government level, most recently in spring 1989 for the period from 1991 to 1995, remains vitally important to the GDR even after the entry into force of economic and monetary union.[60]

No one knows exactly how, and at what cost, private enterprises with a market-economy orientation are to handle contracts that have been concluded by the State in a planned economy, for political reasons, and without regard to price rules. The loss of the GDR, both as economic partner and as bearer of Marxist-Leninist hopes

---

60. Maria Haendcke-Hoppe, "Der Osthandel der DDR. Standbein und Hemmschuh auch nach dem 1. Juli?" in *Deutschland Archiv*, 6, 1990, 819.

of a competitive "real socialist" industrial society, hit the USSR and the modernization of the economy being aimed at by Gorbachev in a particularly sensitive spot. This was also the main reason both for Soviet pressure for the early signing of a comprehensive cooperation agreement with united Germany and for the economic dimension of the Kohl-Gorbachev agreement of July 1990, which was described by one economic journalist in the snappy formula "Credits Instead of Chaos."

One day after the signing of the Two-plus-Four agreement on the external aspects of German unity, and thirty-five years to the day from the start of diplomatic relations between Bonn and Moscow, Federal Foreign Minister Genscher and his Soviet counterpart Shevardnadze initialed in Moscow a "comprehensive agreement" on close cooperation in all spheres and on renunciation of the use of force and of territorial claims, the conclusion of which had been announced on the occasion of the mid-July Kohl-Gorbachev meeting in the Caucasus. This new treaty (signed in Bonn two months later) replaces the Moscow Treaty of 1970, continues the joint declaration from Gorbachev's 1989 visit to Bonn in changed circumstances, and is to set up the framework for the next twenty years for "good neighborliness, partnership and cooperation" between Germany and the Soviet Union.

Treaty on good-neighborliness, partnership, and cooperation between the Federal Republic of Germany and the Union of Soviet Socialist Republics, 9 November 1990 (analysis and text extracts)

In the Treaty, Bonn and Moscow confirmed the resolve "to take up from the good traditions of their centuries of history" and "rise to the historic challenges at the threshold of the third millennium" (preamble).

Both States "mutually respect their sovereign equality and territorial integrity and political independence;" they accept the principle that "any war, whether nuclear or conventional," must be "resolutely averted and peace preserved and constructed" (Article 1). They undertake "to respect the territorial integrity of all States in Europe in their present frontiers without restriction" and declare "that they have no territorial claims against anyone" and regard "the frontiers of all States in Europe as inviolable, today and in future" (Article 2).

An essential component of the Treaty is the obligation of both parties to resolve disputes exclusively by peaceful means and never to use any of their weapons on any occasion, "unless for individual or collective self-defense." They will "never and under no circumstances be the first to use armed forces against each other or against third countries." All other States are called upon to associate themselves with the commitment to non-aggression. Should one of the two parties be attacked, "the other party shall not provide the aggressor with any military or other assistance and shall take every measure to settle the conflict, applying the principles and procedures of the United Nations and other collective security structures" (Article 3). The States party confirm their will to disarmament, with the object of creating a stable balance in Europe at a low level, "sufficient for defense but not for attack" (Article 4).

Regular consultations "at the highest political level" are to take place "as often as necessary, but at least once a year." The foreign ministers will meet twice a year and the defense ministers too will have regular meetings.

For the first time, the rights of Soviet citizens of German nationality are laid down in an internationally binding document: "Soviet citizens of German nationality" and Soviet citizens resident in the Federal Republic "who wish to preserve their language, culture or tradition shall be enabled to develop their national, linguistic and cultural identity" (Article 15). The Treaty, "not directed against anyone" (Article 21), applies initially for a period of twenty years. Thereafter, it shall be extended successively for five years unless one of the signatories gives one year's notice of termination.

This general Treaty serves as an umbrella for three further treaties: one on the presence and withdrawal of Soviet troops; the transition treaty, which settles financial provisions; and the treaty on economic cooperation. The document, binding in international law, was signed in Bonn by Federal Chancellor Kohl and President Gorbachev on 9 November 1990, just one year after the fall of the Berlin Wall. The Federal Republic will, according to the accords in the transition treaty, grant the Soviet Union, by the end of 1994, financial assistance of DM 12 billion and an interest-free loan of DM 3 billion with a term of five years for maintaining their troops on ex-GDR territory and for withdrawing its soldiers; this will mean an additional burden on the Federal budget of DM 1 billion for bank interest. Bonn justifies this financial aid as the cost of regaining the sovereignty of the united Germany and as an investment in Germany's future.

The process of German unification is accompanied by the creation of a completely new relationship with the Soviet Union. The political challenge for the German government is to bring about the new relationship with Moscow in such a way that no doubt arises as to the reliability of the German contribution to the consolidation and further development of the European Community. For the alliance membership of united Germany, again, the position is that the newly emerging loyalties toward the Soviet Union are unproblematic only as long as the relationship between the two superpowers continues to normalize, as long as cooperation between them (proven since summer 1990 in the Gulf crisis as well) increases and Europe continues to integrate.

Berlin: Center or Periphery?

In the opinion of many Germans, and not only in the East, the Europe now to be shaped cannot end at the boundary to the binding recognition of which Poland raised a justified claim. The countries that generated the democracy movement, which generated the chance for Germans to overcome division, must not be fenced off, but must be able to sense the new Germany, which they perceive with some apprehension, as a bridge to the peoples of the European West.

What is to be the capital of the united Germany? Since the Wall was broken through on 9 November 1989 this question has been stirring hearts. It played an important part in negotiation of the treaty on German unity and had been answered to the effect that Germany's capital is Berlin. The decision on the location of parliament and government has been eventually taken by the Bundestag on 20 June 1991. For the Berlin *Tagesspiegel* this choice should be made neither to favor Berlin local patriotism nor to pander to Bonn's calculations about possible removal costs and other inconveniences:

> The decisive point is what capital can enable the future Germany best to play the role accruing to it in Europe. From the viewpoint of this requirement, everything is in favour of Berlin, with a consensus that crosses the frontiers and embraces the major parties. Its implementation will take time, but the signals must be set in good time. The shift from Bonn to Berlin would not mean any move away from the Community Europe with which we are so closely linked by democratic values, culture

and economics, but would correspond to the meaning that will go to this city in the historical shift in Europe.[61]

The political position of the city in Germany and Europe had in the 1980s continually been a topic of debates, among which those at the Aspen Institute in Berlin played a prominent part. Shepard Stone, its cofounder and first director, who in the fourteen years of his directorship from 1974 to 1988 made the Institute a unique meeting point in the divided city, created in 1986 a working group on "Berlin — Germany — Europe," that became the venue for an ongoing debate on present and future perspectives for Berlin among politicians, diplomats, journalists, scholars, and leading figures of cultural and economic life, as well as for the representatives of the three protecting powers. In the volume written by Shepard Stone's friends in spring 1988 on the occasion of his eightieth birthday, Alexander Schwan, political scientist and professor at the Free University of Berlin and one of the participants in the working group, put down some thoughts on Berlin's role, thoughts that outlive the death of their author and of Shepard Stone:

> West Berlin belongs very firmly and very vigorously to Western, democratic Europe, to Western, democratic culture. The better it is at its own activities directed towards that, the more clearly does the city's exposed and at the same time central position in Europe stand out. West Berlin is today and in the future a cornerstone of the consciousness of intimate connection among the German nation, free democracy and European integration — after all the bitter experiences of our history in which the German capital bore its heavy part.
>
> If from this context — and from it alone — a prospect for a free Europe as a whole and a reunification of Germany in freedom is to grow, then Berlin could at once become not only and primarily again the "capital," but more of a European "federal city," alongside and along with such other cities as Brussels and Prague.
>
> The city must, in view of its special position and role, ever anew produce very special achievements. It will naturally fall behind such requirements occasionally, and in times of confusion and scandal even grossly so. Yet it has accomplished much, not least thanks to necessary assistance from outside. In the postwar period it never stood only for its own freedom, but for freedom in Germany and Europe as such.[62]

61. "Die Deutschen im europäischen Wandel," in *Der Tagesspiegel*, 13 May 1990.

62. Alexander Schwan, "Berlin und die deutsche Frage," in *Ein Buch der Freunde. Shepard Stone zum Achtzigsten* (Berlin: Siedler, 1988), 284f.

Two statements, which in the postwar period symbolized Berlin's role as the "beacon of freedom," are closely linked with the two crises that threatened the isolated city's survival. On 9 September 1948, when citizens in the Western part of the city defied Stalin's grip in the winter of the blockade, Social Democrat Ernst Reuter, town councillor and later governing mayor, in an impressive speech on Republic Square to 300,000 Berliners, placed the destiny of the besieged city in the international context.

Speech by City Councillor Ernst Reuter on Republic Square, Berlin, 9 September 1948 (extract)

Peoples of the world, peoples of America, Britain, France, Italy, look at this city and realize that you must not abandon this city and this people, cannot abandon them! ... We have done our duty and shall continue to do so. Peoples of the world, do your duty likewise, and help us in the time that faces us ... with that steadfast, unshakable commitment to common ideals that alone can guarantee our future, the future of all of you.

The West Berliners were then the first Germans who were convincing as democrats, and it was also in Berlin that for the first time the change from victors and vanquished to allies came about. During the blockade, Allies and Germans experienced daily that they were in the same boat and were dependent on each other.

When a decade later between 1958 and 1962, Stalin's successor Nikita Khrushchev once again sought to squeeze the Western powers out of Berlin through ultimatum demands, it was U.S. President John F. Kennedy who on 26 June 1963, when the crisis was overcome, paid tribute to the Berliners on the square before the Schöneberg Town Hall (today Kennedy Platz), and encouraged them to stand firm.

Speech by U.S. President John F. Kennedy before the Schöneberg Town Hall in Berlin, 26 June 1963 (extract)

What is true of this city is true of Germany. Real lasting peace in Europe can never be assured as long as one German out of four is denied the elementary right of free men, and that is to make a free choice.

In eighteen years of peace and good faith this generation of Germans has earned the right to be free, including the right to unite their families and their nation in lasting peace with goodwill to all people.

You live in a defended island of freedom, but your life is part of the main. So let me ask you as I close, to lift your eyes beyond the dangers of today to the hopes of tomorrow, beyond the freedom merely of this city of Berlin and all your country of Germany to the advance of freedom everywhere, beyond the wall to the day of peace with justice, beyond yourselves and ourselves to all mankind.

Freedom is indivisible, and when one man is enslaved who are free? When all are free, then we can look forward to that day when this city will be joined as one and this country and this great continent of Europe in a peaceful and hopeful globe.

When that day finally comes, as it will, the people of West Berlin can take sober satisfaction in the fact that they were in the front line for almost two decades.

All free men, wherever they may live, are citizens of Berlin. And therefore, as a free man, I take pride in the words: Ich bin ein Berliner!

The Berlin crisis was, like the Cuba crisis, a trial of strength between East and West in which whoever yielded lost worldwide and in which far more was involved than the viability of the "island in the Red Sea," as people then called it. But West Berliners played a part in it too, because they displayed their will to stay with the West with the same resolve they had shown during the blockade.

The city acquired merit in subsequent decades simply from its absurd existence: even and especially in the hours of hopelessness, Berlin acted as a bond between the Germans in East and West. Without divided Berlin, the alienation would have bitten less sharply, division been felt less painfully. In the autumn of 1989 it was then the citizens in the Eastern part of the city who liberated themselves from their Stalinist governing party and helped the failed rising of 17 June 1953 to a happy, if belated, resolution.

This time it was the Czech Václav Havel who most convincingly took up the tradition of great words, which particularly in Berlin have always been great politics too. Barely a hundred hours after his election as President of Czechoslovakia, he made his first flight abroad — to his German neighbors, for which in early 1990 two landings were still necessary. The long-persecuted civil rights activist had his own priorities: he cheerfully set protocol aside and asked the waiting journalists and photographers to understand that for him it was "more important to go and see the Berlin Wall than stand before a camera." A quarter of a century after the U.S. President, he took up Kennedy's famous phrase and in a short improvised address sketched out his vision of the future of a Europe without walls.

Speech by Czechoslovak President Václav Havel at the Brandenburg Gate, Berlin, 2 January 1990 (extract)

Many years ago, President John F. Kennedy visited the Berlin Wall. He said then: "ich bin ein Berliner." I wish to take the liberty of repeating that sentence in a new time, in a new context. For I feel myself a Berliner in the sense that in the period of my presidency I shall within the scope of my influence and my possibilities seek to tear down all barriers, all walls, all wires, that separate and divide Europe.

On that occasion Havel explicitly thanked the GDR for having started tearing down the Wall. How infinitely long ago seemed the time when the following Honecker joke, at the time indisputably a sensitive seismograph to the events and the mood in the country, was being hawked around the GDR. It goes like this: The wall in Berlin is to be made higher. Why? Erich Honecker's building society savings have matured, now he wants to invest them. The particular point of this somewhat cruel joke is that in his capacity as then Secretary to the Central Committee for security questions Honecker had in fact been a sort of building master for what in GDR jargon was called the "anti-fascist protective bulwark" and had in the night of 13 August 1961 not ceased to look after things at various points on the border and make encouraging speeches to the building gangs.

The Wall stood for precisely 10,315 days. On 10 November 1989, Berliners from both parts of the city gathered in front of the Schöneberg Town Hall to celebrate their regained freedom together. On that occasion Berlin's governing Mayor, Social Democrat Walter Momper, coined the phrase about the Germans as the "happiest people in the world" that went down in the history of the peaceful November revolution.

Speech by governing Mayor Walter Momper before the Schöneberg Town Hall, Berlin, 10 November 1989 (extract)

Today is a great day. The wall no longer divides us. . . .This is the moment we have so long awaited. For 28 years, since the building of the Wall on 13 August 1961, we have longed for this day and hoped for it. We Germans are now the happiest people in the world.

But in this hour of joy we also recall the many dead and the many injured, the misery and the suffering, that this wall cost. May it never, never be repeated.

The border that long tormented us yesterday lost its divisive character. Freedom to travel is a human right. The GDR citizens took that right, that human right, yesterday. Just as in the last few weeks they have taken the right to shake off tutelage and shape their country themselves. It is a fascinating chapter in German history that is now being written in the GDR. This chapter of history is being written by the people of the GDR themselves. We congratulate the citizens of the GDR, men and women, on their peaceful, democratic revolution.

But it is not just since 1989 that 9 November has been a prominent date in German history. It was on 9 November 1918 that Philipp Scheidemann proclaimed the first German Republic from the balcony of the Reichstag. The 9th of November 1938 is one of the blackest days of the German past: the "Reichskristallnacht." By 11 November, 91 Jews had been killed — 80 of them in Berlin alone — and over 26,000 dragged off to concentration camps.

A bare month after the fall of the Wall, *Die Zeit* asked an American and a Frenchman what they felt at that moment and whether, in their view, the old Germany was returning. Both statements give a representative picture of the varying reactions to this historic event that could be found in the media in those days.

For Elie Wiesel, an Auschwitz inmate and 1976 Nobel Peace Prize winner now living in New York, the fall of the Berlin Wall raised very mixed feelings, culminating in the question whether Germans were engaged in forgetting the past:

> The fact that this astonishing event took place nowhere else than Berlin lent it additional significance. Fifty years before, this was the capital of absolute evil in history; today it has suddenly become a symbol of hope. If something like this is possible, I thought to myself, one need

not abandon hope for similar developments in other parts of the world
— say the Near East.

Then as so often, my feelings were squeezed out by political
considerations. Editorial writers and experts raised the obvious questions: What comes next? Will this unforeseen course of events lead to
the reunification of Germany? If so, when? What international repercussions will that have? Will a united, powerful, new Germany be able
to free itself from the demons of conquest that once dominated the
old Germany? I cannot conceal the fact that particularly as a Jew I
am concerned at that, indeed worried. Whenever Germany became too
powerful, it succumbed to the temptations of ultra-nationalism. . . .

The trend is towards normalization of political consciousness and
of history. If this development continues unobstructed, will it not lead
to the quite natural desire to close the chapter of the past? Is the course
of events not too quick? Is there not a danger lurking in the acceleration
of history?[63]

For Frenchman Dominique Moïsi, born after the Second World
War and a frequent visitor to Germany and particularly to Berlin
as deputy director of the Paris Institute for International Relations
(IFRI), the breaching of the Wall was a moment of happiness he
had long waited for. For him too the twelve years of barbarism
that took his father for two years to Auschwitz and Mauthausen
remain unforgotten, yet these darkest years of German history
have not wiped out everything else:

Germany can regain its identity only in unity. It has to overcome the
three traumatic experiences of Nazi rule, war and division. It can only
leave the present crisis of its cultural identity and the arrogance of its
economic power behind it if it finds its way to another, comprehensive,
political, cultural and economic identity. And it will manage that only
if it makes the experience of unity and at the same time understands
that unity as a culmination of European unity. Europe needs a Germany
that is stable, strong and at harmony with itself. For that it has to
be one Germany.

Berlin must again become one of the great capitals of the European
mind. If Auschwitz is to rest in peace, intellectual life and intellectual
brilliance must again fill the heart of Berlin. In the divided city, the
victim of German overbearingness and of the Cold War, there was in
one half too much artificial illumination and in the other too much
gloomy oppression. Now that reunification is already taking place in

63. Elie Wiesel, "VergeBt Ihr die Vergangenheit?" in *Die Zeit*, 15 December
1989.

minds, Berlin, the obvious capital of the new Germany, should become
a bridge between the two parts of Europe. At the same time, however, the city should also be a place from which Europe can send a
signal of hope to the third world.[64]

A bare six months later, now in the midst of the fiercely raging
"capital dispute," the *Bonner Generalanzeiger* asked Germans and
foreigners for their opinions. From east of the Elbe, remarkably,
none of the contributions asked for had arrived by the deadline,
although according to all opinion surveys Berlin had an overwhelming majority of GDR votes for itself as the site of the future
German capital. In a representative survey by Infratest, which was
given great emphasis by the Bonn newspaper, only 32.3 percent
of Federal citizens voted for Berlin, while 48.7 percent were in
favor of Bonn. In a leading article, Friedhelm Kemna, who has
also lived for many years in Berlin as a journalist, arrives at his
judgment:

> Much is in favour of the view — and quite a few writers in this special
> supplement on the capital question take the same line — that a tradition
> upheld for over four decades by the Federal Republic of Germany of
> Bonn as the Federal capital ought to be maintained, in its historically
> unexampled democratic virtue and efficiency, for the whole of Germany
> too. These views also include, if it were possible, division of the functions
> of capital. The question is whether the town on the Rhine might not
> be the more seemly order of magnitude for the profile of a European
> Germany that should be aimed at than Berlin.
>   Yet this reference must beware of the simultaneously spread and his-
> torically false argument that as capital Berlin represented only the dark
> sides of German history. Berlin was also the capital of the Resistance;
> it was Berlin that on behalf of the whole of Germany kept the German
> question open. Assigning Berlin the rank of political capital too in a
> united Germany was the object of countless solemn proclamations
> throughout four decades.[65]

Here a real fact is addressed that in the debate on Berlin's future
role — German capital in the geographical center of Europe or
European metropolis on the periphery of united Germany — has
an importance that should not be underrated. It is an old

---

64. Dominique Moïsi, "Das Glück, zu sich selbst zu finden," ibid.
65. Friedhelm Kemna, "Es gibt mehr als eine Antwort," in "Die Hauptstadtfrage,"
Sonderbeilage des *Bonner Generalanzeiger*, 9 October 1990.

commonplace of political science that it is not the facts of history that are the decisive point, but the idea that people form of the facts. Seen that way, the "pictures in heads" of Berlin as a symbol of the "Reich," filling its neighbors in East and West first with fear and then in two world wars with terror and disastrous catastrophes, are just as much a reality as the Berlin of the Resistance that closed itself against the brown future of the first Hitler years no less stubbornly and lastingly than did the Rhinelanders in Cologne and Bonn.

Among the remarkable features of this debate is, however, that it was taking place at all. For as long as unity was expected by most to be coming at the Greek calends, everyone took it that Berlin was the "capital-in-waiting," and politicians of every color spoke of the objective of a single Germany and its "indivisible" capital, Berlin. The city that through its staunchness for ties with the West during the blockade became the midwife of the Western State, the Federal Republic, also embodies a piece of hope for the people of the ex-GDR, a last vestige of identity worth conserving. In a very sensitive commentary for the *Süddeutsche Zeitung*, Hermann Rudolph, a journalist born in Oschatz, Saxony, and author of several books on GDR society, has this to say:

> Above all, to be sure, the revolution of the autumn of 1989 would be robbed of a good part of its historic significance if Berlin did not become the capital again. If the future greater Germany were to remain primarily oriented to Bonn it would ultimately amount to unity being summed up in the Federal Republic's being augmented by the GDR. It would be a sign that the citizens of the Federal Republic were at bottom not prepared really to take up the challenge that unification means for them too: to shake up their existing views of life and open up to the experiences, views and demands of those with whom in future they will, as GDR Prime Minister de Maizière said in his government statement, form a "genuine community."[66]

At the end of his committed plea for Berlin, however, Rudolph made the critical statement that the city had not been unaffected by the years of being shunted into the waiting room of history. Over the decades, the claim to become German capital again had

66. Hermann Rudolph, "Hauptstadt fur die Einheit," in *Süddeutsche Zeitung*, 21–22 April 1990.

been undermined by being wrapped up in itself, by its narrowness; indeed, despite all its atmosphere of a metropolis, by its wearisome provinciality. But that very thing has also been a reason for the attractive power that a divided Berlin exercised on many intellectuals, if one is to believe Bernd Wagner, who lived almost a decade as a freelance writer in the Eastern part of the city before moving in 1985 to West Berlin. Wagner, coeditor of *Mikado*, probably the most important of a whole range of *samizdat* literary magazines, which since the early 1980s ventured forth in the GDR below and outside the censorship, stated the following:

> I am afraid, I wish to say, that the flourishing island I live on may stop being an island; fear that West Berlin, the only place in Germany I can live in, will no longer exist any more; that the floe under my feet will break up, the ice melt, we shipwrecks that thought we had already been saved again be thrown out to sea and have to swim like all the rest....
>
> I want everything to stay the way it is, I wanted to say. I want no change, I do not want any changes any more except the ones I make myself.
>
> I do not want history to start again from the beginning, I want it to stand irrevocably still, I want once and for all to have Stalinism over there and Batman over here; I do not want unity, I want differences, I want the separation of Europe into a first and a second world and I want to belong to the first.
>
> I want the Wall, I need it, for I am defenseless. I am afraid, I wanted to say, that the boundary between the realm of the old and the new, of evil and good, will fall away; the boundary that remained even when I confused the realms, and the labels along with them.[67]

In a forceful plea for Berlin as capital of a united Germany, none other than the Federal President, made honorary citizen of Berlin on 29 June 1990, entered the debate that day. For the first time since the division of the city in 1948, it was not only the Senate and the House of Deputies that conferred that high distinction. It was specifically the Senate and the magistracy, the House of Deputies and the Assembly of City Councillors jointly, that made Richard von Weizsäcker an honorary citizen of the whole of Berlin. At the ceremony, held neither in the Schöneberg Town Hall nor the Red Town Hall

---

67. Bernd Wagner, "Blitzschlag, Angst und Vaterlandsliebe," in *Mein Deutschland findet sich in keinem Atlas, op. cit.,* 102f. (note 3).

but in St. Nicolas's Church in the center of Berlin, the Federal President pleaded for Berlin as the logical culmination of the process of unification.

Speech by Federal President Richard von Weizsäcker on the occasion of conferment of the Honorary Citizenship of Berlin in St. Nicholas's Church, 29 June 1990 (extracts)

What is Berlin to be in Europe, above all, what is it to be in Germany itself? That is the core question that concerns all of us. It is the question of the capital. . . .

Our interests and our responsibility as Germans are and remain firmly rooted in our irreversible ties to the West. That is the very reason why they are aimed at security and peace for the whole of Europe and at East-West cooperation in all spheres. The more open a city is to that and the more it has to offer for that, the better qualified it is, from foreign-policy viewpoints too, to be the capital. . . .

Nowhere was the division so lived through as in Berlin. Nowhere else can we today so emphatically meet the task posed us by the coming unity, namely to ensure that things will not lastingly remain at the co-existence of two parts of the population with completely different burdens. Only in Berlin do we truly come from both parts, yet still are one. That is the great opportunity for a healthy, gradual growing together. Politics must daily share that experience directly, since it bears the responsibility for ensuring that our unification is lastingly successful.

"*Fühlst Du nicht an meinen Liedern, dass ich eins und doppelt bin*?" "Can you not feel from my poems that I'm one, but also two?" asked Goethe in a famous poem from his *West-Östlicher Diwan*. For the last forty years this has been an apt description of German identity. Politically divided for the foreseeable future, yet one in culture and history: having to live with this tension, like the curiously grown-together leaves of the *Ginkgo biloba*, the maidenhair tree, described in the poem. That was what made the special difficulty of being a German. Now that both parts of Germany have "the chance of healthy, gradual growing together," it is decisively important for the unification to be experienced and understood not only by Germans, but by all Europeans, also as an opportunity for the harmonious growing together of their divided continent.

5

Germany in Tomorrow's Europe

German unification changes essential parameters of the political landscape of postwar Europe based on division, the status quo, and opposing alliance systems. The new all-German polity must be fit into the newly emerging configuration of the Old Continent in such a way that it is felt by its neighbors, and by the other powers involved with Europe, to be a factor for stability, not for uncertainty.

It is at the geographical center of Europe, where the major point of military presence still lies, in Germany in particular, that the central construction of the new security structure will have to be erected if the whole is to stand up. This assigns a central importance to the European Community as a cornerstone and coordinating body in the system of European relations. Certainly, there are other foreign policy forums where Germany is also represented, but no other organization has the degree of combination of structure, ambitions, and action that the European Community does.

A clear consensus has emerged since the end of 1989 that the process of regaining German unity is also to be understood as a European issue and must therefore be seen in connection with the integration of Europe as a whole. It is important to keep in mind here that the German question did not begin its career as a cardinal problem of international European politics at the end of World War II. The national unity of Germans was never something given in history; it was always a problem, and what was to count as "Germany" has been in controversy for much more than forty-five years.

For the last three hundred years, there has never been a period in which Germany was not an essential part of the European system of States, either through its formal alliances or in more indirect ways. The German question emerged as a wider European issue with the Peace of Westphalia in 1648, which granted an international legal framework to the Holy Roman Empire of the German Nation, a fragmented grouping of territories large and small, governed in a variety of ways, including through foreign influence. A neutralized Central Europe, one without a political power focus, remained a first principle for the preservation of peace until the beginning of the nineteenth century. At the Congress of Vienna in 1815, after the collapse of Napoleon's policy of European hegemony, the Great Powers again agreed on a rearrangement of German States in a new, looser grouping, the German Confederation, which they would guarantee.

From the post-Napoleonic German Confederation, with its rival centers of Austria and Prussia via the Central European hegemony of Bismarck's Reich and its failed containment by the Treaty of Versailles, to Hitler's claims to world domination, the German question has remained a problem for Europe. It is only at the end of this century that a real chance has come into being for a solution to this question favorable both to the Germans and to Europe as a whole.

The Germans in the European Community

The Chinese ideogram for the concept "opportunity" means "crisis" as well. This association serves well to describe how political developments in Germany and the breakup of Eastern Europe have interacted. It also leads one to the conclusion that the political actors of our day may one day be measured by how they exploited the opportunities of this crisis. This is true first for the process of rethinking alliances, which has been under way since early 1990, and second, for the European Community as well, which is now faced with the twofold challenge of incorporating the ex-GDR into the Brussels Treaty framework and of reshaping its relationships to the reforming countries of Central and Eastern Europe.

Western Europe, in its manifestation as the European Community, sees itself faced in the 1990s with a massive creative task for which it is only partly prepared. The completion of the internal market that is planned for January 1993, and the leading role that the July 1989 Paris world economic summit of leading Western industrial nations entrusted to the European Commission with regard to measures of cooperation with and assistance to the democratizing COMECON

States, remain important milestones in coping with these tasks. The joint Franco-German initiatives in 1990 and 1991, for acceleration of political union and for a common foreign and security policy for the European Community, are still further signs of growing awareness of pan-European issues. If this historic opportunity to strengthen the Europe of freedom and democracy is not to be foregone, it is indeed time to sketch out a map for a qualitatively new stage in Community policy.

That developments in Germany are of fundamental importance for the Community is documented also by the fact that at a special 28 April 1990 summit in Dublin the consequences of German unification for Community policy were discussed. There it was the line of European Commission President Jacques Delors that won out; he had already spoken earlier in favor of regarding the GDR — "as one of the family" — as a "special case" among the States of Central and Eastern Europe. The Dublin resolutions proved the Community's capacity to keep pace politically even with such headlong developments as those within Germany and in East and Central Europe as a whole.

Presidency Conclusions of the Special Meeting of the European Council, Dublin, 28 April 1990 (extract)

2.
The Community warmly welcomes German unification. It looks forward to the positive and fruitful contribution that all Germans can make following the forthcoming integration of the territory of the German Democratic Republic into the Community. We are confident that German unification — the result of a freely expressed wish on the part of the German people — will be a positive factor in the development of Europe as a whole and of the Community in particular.

3.
A point has now been reached where the continued dynamic development of the Community has become an imperative not only because it corresponds to the direct interests of the twelve Member States but also because it has become a crucial element in the progress that is being made in establishing a reliable framework for peace and security in Europe. The European Council therefore agrees that further, decisive steps should be taken towards European unity as envisaged in the Single European Act.

German Unification

4.

We are pleased that German unification is taking place under a European roof. The Community will ensure that the integration of the territory of the German Democratic Republic into the Community is accomplished in a smooth and harmonious way. The European Council is satisfied that this integration will contribute to faster economic growth in the Community and agrees that it will take place in conditions of economic balance and monetary stability.

But the special summit in Dublin also made clear that we are in a transitional period, in which national and Community policy motives are intertwined. Support for German unity — that is, for the German national State — was unanimous; yet, it was not only the British who shied away from the great possibility of using this event as the occasion to define a thoroughly new political constitution for Western Europe. For American journalist Elizabeth Pond, in the 1980s European correspondent for the Boston *Christian Science Monitor*, Germany in particular is especially well-prepared for the "postnational Europe":

Germany — the "belated nation," the political dwarf with a chronic identity crisis: Germany is leading the trek into the European future. Along that road, its own situation may be normalized and at the same time a European unity emerge, as under Charlemagne, but now a decentralized, federative, postnational unity. . . .

Seen this way, a de-nationalized and decentralized Federal Republic brings far better preconditions for the new era of a supranational Europe of the 1990s than does France or Britain, not to speak of the Soviet Union. The Germans in 1945 lost their sovereignty and their national pride. They already have that painful loss behind them, as the European Community gains in power and influence. . . .

Germany's time has come. Despite its past, it is the heir of the Enlightenment and of the West. In these turbulent months, the country had a concept of its political goals and pursued a prudent foreign policy to secure those goals. Germany has finally found its identity in Europe.[68]

The process of incorporation into European integration and the renunciation of nation-state thinking will certainly be a decisive

68. Elizabeth Pond, "Aufbruch mit neuer Identität. Deutschland ist für das postnationale Europa gut vorbereitet," in *Die Zeit*, 3 August 1990.

test of the Federal Republic's self-image as a State; a self-image that now must be conveyed to unified Germany. But there is also a need for the European Community to prove its ability to adapt to the increased economic and political power of one of its members.

The political debate on the risks that might arise from German unity is clearly dominated by the fear that the new Germany, with the economic power of 80 million people, might take a still stronger position in Europe than the old Federal Republic of Germany. Here it is mostly political weight that is meant, the weight that the biggest partner, in economic terms, to integration could bring to bear in Community decisions — especially because the final goal of integration is political union. These fears were articulated in a particularly blunt way by then British Minister for Trade Nicholas Ridley, when in a 14 July 1990 interview with Dominic Lawson, editor-in-chief of the respected Conservative weekly *The Spectator* and son of Margaret Thatcher's former Chancellor of the Exchequer Nigel Lawson, he said the "unsayable about the Germans" — as the article's title ran. The title page of the magazine was illustrated with a caricature of Federal Chancellor Kohl with a black Hitler forelock and Hitler toothbrush moustache.

Interview by British Minister for Trade and Industry Nicholas Ridley with Dominic Lawson in "The Spectator," 14 July 1990 (extracts)

[European monetary policy] is all a German racket, designed to take over the whole of Europe. It has to be thwarted. This rushed take-over by the Germans on the worst possible basis, with the French behaving like poodles to the Germans, is absolutely intolerable. . . .

When I look at the institutions to which it is proposed that sovereignty is to be handed over, I'm aghast. Seventeen unelected reject politicians. . . . with no accountability to anybody . . . .who are pandered to by a supine parliament . . . .the idea that one says, "Okay, we'll give this lot our sovereignty," is unacceptable to me . . . .You might just as well give it to Adolf Hitler, frankly . . . .

We've always played the balance of power in Europe. It has always been Britain's role to keep these various powers balanced and never has it been more necessary than now, with Germany so uppity . . . .Being pushed about by a German would set off utter indignation here, and that would be quite understandable too.

Sir Ralf Dahrendorf, former German European Commissioner, later Director of the London School of Economics, and today, as Rector of St. Antony's College, Oxford, very well acquainted with political realities in Britain and Brussels, believes like most commentators that Ridley's views are not entirely alien to the then Prime Minister's immediate circle, regarding them as the minority opinion, since the Conservatives are also looking for a way to combine national interest and European destiny effectively. In the view of this learned economist and social scientist, the real problems lie elsewhere:

> The much tougher question is instead whether united Germany will still have the same interest in the European Community as the old Federal Republic. Is a new Washington — Bonn — Moscow axis perhaps forming here? and does Mr. Pöhl's two-stage Europe not exclude Britain in order to sustain the DM area? How serious really is German policy towards Europe? Does it not mean that European integration is ultimately the most important guarantee of a peaceful future for the continent?
>
> Today it is clear that Mrs. Thatcher cannot put the questions of Europe's structure that way. Her picture of the world derives from another epoch. . . .
>
> The British voice is missing in this year of reconstruction and new construction. In any case, there are not exactly many voices worth listening to. Germany is confusing its friends; France is abashedly silent; from Britain it is again primeval noises that are to be heard. All this has not for the moment had any dramatic effects, but it is disruptive in a process that could open up so many opportunities.[69]

A similar confusion of feelings can also be diagnosed in the Italian Gianni De Michelis, whose country took over presidency of the Community in the second half of 1990. De Michelis, who is Socialist Foreign Minister for the Christian Democrat Prime Minister Giulio Andreotti, had already taken a very headstrong step in Ottawa in February 1990 in calling — only to be disavowed a little later by the Prime Minister — for Italy's inclusion in the Two-plus-Four talks. Andreotti himself had caused a furor on 13 September 1984 at the communist "Unità" festival with his committed plea for the permanency of German double statehood when, referring to the danger allegedly threatening South Tyrol

---

69. Ralf Dahrendorf, "Schrille Töne von der Insel. Die Ridley-Affare zeigt erneut: Margaret Thatcher hat mit Europa nicht viel im Sinn," in *Die Zeit*, 20 July 1990.

of pan-Germanism, he said with cutting clarity: "There are two German States, and there should continue to be two German States."

Following a meeting of Christian Democratic heads of government of Community countries in Pisa, Andreotti by contrast assured the press on 6 February 1990 that, converted by recent events, he was "absolutely certainly" in favor of German unity and also understood the haste with which Federal Chancellor Kohl was striving for it. Gianni De Michelis, who in the spring of 1990 had spoken about the relationship between "stability and integration in Central Europe," seemed to share this new optimism of his head of government only in a conditional way.

Article by Italian Foreign Minister Gianni De Michelis in NATO Review, May-June 1990 (extracts)

In the place of our familiar, and therefore reassuring, adversaries, are we now to find ourselves face to face with some rather disquieting friends?

The old world was familiar territory to us, while today's is full of uncertainties, resulting from the disappearance of traditional points of reference . . . .

The current situation has become increasingly uncertain as a result of the Soviet Union's internal problems, as formidable as its geographic size, and the accelerated pace of the German unification process, which continually brings new surprises, due to the numerous implications for domestic and foreign policy . . . .

The idea of integration must, therefore, be extended to include the Europe of the Slavs, of the Danube region, formerly Hapsburg, and of the Balkans. A Europe of the Twelve is not enough; but nor do we want to create new axes, new hegemonies or new national alliances.

The fear of being politically marginalized, of becoming no longer the shapers of policy but the recipients of the decisions of the "others," seems to be the common denominator of many prominent anti-German statements in recent times. Who really won the war? The question is still being asked. In a Europe in which the relationships of forces are no longer primarily determined by the confrontation between blocs and the security-policy dependency for Germans bound up with it, economic strength counts more than ever.

On 1 July 1990 the German monetary union came into force, and on the same date, the first stage on the road to European monetary union began. In the categories of politics, these are two almost incomparable processes; in their economic interactions, however, the two events are closely interconnected. If the experiment of German monetary union were to be burdened with rising inflation rates, an unacceptable impact on employment, or even unsupportable budget deficits, this would also weaken the internal market and the common economic area in Europe now in the process of formation. To the extent that German monetary union is a success, on the other hand, it will contribute to the rate of integration in Europe.

In the report on the impact of German unification on the Community that British Labour MP Donnelly presented to the European Parliament on 12 July 1990, this connection was brought out clearly: the German unification process has decisively contributed to the regained dynamics of European unification; it will, however, in the coming months and years present sizeable challenges to the Community.

Interim report of the Temporary Committee of the European Parliament to consider the impact of the process of German unification on the European Community, 9 July 1990 (extracts)

German unification: overall assessment of the impacts, and general considerations

12. The evidence taken by the Temporary Committee has demonstrated that the process of German unification is a highly uncertain, but nevertheless manageable one. The uncertainty is due to the entirely unfamiliar situation of converting a centrally planned economy into a market economy, a process which is also taking place in other Eastern European countries, but which will have to occur earlier and quicker in East Germany than elsewhere . . .

13. The process also appears to be a manageable one in terms of the impacts on the European Community. The legal and constitutional problems posed are unique ones, in that there has never been a considerable increase in the territory and economic weight of the European Community except by means of a formal accession by a third country after lengthy negotiations. . . .

14. The evidence taken by the Committee has shown that the balance of advantage to the Community of the process of German unification is likely to be very considerable. . . . Moreover, the current GDR's accession to the Community will act as an important bridge between the Community and

Eastern Europe and the Soviet Union, both in the political and economic fields. . . .

15. The outlook in the medium and long term is a promising one. In the shorter term, however, German unification will pose a number of problems, both within Germany and for the Community at large. . . .

Difficulties in integration into the Community were, moreover, perceived by the last GDR government as well. While the Commission wished to put incorporation of the GDR into legal acts with definite exceptions and transitional rules before the all-German elections in early December 1990, then Foreign Minister Meckel, at a working lunch for a session of the Council of the European Communities on 16 July 1990, put forward the view that over hasty incorporation of the GDR into the Community might still further increase the already great difficulties in the GDR's merger with the Federal Republic. A study done by two members of the East Berlin Institute for Politics and the Economy (IPW) before the special Community summit in April 1990, moreover, reached the conclusion that the image of the Community in the GDR was still for the most part vague, and that there was considerable ground to be traveled here:

> The political forces and the public of our country really started only recently to realize that the economic and monetary union being aimed at and national unification with the Federal Republic are closely bound up with the question of future European Community membership for the present GDR. In the GDR — as firstly also in the Federal Republic — the pressing tasks of merging the economies of the two States were initially seen as a German-German problem. In the programmatic documents that the parties and citizens' movements adopted in preparation for the elections to the Volkskammer on 18 March, the demands for restoration of national unity and for a European setting for the German unification process, in various variants, were mostly placed in foremost position. Few of these documents, however, explicitly mentioned the European Community. This all points to how little the European Community, as a system of integration and interpenetration among its Member countries, including the Federal Republic, and as the core of the Europeanization process among the economies, societies and States of our continent, is present in the traditional economic, political and social reality of the GDR and of the awareness of the parties and movements and of the citizens of our country.
>
> Poorly-developed perception of the Community is proving a shortcoming that may weigh increasingly heavily on the GDR.[70]

This pessimistic estimate does not, however, coincide with the findings of recent polls, which, as part of the regular opinion surveys by the European Commission, now cover the ex-GDR too. According to the spring 1990 *Eurobarometer*, 88 percent of the citizens of the GDR thought that Community affairs were important for their own future, 83 percent supported the present efforts at unification of Western Europe, and 65 percent would very much regret failure of the European Community.

A survey made simultaneously in the Federal Republic also contains remarkable statements on the relationship between efforts at unification and ties with the West. While three-quarters of Federal citizens (77 percent) were in favor of unification of the two German States, this favorable attitude declined markedly (to 24 percent) if this unification were to be made dependent on withdrawal from NATO, and only 4 percent would be prepared to sacrifice membership in the European Community for the sake of German unity. These findings are an encouragement to all those who, like André Fontaine, then director of *Le Monde*, believe in the possibility and necessity of a "European Germany," even if this belief is not entirely free from doubts and afterthoughts:

> At the beginnings of the work of European unification, in the middle of the Cold War, when talk was only of "containing" the Soviet Union, Robert Schuman made no secret of the fact that one of the main goals of his policy of European integration was to contain Germany too. The Federal Republic, which had come into being only a few months earlier on one of the biggest fields of ruins in history, reminded one at the time more of a beggar-woman waking from profound unconsciousness. If there was any point even then in "containing" it, then that necessity would today be several times greater, now that it is crowning its economic triumph by annexing the GDR without striking a blow!
>
> This triumph has not yet turned Helmut Kohl's head, and he is seeking to calm his neighbours by calling on them to "tie in" his country and give it a "European roof". . . .
>
> The only policy still open to France if it is to prevent a German Europe is to support the efforts of all those who — with the Chancellor and his friend Delors at their head — are fighting for a European Germany:

---

70. Gert Schimansky-Geier and Norbert Lehmann, "DDR und Europäische Gemeinschaften (I)," in *IPW-Informationsdienst*, 1, 10 May 1990.

a Germany whose sovereignty would be sufficiently limited to reduce the risk of its dominating the continent to the minimum conceivable.[71]

This attitude is, moreover, supported by a broad majority in the Community Member States. In the *Eurobarometer* survey in spring 1990, a clear majority (71 percent) was still in favor of unification. The smallest assent figure is among Luxemburgers (52 percent) and Danes (56 percent); the largest among Spaniards (81 percent) and Italians (77 percent); the proportions of French (66 percent) and British (64 percent) are somewhat below the weighted average.

The citizens of the Member States are, in a plurality (43 percent), of the view that a united Germany would not face the Community with greater problems, while 23 percent assume that it would hinder the process of European integration. A further 24 percent have not yet thought about it.

Compatibility with Europe and Unity

The question of what size of Germany would be acceptable to its immediate and more distant neighbors, runs like a red thread through the debate on the Germans' role in Europe. This is a question posed put not only by others to the Germans, but also by Germans to themselves. A downright classical formulation of the problem can be found in a speech by Christian Democratic Federal Chancellor Kiesinger given before the Bundestag for the "day of German unity" on 17 June 1967.

Speech by Federal Chancellor Kurt Georg Kiesinger for the day of German unity, 17 June 1967 (extract)

Since . . . the point is to think about the German problem seriously and honourably, we must not duck the question of how this policy of ours of détente as a precondition for overcoming the division of our people can be combined with our Western alliance and with our efforts towards European unification. Does the one not exclude the other? Is there not a tragic contradiction here in the thinking and feeling of our whole policy? Germany, a reunited Germany, has a critical size. It is too big to play

71. André Fontaine, "Une Europe du possible," in *Le Monde*, 6 July 1990.

no part in the balance of forces, and too small to keep the forces around it in equilibrium by itself. It is therefore in fact hard to conceive how Germany as a whole could, if the present political structure in Europe continues, join one side or the other without further ado. For that very reason, the growing together of the separate parts of Germany can only be seen as imbedded within the process of overcoming the East-West conflict in Europe.

Barely ten years later, Federal President Scheel, who as an FDP politician and Foreign Minister in the first Social Liberal coalition helped to put a decisive stamp on the *Ostpolitik* of the 1970s, took a stance in the Bundestag on the same occasion. This was at a period of disillusion in German policy, when the Honecker regime was adopting a restrictive interpretation of the Basic Treaty and at the same time pursuing a rigid policy of demarcation. This rigidification was reflected in particular in the constitutional amendment of autumn 1974, in which any reference to the existence of a German nation in two States and the vision of a later unification was deleted. The distance thus taken from the concept of the unity of the nation, combined in the text of the 1974 Constitution with a consistently upward valuation of ties with the USSR and the Socialist Community of States, was interrupted only briefly by Honecker when on 15 February 1981 he surprisingly spoke of a unification of the two German States under the aegis of socialism.

Speech by Federal President Walter Scheel on the twenty-fifth anniversary of the day of German unity on 17 June 1978 (extract)

We certainly do not want to return to a state of political feeling, thinking and acting that isolated our people in democratic Europe. That Europe felt fear of, since it continually had to watch out for irrational decisions as a result. We do not, of course, wish to return to forms of government, to concepts of the State, that prevailed in the Holy Roman Empire, in Wilhelmine Germany or even in the so-called "Third Reich". . . .

Our struggle for unity is not a dusty, backward-looking romanticism about the Reich — unity is a forward-looking goal of peace for Europe. We are striving for unity in order to "serve the peace of the world as an equal partner in a united Europe."

These words of the Basic Law make it clear that the old-style nation-

State, jealously watching over its sovereign rights, is not the goal of our struggle for unity. . . .

A bare seven months after the breaching of the Wall, and two months to the day after the first free elections in the GDR, one decisive milestone on the road to national unity was achieved in Bonn with the signature of the State Treaty on economic, monetary, and social union. It is rather unique in history for a State to commit itself, at great risk, employing all its ever-cherished monetary stability, to the economic and financial rehabilitation of a neighbor. Other East European peoples who, like the GDR, were economically ruined under the banner of Marxism-Leninism are in a less fortunate position, even if the Federal Republic, within the limits of its possibilities and in the interest of an integrating Europe, will give assistance there as well.

Bonn's commitment to the GDR was justified by the continued existence of a single German nation and a single German people denied by Honecker's SED, which after forty years of forced division has found the road to unity. On the occasion of signature of the Treaty in the Palais Schaumburg in Bonn, the Federal Chancellor and the GDR Prime Minister also recalled the European dimension of this — in Helmut Kohl's words — "historic moment in the life of the German nation."

Statements by Federal Chancellor Helmut Kohl and GDR Prime Minister Lothar de Maizière on signature of the State Treaty in Bonn on 18 May 1990 (extracts)

Statement by the Federal Chancellor

This historic day of signature of the Treaty on economic, monetary and social union also starts a new period of European history. We are at the same time setting ourselves a great task of creation. Its success is of great importance for the future of the whole of Europe, well beyond the borders of Germany. . . .

At the end of this century that has brought so much suffering to humanity, we Germans are being offered a unique opportunity — the opportunity to "attain the unity and freedom of Germany in free self-determination" and "serve the peace of the world in a united Europe." That is the mandate of the Basic Law. That is also what our neighbours expect of us. We wish to be German Europeans and European Germans.

Let us take advantage of this opportunity; let us take up our duty. I call upon Germans in East and West to create together the united Germany in a united Europe.

Statement by the Prime Minister of the GDR

This is an important day for us today. It is the beginning of actual achievement of the unity of Germany. The economic, monetary and social union makes the process of unification irreversible. What we are today taking is a decisive step towards our goal: to complete the unity of Germany in freedom, in a European peace order. . . .

Among us, too many are becoming pusillanimous before the undoubted mountains of problems that face us. Perhaps we Germans should in this issue too not be so concerned with ourselves, but look towards Europe. I am convinced that the outcome of the unification process will not leave any German the poorer, but that things will go better for us all jointly. Nor will that be at the expense of Europe, but to the benefit of a joint European development in peace, freedom, prosperity and social justice.

It is striking that both politicians avoided Gorbachev's image of the "common European house," long bandied about particularly in German-speaking countries and probably already cited to death. This withdrawal from Utopia, which can also be seen in the Soviet Union itself — quite apart from the reforming countries in Central and Eastern Europe — seems to be symptomatic of a new stage in international relationships: the search for practical solutions now takes primacy. In the joint German-Soviet declaration of 13 June 1989, which was signed at the conclusion of Gorbachev's State visit to Bonn, the two concepts of a "European peace order" and a "common European house" still stood side by side on an equal footing. One year later, at the German-Soviet meeting in the Caucasus, the Soviet President said laconically — in German — that they had "just been doing *Realpolitik*."

United Germany remains an integral component of the Western alliance and of the European Community, which does ultimately intend to develop toward political union, toward the limitation of national sovereign rights. Seen that way, it is not Gorbachev's blueprint but the Community as a "European house" capable of expansion that offers the model for the future architecture of the continent. This fact is reason enough for Parisian expert on Germany and convinced European Jean François-Poncet, General Secretary at the Elysée Palace under President Giscard d'Estaing, then Foreign Minister, and today Senator, to accept unification and the accompanying external circumstances in a relaxed fashion. In an interview with the weekly *Der Spiegel* on 23 July 1990 he presented his opinion:

> There are two possibilities here: either Europe falls back into a policy of nationalism and a Germany freed of all commitments cooperates sometimes with France, sometimes with the Soviet Union. Europe would then be back more or less where it was in 1913, minus the risk of war. We want a different Europe, while at the same time we understand that Germany, in the interest of reunification, should make treaties with the Soviet Union — as long as that is not at the expense of Europe....
>
> If we take the lessons of history, we shall build Jean Monnet's Europe, not the Europe of Rapallo....The times are past when it was thought that France would dominate Europe politically, and Germany economically. The French should not even start to ask whether Germany weighs a little more or a little less, and vice versa. That would be a tragic fallback, if not to the year 1913, at any rate to 1922, the year of Rapallo, and that also means a fallback into European powerlessness.[72]

While the Frenchman François-Poncet wished to show by his analogies with 1913 and 1922 that Europe was now dealing with an utterly changed Germany, the position of well-known American historian Gordon A. Craig a few days after 9 November 1989 looked decidedly more pessimistic. The Scots-born adviser to several U.S. administrations nevertheless qualified his statements by pointing out that history was in a way like a large wardrobe in which one could scrabble for whatever fit the particular occasion:

> But I would go so far as to say that many people are convinced that the Germans have an occasional breakdown; and that this is attributable to the dark abysses in their souls, to their constant inclination to ask themselves who and what they are and what they are living for. On top of that is their feeling that nobody loves them. Hence the tendency to make big triumphs out of tiny victories; in short, to exaggerate. But we ought not of course to forget that much has changed in the last forty years....
>
> The mystical reverence shown towards the State has gone; the relationship between citizen and government has become more pragmatic. The politics of mysticism and the mythologies have been driven out. This is real democracy. To be sure, under the influence of very strong emotion, of a powerful upsurge of feeling such as with sudden reunification

72. Jean François-Poncet, "Zurück ins Jahr 1913?" in *Der Spiegel*, 23 July 1990.

with the awareness that they all belong together again, a spark might leap over. The surge towards a shining horizon behind which all possible promises lie concealed might perhaps start again.[73]

At the end of his statement, Craig declined, in reply to a question by the interviewer, to rule out the possibility of Germany's aiming at predominance in Europe by peaceful means. Similar views were evidently also discussed in a small circle of experts on Germany who came together in the spring of 1990 at Chequers, the country residence of the British Prime Minister, in spring 1990 to do some thinking on the future of Germany and the future of Europe. Margaret Thatcher had invited experts on Germany Gordon Craig and Fritz Stern from the United States and Lord Dacre (Hugh Trevor-Roper), Norman Stone, and Timothy Garton Ash from Britain, to spend a day discussing with them such themes as "Who are the Germans?" "Have they changed?" and "What consequences will unification have for Europe?"

The minutes of that meeting on 24 March 1990, written by Charles Powell, Mrs. Thatcher's chief foreign-policy adviser, read in part like a prewar treatise on national psychology and the German national character. The psychogram is not exactly flattering. The Germans, say the findings, are not concerned with the feelings of others, are plagued by fear, are bragging and pushy but want to be loved, suffer from an inferiority complex and self-overestimation, wallow in self-pity, and kick over the traces. But the Germans, it continues, no longer believe that the world should hang on the Germans' lips. They have no territorial claims and are no longer militaristic.

This summary, in the view of historian and journalist Timothy Garton Ash, present at Chequers, reflects more the writer's image of Germany than that of the expert. Mrs. Thatcher herself, argues Oxford professor Norman Stone, close to the Conservatives, is understandably caught in the trap of an image of Germany created in the twentieth century; but she had been convinced at the meeting that Germany was now a very good country that could teach the rest of the world a lot. This no doubt also explains the rather strange policy recommendation at the end of the minutes that one should be "nice to the Germans":

73. Gordon Craig, "Zu groß für Europa?" in *Der Spiegel*, 13 November 1989.

It still had to be asked how a cultured and cultivated nation had allowed itself to be brainwashed into barbarism. If it happened once, could it not happen again? Apprehensions about Germany did not relate just to the Nazi period but to the whole post-Bismarckian era, and inevitably caused deep distrust. The way in which the Germans currently used their elbows and threw their weight about in the European Community suggested that a lot had still not changed . . . .

There were differing views over how genuine the Germans were in saying they wanted a more integrated Europe in parallel with German unification. Was it just a tactic to reassure others? Or a genuine desire to subsume the latent nationalist drive of a united Germany into something broader? . . .

The overall message was unmistakable: we should be nice to the Germans. But even the optimists had some unease, not for the present and the immediate future, but for what might lie further down the road than we can yet see.[74]

On reading this report, one is inclined to agree with the analysis by Gebhard Schweigler of the Foundation for Science and Politics in Ebenhausen near Munich, who gives weighty reasons why despite high assent in opinion surveys, the West Germans' enthusiasm for unification is kept within limits. The question of the national awareness of Germans has been one of his specialities since he took his doctorate on the subject in the early 1970s at Harvard University.

In a commentary for the *Süddeutsche Zeitung* in late May 1990, Schweigler saw, in addition to a lack of willingness on the part of FRG citizens to bear the material costs of unification and a diffuse unease at the fact that 16 million Germans in the GDR were now to decide what almost 80 million Germans ought to do, two further motives, ones fed by the international dimension of the German question. To the question as to whether unification, of which one was in favor in principle, should take place now and immediately, especially if the price was still unknown, there are in Schweigler's view two ways to answer that, and which for many FRG citizens do not hold water:

---

74. The minutes of the meeting were reproduced a few days after the Ridley interview in the *Independent on Sunday* for July 15, and one day later in *Der Spiegel*, and Garton Ash's and Stone's positions in the *Frankfurter Allgemeine Zeitung* for 18 and 19 July 1990.

The nationalist answer — because Germany must be as big and strong and powerful as possible — is seldom heard. The future economic and political power of Germany is even if anything on the debit side of reunification. Why needlessly arouse neighbours' envy, discontent and fear? . . .

Of greater importance might be the nation-State answer: all Germans must live in one State and determine their destiny in it themselves. But against this answer is the current rhetoric in the Federal Republic which has for years been stressing the end of the nation-State in Europe. The Germans (in the West) have long pledged themselves to the goal of having their nation-State dissolved in a united Europe. . . . It can, then, be hardly surprising if Federal citizens today respond with uncertainty and confusion to the demand that all Germans ought to live in their own State.[75]

A few months earlier, the liberal Munich daily had used the Federal Chancellor's phrase, which has since then become commonplace, that the German question concerned "not only the Germans," as the occasion to ask authors — from East and West, from the Federal Republic and the GDR — to comment. "How can *what* Germany be fit into *what* Europe?" was the question answered by sociologist and freelance journalist Wolfgang Pohrt with the lapidary statement "Together we are intolerable." As a regular collaborator on the left-wing magazine *konkret*, Pohrt had made a name for himself in the early 1980s with his sharp attacks on the West German peace movement, which he accused of having turned into a "German national arousal movement."

United, Germans will feel even more the ones again robbed of a place in the sun, who have to conquer their living-space for themselves. For the West Germans will be worse off in a reunited Germany than they were ever accustomed to; and the GDR Germans not nearly as well off as they had expected and had seen.

Reunited Germany would, accordingly, be a society of the disappointed, loaded with resentment, railing against destiny, God and the world with the motto: "Together we are intolerable, and that is the others' fault."[76]

---

75. Gebhard Schweigler, "Reißt zum Schluß auseinander, was zusammengehört?" in *Süddeutsche Zeitung*, 31 May 1990.

76. Wolfgang Pohrt, "Gemeinsam sind wir unausstehlich," in *Süddeutsche Zeitung*, 28 February 1990.

The popular East Berlin cabaret "Distel [Thistle]," whose 1990
program "Mit dem Kopf durch die Wende [a pun: with your head
through the wall/your head through the turning-point]" was invariably sold out, tried in its own way to portray the changes, expectations, and fears of Germans and of their neighbors. One of the
most successful passages showed the wet-behind-the-ears couple
"BR-Detlef" and "DD-ERna" [the Federal Republic and the GDR]
wanting to rent a flat together, with lots of envious, fearful, and
sharp-eared neighbors.

Denial of and skepticism about a united Germany also permeate
most articles in a political collective volume, which came out as
the first German-German joint enterprise by two publishing houses,
from Frankfurt am Main and Leipzig, in the spring of 1990 under
the nostalgic title "Nothing will ever be what it used to be again."
The book was originally to be called "GDR, the hope," but by the
end of 1989, the working title had, to the bitter disappointment of
editors Blohm and Herzberg, who live in the two halves of Berlin,
"been given a big question mark." For they saw the publication as
an attempt to set a debate across the frontier going among the Left,
specifically those who "could not accept a mere *Anschluss* of the GDR
to the Federal Republic." Vicar Friedrich Schorlemmer, theology
lecturer in the Wittenberg divinity seminar, cofounder of "Democratic
Break," and now an SPD member, who had in December 1989 been
awarded the Carl von Ossietzky Prize of the West Berlin International
League for Human Rights, had the following to say about the national
question:

> We have brought down the Big Brother system, and now we are all
> really confused and do not want you over there in the Federal Republic
> to make a system for us. In the ante-room of hope lurks worry. Where
> are things to go, where will they go? (and there I can already hear
> the worried voices of the Jews and the Poles). . . .
>
> We still have time to combine the unity of Germany with the unifi-
> cation of Europe, not the other way around! Part of that is compre-
> hensive disarmament. Who if not the Germans should have a vital
> interest in demilitarization, since after all both countries are integrated
> into opposing military alliances and both territories are the most explo-
> sive arsenals. We Germans have a natural interest in peace, as all
> Europeans have a natural interest in never again having Germany militarily
> strong. . . .
>
> I would be pleased if in the two German States we could agree always
> to put peace before unity so that we can finally secure unity in peace.

If we gain a European peace order, that would be a gain in which no one would lose, but everyone would win — and no one would need fear us Germans any longer. Humanity reaches further than the flags of our country.[77]

In bringing "the worried voice of the Jews and the Poles" into his plea for national self-restraint, in support of his thesis, Vicar Schorlemmer no doubt had in mind the special sensibility of those hardest hit by Hitler's annihilatory plans. An impressive example of the readiness to take the "new Germany" without prejudices was given by Richard Cohen, the respected *Washington Post* columnist, on 6 December 1989, at a time when national unity by no means seemed inevitable:

Of course, no one can ignore what happened the last time Germany was unified. It produced Adolf Hitler, World War II and the Holocaust . . .

But a lot has changed. For almost half a century, West Germany has been a democracy — an integral part of the democratic West . . . Germany justifiably still remains on parole. But if a united Germany is ever to take its place among nations it has to be allowed to act much like any other nation. To treat it differently, to feed a German sense of victimization, would only repeat the mistakes of the past.[78]

The Franco-German Relationship Put to the Test

"Nothing will be the way it was again" is also a suitable description of the Franco-German relationship at the beginning of the new decade, if for different reasons. Many French diplomats and politicians are indeed, in view of the headlong changes in the neighboring country, beset with the woeful feeling that the Franco-German relationship will never again be what it was.

In September 1989, a translation appeared in France of Ernst Weisenfeld's very balanced analysis of French attitudes to the question of German unity since the end of World War II, which

77. Friedrich Schorlemmer, "Die Menschheit reicht weiter als die Fahnen unseres Landes," in Frank Blohm and Wolfgang Herzberg, eds., *"Nichts wird mehr so sein, wie es war," Zur Zukunft der beiden Republiken* (Frankfurt/M: Luchterhand; Leipzig: Reclam, 1990), 45ff.

78. Richard Cohen, "No Double Standard for Germany," in *Washington Post*, 6 December 1989.

was at the same time a plea for a joint security policy, for a policy toward the East, and for a continuing cooperation within Europe. Since 1951 the Paris correspondent and for years director of the French studio of the German television station ARD, now editor-in-chief of the journal for Franco-German dialogue, *Dokumente*, Weisenfeld described the attitudes of the French shortly before the Wall came down like this:

> Many Frenchmen are not easy with the idea that the self-determination of the Germans could lead to the reunification of 80 million people. Nevertheless, the great majority is today prepared to grant the Germans the self-determination they are calling on for Poles, Czechs, Hungarians and Romanians, without shrinking. . . .
>
> However, what they expect first of all from the Germans is patience. With their demand for unity, they ought not to anticipate too much of what is perhaps again possible in maybe fifty or a hundred years as regards possibilities of State structures in the heart of Europe. All empires some day break up. That is France's starting-point when it thinks about future systems in Central Europe too. What is important to it is to be involved in creating this system on principles to which it feels committed. These include the self-determination of all peoples of the area — including the Germans, including their right to unity. But not, pray, too much unity; at least not unity that has to become a danger to others. Otherwise, let time bring counsel. . . .[79]

It is precisely this attitude that is reflected in a number of statements shortly before 9 November 1989. Six days earlier, President Mitterrand, at a joint press conference with Federal Chancellor Kohl concluding the Franco-German summit, made the famous statement "I am not afraid of reunification," and added that the German striving for reunification was legitimate, "if they want it and if they can get it."

On 8 November, Mitterrand's political rival, Paris Mayor Jacques Chirac, at a talk to the French Institute for International Relations (IFRI) illustrated the "overcoming of Yalta" with the statement that France should tolerate no doubts of the fact that it was in favor of German reunification "if this was demanded by the Germans themselves." One day earlier, Foreign Minister Roland Dumas had taken the budget debate as the occasion to describe

---

79. Ernst Weisenfeld, *Quelle Allemagne pour la France?* (Paris: Armand Colin, 1989), 220.

the tasks of French policy in the light of the revolution in East and Central Europe. He called 1989 "a year of hope" and spoke of "major construction projects" for 1990, the first and most important of which lay in the area of East-West relations in Europe. A mere forty-eight hours later the Europe without walls and without divisive frontiers, the outlines of which Dumas had sketched in his speech, was to become a reality in the heart of the continent.

Speech by French Foreign Minister Roland Dumas to the National Assembly on 7 November 1989 (extracts)

The developments in the East are neither an accident nor a revenge of history. They are an expression of the strongest feeling lying deep within the human soul: love of freedom. . . .

One thing is certain: their aspiration to come together is legitimate. That is true for the German nation as it is for any nation that fate has divided. . . .

A new Europe is coming into being before our eyes. The Europe of the year 2000 will no longer have any similarity with the Europe of the division at Yalta. It is the wish of its peoples that that should be. With their silent marches in Dresden, in East Berlin, in Leipzig, in Prague, in Sofia, after those of Gdansk and Budapest, they are laying the foundations of the new building in which Europeans will find themselves again. History will then ensure that the walls will fall and the frontier barriers be lifted, since Europe will have become itself again.

Only a month later, the note of new departures, perceptible in Dumas's speech, was dampened by concern that developments in Germany could run too quickly and too much out of control. The President of the Republic was deeply offended when Kohl announced his Ten Point Programme, without consulting or even informing France. The Chancellor found it remarkable that Mitterrand should hastily announce a visit to the GDR, even before Kohl had agreed upon a date.

Suddenly, the behavior pattern described in a bitter comparison by editor-in-chief of *Die Zeit*, Theo Sommer, on 15 December 1989, applied to France as well: "Every pious Christian wishes to get to heaven, but none of them want it to happen too soon." By this the journalist was referring to the fact that the French

President — and President-in-Office of the European Community — had made it clear to the press, following the European Council's meeting in Strasbourg, that the Germans' desire for unity had to take second place to the requirements of European integration.

Press conference by French President François Mitterrand in Strasbourg, 9 December 1989 (extract)

I believe that these two movements (German unity and European unity) fit in to the becoming of Europe, but not just any time or anyhow . . . . I would say right away that it would be wise to develop, strengthen and accelerate the structures of the Community before any further steps. The Community acted on most countries in the East that are on the road to freedom and democracy like a breakwater and a magnet.

Had it not been there, things would not have happened the same way. There would have been a rapid approach to European anarchy, such as we knew before the 1914 War. . . . If the Community is first strengthened, the movement of peoples and States that do not belong to it will organize around this reality. The new German equilibrium that Germans are aiming for will fit into the European equilibrium, since the Community must not only strengthen itself. . .but must also continue to develop a new form of relations and of cooperation with the countries of the East and particularly the Soviet Union. . . .

That is why strengthening the Community takes priority among the factors that I have been putting forward for several weeks now; that is why I insist on the government conference. It is the sole objective link that can be seen between the various points we have touched on today.

Public opinion in France, however, differed considerably from the more reticent attitude of the political leadership. In a Franco-German opinion survey in mid-September 1989, when television pictures from the embassies in Prague and Warsaw were making the whole anomaly of the German situation vivid, almost four-fifths (79 percent) of those polled in France regarded German unification as legitimate, while the German partner, at 68 percent assent, lagged behind this record figure.

In a telephone survey for the conservative Paris daily, *Le Figaro*, on 9 and 10 November 1989 — the publication date was 13 November — it emerged that for 70 percent of the French, unification of the two German States was not an obstacle to European unification and, in any case, 60 percent were convinced that German unity was also a good thing for France. The discrepancy between public opinion and representatives of the "classe politique" caused Jean Hohwart, diplomat, expert on Germany, and author of a book published in 1988 by the highly-regarded Paris Foundation for Defense Studies (FEDN) on "Franco-German Necessities and Defense in Europe," to make the following commentary:

> Not all that long ago, the argument of European unification was being used to anchor the Federal Republic into the West, although it was already one of its essential constituents. Today it is really being used more to prevent Germany becoming too powerful within the West. As if one did not know that it has had economic pre-eminence in the Community and in the world for a long time now; as if one were refusing to see that its political weight has steadily grown over the course of the last decade, in consequence of its economic power, but also because of our own failure; as if only the newly added 16 million East Germans would be achieving what 60 million West Germans have already created. Does this not show quite clearly that the reasons and arguments of a good part of our intelligentsia are based not on rationality, but on emotional logic and on processes that rather more resemble Freudian repression?[80]

Of course, the wish to tie in and control Germany has much to do with the process of European unification, but it suc- cumbed early on to the nature of things and was always part of the effort at closer integration of Western Europe. For Germans, this connection between their unity and common Europe is accepted and taken on board, but from a thoroughly positive position. For them, Europe is a necessary alternative to the absolute rule of the nation-State that they themselves pursued *ad absurdum*.

Nor is unity the outcome this time of "Blut und Eisen" as with Bismarck's foundation of the Reich; rather, it is the by-product of a democratic uprising against a Stalinist type of dictatorship. Even in early autumn 1989, when young GDR refugees were telling the cameras the reasons why they had left home, family, and possessions, they were proving that they take as an inner law the

---

80. Jean Hohwart (pseudonym), "Pour un autre regard sur les évènements d'Allemagne," in *Le Trimestre du monde*, 1, 1990, 74.

freedoms that the West once conveyed to the beaten Germans as a guarantee against a return of totalitarian dictatorship.

On the afternoon of 17 January 1990, a few hours after Commission President Jacques Delors had spoken in his Strasbourg speech of the GDR's European "vocation," Federal Chancellor Helmut Kohl was a guest of the *"Bureau international de liaison et de documentation"* (BILD) and of the *"Institut français des relations internationales"* (IFRI), to give a talk on "The German Question and European Responsibility." On this occasion he dealt particularly with two issues that at the time dominated public debate in France: the border guarantee for Poland and the connection between German unity and European unification.

Speech by Federal Chancellor Helmut Kohl on "The German Question and European Responsibility" in Paris, 17 January 1990 (extracts)

The Germans — and no one should doubt this — have no intention to unleash on tomorrow's Europe a frontier debate that would inevitably endanger the European peace order we are jointly striving for.

The Germans want a lasting reconciliation with their Polish neighbours, and part of this is that Poles must have the assurance of living in secure frontiers. No one wants a second expulsion following the horrors of the expulsion that Germans have had to bear on their own bodies.

That is why no one wants to link reunification with the shifting of existing frontiers — frontiers which in a future Europe of freedom will in any case lose importance. . . .

In reality there is no contradiction between German unity and European integration. They are not competing but concomitant mandates of the Basic Law, in the preamble to which the German people are called upon to ". . . preserve their national and political unity and to serve the peace of the world as an equal partner in a united Europe."

The Federal Republic of Germany will accordingly not — as is here and there claimed — become a "problem case" in the European Community. . . .

The Federal Republic of Germany will stand by its European responsibility with no ifs and buts — for it is particularly true of us Germans that it is Europe that is our destiny!

Precisely because unity is the fruit of a wide-ranging European process and not solely of German effort, Germany and France ought to ensure that it does not end in a "retreat to the nation-State." This is the firm conviction of German-born French expert Joseph Rovan, who, just forty-five years ago, gave decisive impetus to Germany's rapid inclusion in the circles of the European democracies through his concept of "the Germany we deserve":

> Despite the advances of European integration, nation-State thinking, and particularly the feeling of the nation-State, has not disappeared in France any more than among Germans. In times of rapid change (and changes frighten most contemporaries), the nation appears to many as a sure value in the midst of unfathomable abysses. The absurdity of the idea that a French or German nation-State could in the 21st century lead an independent existence in between the great powers has scarcely reached the general awareness, and is not being presented with the necessary force to the citizens even by responsible politicians, who with few exceptions are tied to the national perspective. . . .
>
> For French fears, as for German agitation, there is no other solution than acceleration and deepening of the process of integration of the Twelve, which unfortunately depends not only on Germans and French people; it does, though, largely depend on their initiative. The German side must understand that these feelings are, first, historically understandable, and second, can be assuaged only by more European integration. The French side should see that only Jean Monnet's method of mutual linkage of national interests of one side and the other can prevent a chaos that would bring dangers to all concerned.[81]

Looking at it from this viewpoint, one may regret that on 22 December 1989 the French President left East Berlin only a few hours before the Brandenburg Gate — the monument that for decades had been a particularly spectacular symbol of the absurd division of the city — was opened. Was that not a missed historic opportunity to display Franco-German solidarity to the world? Or did France's status as victor and protective power oppose such a gesture, which would have been quite in the tradition of the symbolic acts at Rheims Cathedral and at Verdun? After all, eleven days previously, at Soviet request and for the first time since signature of the Four Power Agreement in 1971, the "Big Four" had met in the Allied Control Council building in Berlin to discuss the new position in their sphere of responsibility.

In ensuing months, German efforts to be rid as quickly as possible

---

81. Joseph Rovan, "Rückzug auf den Nationalstaat? Wieder einmal eine deutsch-französische Krise," in *Frankfurter Allgemeine Zeitung*, 8 February 1990.

of the vestiges of Allied responsibility, particularly in Berlin, as well as some of the accents of impatience and ingratitude in connection with the new role of Berlin as a future capital, conversely aroused irritation on the French side. In a pointed contribution to the June 1990 special issue of the Bonn *General-Anzeiger* on "The Capital Question," Alfred Grosser also took a position on Berlin's symbolic value in the relationship of Germans with their neighbors. He warned Germans to display greater sensibility in dealing with the Western powers, which had been particularly indispensable for decades:

> Here the point is particularly the future symbolic value of Berlin. This had already changed dramatically in June 1948. For the victors of 1945, until then Berlin had embodied Prussianness and Nazism, which was unjust in two respects: Prussia had many more positive features than was believed, particularly in France (and is indeed still sometimes believed today), and Hitler was certainly not exactly the embodiment of Berlinishness! At any rate, Berlin suddenly in June 1948 became a symbol of freedom — of threatened freedom, of freedom worth defending. The Western occupying powers became protective powers, and the West Germans — Berliners included — became partners in the cause of freedom. And then, from 13 August 1961 to 9 November 1989, the Wall became the symbol of the sharp division between freedom and unfreedom.
>
> At the same time, however, Berlin's Four-Power status retained another symbolic value: when in May 1972 the joint resolution of the Bundestag described the Four-Power system as desirable and to be retained, this was because the Four were the last bond around the unity of the German nation. Today the triune Moor of West Berlin has done his duty, so let him go: a united Germany no longer needs the Four, nor the protection of the Three for West Berlin.
>
> Yet the speed of forgetting is somewhat preoccupying. Berlin the capital, as a symbol of regained freedom for the Germans in the GDR, and for the Poles, the Hungarians, the Czechs: that is the way it should be in a foreseeable future. But not Berlin the capital in a Germany that forgets all the past, and raises power-claims to East and West! ...
>
> Bonn or Berlin, the moral obligation remains to think of others too. As a well-meaning but concerned friend from outside, one may express the fear that this is not being fully recognized.[82]

82. Alfred Grosser, "Die moralische Verpflichtung bleibt," in *General-Anzeiger*, 9–10 June 1990.

This warning from the country of the "hereditary friend" (a phrase coined by Alfred Grosser) meets with thorough understanding in the Federal Republic and corresponds with a particular sensitivity found in the French attitude. The future of Franco-German cooperation, which less than a generation ago was treated by Jean Giraudoux as "the only serious question in the world," also concerns politicians like Helmut Schmidt, who in the 1970s, along with Valéry Giscard d'Estaing, practiced the embrace be-tween Frenchmen and Germans as a kind of "dream couple."

Moreover, on 14 February 1990, both statesmen had approached their respective countries in a joint initiative and declared political union of Europe to be a priority task for Franco-German cooperation. As the Mitterrand-Kohl initiative was to show on the eve of the Dublin EC summit, this idea was also fully in line with the wish of the governments in Paris and Bonn. In the interim, the former Federal Chancellor had repeatedly taken a position of recalling the importance of France on the European dimension of the German question, stating for instance on 9 March 1990 in *Die Zeit*:

The French nation is the only one which in the eyes of all our neighbours can legitimatize German unity....

For decades the French have been our friends — from Monnet and Schuman via de Gaulle up to Giscard d'Estaing and Mitterrand. France has become our most important ally. Earlier we took no major step without prior accord with Paris, be it the Helsinki Final Act and its preparation or talks with Brezhnev, the NATO dual decision, the fight against terrorism or the creation of the World Economic Summit or the European Council of Heads of State and Government, or accession of the Mediterranean States to the European Community....

The impending unity of Germany raises questions of far greater importance than those just mentioned by way of example. Nothing today would be more important than continual accord for policy on Germany among the Twelve Community States, for Germany must remain predictable and calculable!

At the end of this dreadful century, our people have yet again been allotted an opportunity. We can take advantage of it for our morally justified goal of State unity only if we commit ourselves to the ethos of a politics soberly guided by pragmatic reason. If we do not, out of solidarity with our countrymen in the GDR, forget solidarity with our neighbors. If no neighbor has to doubt the uprightness of our words, or that they will be kept. And if we join willingly the community of peoples.[83]

German-German Community of Responsibility

Not forgetting solidarity with neighbors for the sake of solidarity with countrymen in the GDR was indeed one of the foremost tasks of Federal German policy after the turn in East Berlin. A few weeks after 9 November, historian Michael Stürmer, director of the research institute of the Foundation for Science and Politics in Ebenhausen near Munich, sought to sharpen his countrymen's view of their European responsibility and conversely look at the German-German rapprochement through the eyes of the outside world:

> For the point is still one of Europeanizing the German question, that is, providing European answers and tie-ins for the German question, and it is the sole point. The present German mouth-to-mouth resuscitation is being perceived by the rest of the world as a passionate embrace, blind to the world. An isolated Germany policy of the Federal Republic would, however, quickly become very lonely and be surrounded by mistrust. . . .
>
> Freedom is the core of the German question: that is what will make it tolerable to Europe and soluble for the Germans. As a State revolution in Europe it will remain blocked, with or without Mikhail Gorbachev. That is why it is also certain that German unification, if it were conceivable and attainable, will take shape only once it turns from being a shake-up in the world political system in the heart of Europe into a factor for stabilization, from a revolution of power relationships to an important sideshow. What follows from this, however, is the method that nothing can be achieved head-on, battering down the European wall with the German head, nor through special German-German deals, and, by the way, nor through Soviet-American arrangements in the geostrategic game, from Yalta to Malta. There remain only the forming of links, the building of trust, assurances, settlements. Never was the time riper for them, never was this process more necessary: particularly for the smooth stabilization of the revolutionary change. The elements are ready; they must be put together. Whether Germans are well-advised here to speak

83. Helmut Schmidt, "Nicht die Chance verpassen, Auf dem Weg zur deutschen Einheit haben wir schon viel Porzellan zerschlagen," in *Die Zeit*, 9 March 1990.

immediately and loudly of German reunification instead of European unification is something that will continue to concern us all.[84]

Only six months later, "mouth-to-mouth resuscitation" had been replaced by a guided therapy of economic, monetary, and social union. For the third time in German postwar history — after Ludwig Erhard's monetary reform in 1948 and the incorporation of the Saarland in the 1950s—a currency conversion was marking the historic break, making the organization of the common polity into an almost substantive implementation of what had already occurred. In the view of economic experts, the lesson to be learned from the two comparable, if not identical, events is that success lies in innovation and competition, not in attempting to retain old structures for social reasons.

This time, however, there is far more at stake: the unprecedented merger of two matured States and economic systems. Both sides complain that there is no time left for reflection, stocktaking, or even growing together; everything is moving far too quickly. And all too quickly, euphoria at the opening of the borders has been overlain by both justified and irrational fears. Reports of mass firings of workers in the ex-GDR stirred fears in the Federal Republic of the later consequences of unity. Uncertainty in the ex-GDR grew in parallel to the constant rise in unemployment figures.

To counter the atmosphere of uncertainty and self-preoccupation, the four leading bishops of the two Churches brought to people's attention the European dimension, which had been somewhat repressed in the previous months in debates marked primarily by economic considerations. With great force, they warned that the attention of Germans, who had for a while been concerned primarily with themselves, should once again be strongly directed outward.

For a common future. Declaration by the leading German bishops, 1 July 1990 (extracts)

A new common task lies before us in Europe and in Germany. It cannot be solved overnight, but is a matter of the long haul. For Germans, much

---

84. Michael Stürmer, "Die Deutschen in Europa. Auf dem Weg zu einer zwischenstaatlichen Innenpolitik," in *Europa-Archiv*, 24, 1989, 727ff.

depends on our remaining aware of the burden of the past, not becoming overbearing and above all sharing the burdens too among ourselves. . . .

It is not surprising if we Germans have for months been strongly concerned with ourselves. Yet the warning is justified: to keep a sense of due proportion and not lose sight of larger problems, albeit remoter from us. It makes a difference here whether a single Germany that has arrived at peace in the heart of Europe turns to worldwide problems, or else a divided Germany, not sufficiently certain of itself, draws its uncertainty and disquiet upon others. In this respect too, the most recent developments among us can go to benefit all peoples.

Outdated nation-State thinking cannot be our way. United Germany must find its place in Europe. From Germany there must now come powerful impulses to European cooperation that at the same time bring the center and the east of Europe, for decades in the shadows, more strongly into view. A German unification that takes the interests of our neighbors into account will not be a barrier to the greater Europe; on the contrary, it will promote and accelerate that development.

The bishops' warning that all Germans should "remain aware of the burden of the past" had been converted into action a few days earlier by the Speakers of the Bundestag and the Volkskammer, Rita Süssmuth and Sabine Bergmann-Pohl. Their joint visit to Israel included young people from the Federal Republic and the GDR. The GDR, apart from Albania, was the only country in the former Eastern bloc that never established relations with Israel and forcibly prevented participation by its citizens in the process of reconciliation with the Jewish State. After the first free elections, the GDR, in its government declaration of 12 April 1990, immediately acknowledged the burden of coresponsibility for the Holocaust. Israel was chosen for the first and only joint visit abroad by the two Speakers in a decision intended to take some of the sting out of German unity in the eyes of Israelis.

In early 1990, a controversy between Israeli Prime Minister Yitzhak Shamir and Federal Chancellor Kohl was sparked by Shamir's statement that even forty years of democracy were not yet a guarantee against a repetition of the past, demonstrating that there are considerable reservations in Israel against German unity. In a sensitive analysis, Ammon Neustadt, lecturer at the Institute of Political Science of the University of Tel Aviv, gave some reasons for this attitude:

In the Jewish consciousness, the memory of the Holocaust belongs among the most important indicators of Jewish and Israeli approaches to the German question. Emotional chords from the past are an integral component of the Jewish viewpoint. . . .

An important aspect in this connection is the symbolic one. The Berlin Wall symbolized not only collapse and division. For broad sectors of Jewry, it acted at the same time as an unmistakeable warning of an epoch not to be forgotten, the unrepeatability of which was at least symbolically guaranteed by the existence of the Wall. Its very ugliness and inhumaneness were supposed to increase the psychological inhibitory threshold against forgetting brought about by time. It created a surface of emotional contact with memories of the one-time deeds of horror . . .

Undoubtedly the change in the German question is also regarded as the end of an epoch that still touches many deep-running feelings. Some are pained particularly now at the feeling of absence of "adequate" revenge, which in any case was always without any prospect and expressed more of a spiritual frustration. The impression exists that it is definitive rehabilitation of Germany that is now taking place, but without a say for the Jews that would emotionally be regarded as just.[85]

That the removal of dual statehood should not come about at the expense of forgetting the past, is a view shared by intellectuals from both parts of Germany. The thesis can be found in a particularly pointed speech given on 1 February 1990 at a congress in Tutzing by Danzig-born writer Gunter Grass, who now lives in West Berlin. His plea against a new "Greater Germany" takes up his arguments of previous years in which he expressed his unease at an unloved Fatherland:

Nightmare opposes dream. What prevents us from helping the German Democratic Republic and its citizens through a just and long overdue equalization of burdens in such a way that the State can also be consolidated economically and democratically and its citizens have less problems about staying at home? . . .

Are comprehensive unity, a larger area for the State, combined economic power, a growth that is worthy of being aimed at? Is it not all instead too much again? . . .

We should be aware, and our neighbors are aware, how much suffering this unitary State caused, what an extent of misery it has brought

---

85. Ammon Neustadt, "Israelische Reaktionen auf die Entwicklung in Deutschland," in *Europa-Archiv*, 11, 1990, 352ff.

to others and to us. The crime of genocide summed up in the word Auschwitz, which cannot be qualified in any way, is a burden on this unitary State . . . .

Anyone reflecting about Germany at present and seeking answers to the German question has to include Auschwitz in his thoughts. The place of horror, standing as an example for all the lingering trauma, rules out a future German unitary State. Should it nevertheless be forcibly brought about, as is to be feared, it will be condemned to failure.[86]

Here there is a direct link to the lively debates of 1960 concerning Karl Jaspers's theses on reunification. Persecuted during the Third Reich and professor of philosophy at Basel after the war, he continually took positions on political and historical questions of the time. In a television interview on 10 August 1960, he aroused violent contradiction with his thesis that German unity had finally been "gambled away" by Hitler's Reich and that there was a kind of moral duty to renounce the transcendence of dual statehood.

The realization that today other responses to the burden of history have also become possible was impressively illustrated by Federal President Richard von Weizsäcker's visit to Prague, fifty-one years to the day after Hitler's invasion of 15 March 1939. The initiative for this highly symbolic meeting had come from Czechoslovak President Václav Havel, who five months earlier, as a playwright and fearless dissident, had been awarded the German book trade Peace Prize in Frankfurt. On that occasion Havel, who was not allowed to receive the prize personally, had already emphatically put forward his view that in the past few decades the "national animosities, prejudices and passions" of Czechs against Germans had evaporated. In an interview with editor-in-chief of *Die Welt*, Manfred Schell, on 10 March 1990, Havel unreservedly supported Germans' efforts to reunify their country.

Interview with Czechoslovak President Václav Havel, 10 March 1990 (extracts)

I have spoken on this in the American Congress, in the Polish Sejm, and

---

86. Günter Grass, "Kurze Rede eines vaterlandslosen Gesellen," in "*Nichts wird mehr so sein, wie es mal war*," op. cit., 228ff. (see note 77).

on other occasions, too. The Germans have the right to unite. But I hope, too, that this will not lead to any complications for the unity of Europe. A united Germany should become the motor of the European unification process.

I have no fear of a united Germany, for I am quite certain that it will be democratic and peaceful, that it will also see its future as being in Europe and that radical forces will have no chance there. But I also understand it when others, perhaps feeling themselves more directly affected than Czechoslovakia by unification of Germany, take a different view....

An order must be created and applied whereby every State can decide freely how it is to regulate its internal affairs. This is also true of its relations to other States. This new order should replace the conditions created by the Second World War. The time of tutelage and dependencies is over. Now it is freedom and self-determination that apply. They will also lead to a higher level of European integration. Of that I am quite certain.

In a moving speech at the meeting in Prague Castle, Havel welcomed Federal President von Weizsäcker as "a representative of German democracy," a messenger of peace, decency, truth, and humanity. Speaking to his countrymen, Havel emphatically opposed anti-German resentment and ideas of collective guilt: "Despising Germans as such, condemning them simply because they are Germans or fearing them on that ground alone, is the same as being anti-Semitic."

In his speech, Weizsäcker thanked Havel for his initiative toward reconciliation and gave assurances that on the road to national unity, Germans would be profoundly aware of their special responsibility for peace in Europe.

Speech by Federal President Richard von Weizsäcker in Prague, 15 March 1990 (extracts)

The newly-won freedom and the trust of the peoples of Europe are opening up to us Germans the way to overcoming the division of our people. This trust is a valuable asset, which we are called upon to cherish and uphold. We are grateful to our neighbors for their acknowledgement of our right to self-determination....

On the road to unity, we Germans are aware of our special responsibility for peace in Europe. Who would not understand it, from a look at the course of European history, at the position of our people in the middle of the continent and thus at our own experiences and interests? We Germans have more neighbors than any other European people. Our location has brought about a historical development always marked by mutual influences and interferences between the neighbors and ourselves. Our history has never belonged to ourselves alone.

Today too, and even more so today, there is no isolated national policy for us. The age in which good patriotism was transformed into wicked nationalism against neighbors and led to destructive European fraternal wars lies behind us. Just as Germans and French have overcome it together, that should be the case between you and us too.....

We Germans very well know how important it is not to allow any old or new concerns arise among our neighbors from our unification. We will and shall take their feelings, the feelings with which they accompany our development, very seriously. We will and shall not only agree our steps through close contact with their governments, but also make them understandable to their peoples. Through our words and deeds, we wish to convince people that unity is not only democratically legitimate, but will promote the spirit of peace in Europe.

Could it be that French poet and diplomat Paul Claudel, who even in the years just after the war had opposed the old thought-patterns of "eternal Germany," was ultimately right? Almost prophetic in retrospect, his courageous "Reflections on Germany" in the spring of 1948, detached the question of Germany's future in Europe from the narrow framework of its traditional image as a foe and gave Germans in their European role a content with which they and the world can live in peace:

Germany, that vast area for criss-cross traffic of all kinds, that giant alluvial plain, was not created to divide peoples, but to bring them together.... It is a great misfortune for Europe and the world that Germany today is having that role taken away from it. For that role really belongs to it. Of all the crimes it has committed, the one it has committed against itself is the greatest....

Germany needs Europe and Europe needs Germany. The issue is not just their existence, but our own existence. Madame de Sévigné once said that she was suffering from her daughter's sore throat. Europe will suffer from Germany as long as Germany has not regained its balance....

In the general interest, it must again be given the possibility to decide about itself and about its immense resources. Above all, it must be given back that inestimable good without which no Christian people can live: the right to prospects for the future, the right to hope.[87]

Even today, the neighbors' attitude is being influenced by memory of what an overweening Germany once did to them. In late January 1990 this concern was made graphically clear by the cover illustration of the London *Economist*, depicting a two-headed German: above, a Bavarian peasant smiles contentedly; below, a grim, armored Prussian militarist is shown with features recalling Bismarck's. The ambivalence of attitudes is emphasized by a twofold question: Germany benign or malign?

A member of the French Academy, Claudel wrote his Reflections on Germany for *A present*, the editorial group which included several leading members of General de Gaulle's resistance movement.

Germany needs Europe, but Europe needs Germany too; that was early recognition of the fact, which applies more than ever, that the Germans and their neighbors need each other and find more strength from togetherness than from enmity. If this ideal is achieved, the outlook is positive that that the "new Germany" will fit peacefully into the Europe of tomorrow.

---

87. Paul Claudel, "Quelques reflexions sur l'Allemagne (8 March 1948)," in *Oeuvres en Prose* (Paris: Bibliothèque de la Pléïade, 1965), 1383ff.

6

Lines of Continuity for United Germany

Q uestions posed concerning democracy in Germany and Germany's national existence in Europe have been answered concordantly through the Two-plus-Four settlement in Moscow on 12 September and the GDR's accession to the Federal Republic on 3 October 1990. A united Germany will now be faced with new questions: what lines of continuity will be decided upon; how will united Germany cope with its role in Europe; and what responsibility will the Germans assume worldwide?

These questions, intensifying with the approach of German unity and in the weeks and months thereafter, have led to diverse answers among Germans and their neighbors. Not for the first time in its history, Germany is self-preoccupied, and the debate on the future orientation of the country in the center of Europe is being pursued primarily by historians and commentators. For decades, Germans had become accustomed to the idea that solution to the German question could no longer be in the form of the nation-State. Now they must cope with the unexpected development that restoration of their nation-State confutes the assumption that it is sufficient to define the Federal Republic as a "postnational democracy."

A further indubitable part of the growing together of the two parts of Germany is reflection on German history, as experienced jointly and separately. Federal State unity is the form in which freedom is becoming a reality for Germans, who until the autumn of 1989, had to do without it. In contrast to events leading to initial foundation of the German nation-State, this time unity cannot be at the cost of freedom; however, once again Germans are not truly prepared to handle a great State. For almost half a century, West Germans have lived with reduced responsibility, reduced risk, and under the protection of the Allies. Under such circumstances, moderate, and at the same time appropriate, use of the new power accruing to them and the presentation of new possibilities through unification could prove difficult to accomplish.

A Trial of Steadfastness for the Germans

On 3 October 1990, when SPD Honorary Chairman and former Federal Chancellor Willy Brandt was asked to draw up a balance sheet on the process of German unification and answer the question as to whether at least approximate success in reconciling the hopes and concerns of either side had been achieved, he gave the following answer:

> I do not think so. At the same time, though, I wonder whether that would at all have been possible. At that time, on the 10th of November, the day after the Wall opened in Berlin, I said that what belonged together was now growing together. Today I would say that what politically belongs together from this 3rd of October onward still has to grow together. On the 10th of November I did not foresee how hectic the process would be, and so I ask myself how far it could actually have been avoided. An ordered transition could scarcely have been combined with the opening of the Wall in Berlin and along the whole German internal frontier. No, the real problems, the economic difficulties, and the balancing out of the differing worlds of consciousness and of experience will keep us busy for a long time yet.[88]

This estimate very clearly reflects the change in awareness in many Germans since the weeks of upheaval in autumn 1989. The restoration of unity after over forty years of division can perhaps scarcely be understood except as an irruption of miracle into politics. Achievement of unification, however, presents the possibility that the complex interplay of attraction and repulsion might spill over into confusion as to whether the Germans really do belong together and whether the desire for a joint State was not overly

88. Willy Brandt, "Ich habe die Hektik nicht vorausgesehen.' SZ Interview with Willy Brandt," in *Süddeutsche Zeitung*, 2–3 October 1990.

hasty. In his introduction to a collection of essays on mental problems associated with approaching unification, Munich historian Christian Meier arrives at the following finding:

> Madness! was probably the most frequent, most typical short comment on what was happening and being experienced in the GDR in those weeks of upheaval in autumn 1989. Fear seems since to have long become a central component in the description of the state of Germans in the East — but perhaps not just them. Alienation might very soon be the major keyword for the mental condition of the growing together of the two German States.... The German uncertainties which were always also, if not indeed primarily, uncertainties on the part of Germans about themselves, have a long history. We are in the process of beginning a new chapter in them....
>
> In view of the size of the future Germany, great expectations will be made of us. A greater responsibility will be the result. The niches of very conditional responsibility into which both German sub-States have been able to fit themselves are no more. But this implies a great challenge. Yet there are great opportunities bound up with it too. These opportunities can be grasped only in the European framework. In general, it is to be hoped that our European neighbors will be speaking up in the "great debate." After all, we are dependent on them. After all, this Germany has to grow together with them, in close accord.[89]

A recent and much listened to voice is that of Britisher David Marsh, Bonn correspondent of the London daily *Financial Times* and author of a book on the Germans that has also been published in the Federal Republic. For him, those involved, and their neighbors, the condition for the success of the operation was the unexpectedness of the course of events and the absence of any concrete plan for accomplishing Germany's unification in freedom. Had it been otherwise, according to Marsh, then both at home and abroad there could have been a great wave of mistrust of the government in Bonn. On the other hand, he feels this lack of preparation for the challenges of unification also contains dangers:

> Bonn has discovered its most successful export item to date: itself.
> But however contradictory this may seem, the moment of triumph is also a time of crisis. Despite the parliamentary whiter-than-white

---

89. Christian Meier, *Deutsche Einheit als Herausforderung, Welche Fundamente für welche Republik?* (Munich: Carl Hanser Verlag, 1990), 9ff.

of the unification treaty, Germany is rushing into unification disorderedly and without knowing where it is headed. Developments have overtaken each other because the GDR State without communism has been unmasked as a power vacuum, and the much-praised GDR identity as a mirage without control by the Stasi. . . .

A real danger would arise only if — as has already happened in history — Germany were to overestimate the possibilities of its European position as the "land in the middle" and underestimate its potential vulnerability. Despite the fading of ideological East-West confrontation, by no means all military risks have been banned from the continent. Germany must of course seize the opportunity of seeking friendship and cooperation with the ailing military colossus of the Soviet Union. It ought not, however, to forget that the process of political decay in the Soviet Union and Eastern Europe that brought in the liberalization of human rights and economic forces bears within it the danger of burgeoning instability, that could exert a fatal effect on the reunited Germans too.[90]

The European instability mentioned by Marsh in connection with the break-up of the Soviet Empire in reality concerns all close and more remote neighbors of the USSR, even if here as well the Germans are particularly exposed. In contrast, things are no doubt different with German national feelings, which in many respects differ from those of other nation-States. American William Pfaff, European correspondent for the *Los Angeles Times*, advocates treating the Germans as a nation "like the others," whose unsolved problems are thoroughly comparable with those of say, the Americans; yet his analysis shows that he is not totally convinced of the correctness of this assertion. As an attentive on-site observer, what particularly struck Pfaff was in fact specifically the etiolated national sense of the Germans, who apparently felt better in their European skin than in their new role:

The whole matter of recovering a German nation after four decades of "provisional" government in the West and puppet government in the East is largely unconfronted. The implication is that national anonymity has been very comforting to the Germans and they are not anxious at all for it to end. . . . They insist that they are Europeans, and secondarily Germans. One result of the events of the past year is that they have discovered how truly they are West Europeans.

90. David Marsh, "Gelungene Operation ohne Plan," in *Frankfurter Rundschau*, 2–3 October 1990.

There is an unspoken conclusion that the West is not only where they belong but want to belong — where they are secure, comfortable, among friends. The East, which a year ago seemed to many Germans a place of big commercial opportunities as well as hazy political alternatives, now gloomily is seen as the pit where millions of marks are going to have to be sunk out of considerations of international duty, not German ambition.[91]

A certain tendency to retreat from history, and therefore from the nation, is similarly discerned in their own country by some German historians. Four years after the "historians' dispute" over the uniqueness of Nazi period crimes, which covered the Germans' relationship to their recent past and also to their present, national unification again seems to be offering an occasion to ponder the past, particularly the recollection of history.

In connection with unification, the Hamburg paper *Die Zeit* asked prominent historians how the past would and must determine the future of the unified nation. Freiburg historian Heinrich August Winkler, who had in earlier works dealt with the relationship between bourgeois emancipation and national unification during foundation of the Reich in the 19th century, answered as follows:

> In no other European country is skepticism about the nation-State so great as in Germany. The reason is plain: nowhere did the nation-State fail so dreadfully as here. The German nation-State, the Reich founded by Bismarck in 1871, destroyed itself before it was occupied by the victors in the second of the World Wars it had unleashed, and ultimately divided. The external decline and fall of 1945 had been preceded twelve years earlier by the internal one. . . .
>
> German unity would not have come about if the world powers and Europe were having to face a new German Reich, the restoration of a sovereign nation State of the traditional type. But that is not on the agenda. United Germany will be no less federalist and no less "multi-cultural" than the existing Federal Republic. Moreover, it is from the outset tied into the European Community and into an Atlantic alliance which is in the course of developing a new, cooperative understanding of European security. These supra-national ties, along with the restriction of military potential and renunciation of ABC weapons accepted

91. William Pfaff, "A Nation, Like the Others, With its Own Unsettled Business," in *International Herald Tribune*, 3 October 1990.

by Germany, are nothing but the political "sine qua non" of reunification. Accordingly, the German nation-State is in part undoing itself in the very process of its emergence.[92]

Certainly, almost no one would have objected to the closing sentence from the Federal Chancellor's address on the eve of the day of German unity: "Germany is our Fatherland; united Europe is our future." In contrast, the thesis of Social-Democratic chancellorship candidate Oskar Lafontaine, that united Germany should see itself as something "provisional" as it will soon be dissolved in a greater Europe, sparked fierce controversy. It is undisputed that the Federal Republic, like other Community Member States, is increasingly bound in its economic and political decisions by framework decisions of the European Community and that its national sovereignty no longer allows going it alone. But Lafontaine, who had already been very reticent about the process of German unification, obviously goes further, as his concept is aimed at taking away the definitive aspect of the outcome of this process.

Speech by Saarland Minister-President Oskar Lafontaine (SPD) to the German Bundestag on 23 August 1990 (extracts)

I have spoken of the obligation to organize the unification process in European fashion. This faces us with the task of coming to an understanding about what we are in future to mean by "nation." There has been so much talk about the national question. But we have to see that the point is, as Carlo Schmid put it here once on 25 February 1972, to build a nation of Europe. . . .

We have to be guided by the concept of nation of the USA, the concept of nation of France or the concept of nation of Switzerland. It will immediately be clear that our Article 116 could not be constitutive for the French Republic, for the United States or even for democratic Switzerland. The thing that is constitutive for belonging to a nation — that is the decisive point, and that means building the nation of Europe — has in future to be that a community of citizens, men and women, recognize the same goals of the constitution, which were already prefigured in the

---

92. Heinrich August Winkler, "Mit Skepsis zur Einigung: Die Westdeutschen müssen nicht nur materielle Opfer bringen," in *Die Zeit*, 28 September 1990.

bourgeois revolution in France. The values of freedom, equality, frater-
nity, which today we would extend by that of sisterhood, are to be found
not within the limits of a national culture; they are instead universalistic
values to which we must commit ourselves if we wish to create the United
States of Europe. . . .

Anyone fixated too strongly on national unity or dependent on it will
all too easily lose sight of the unitary nature of the conditions of life.
The decisive point is first and foremost — this is the political conception
of German social democracy — how the individual fares, how he is able
to live in actual practice. After that we ask the question of State organization;
not the other way around.

Lafontaine's statements came in the special meeting of the
Bundestag on 23 August 1990, after the Volkskammer in East
Berlin had taken the decision to join the Federal Republic of
Germany on 3 October, pursuant to Article 23 of the Basic Law.
German unification is indeed coming about under essentially
different circumstances and conditions than the first German
unification in the 1860s. Today, we are as far from "unification
wars" against neighbors as from the nation-State idea and the
dominant nationalism of 1870, which twice threw Europe and the
world into catastrophe through the expansive exaggeration of World
War I and the lunatic absolutization of Hitler.

The restoration of German unity — in territorially restricted
dimensions, with definitive renunciation of former territorial claims
east of the Oder and Neisse — is this time a part and an outcome
of a comprehensive, peacefully occurring change in political
circumstances on the Old Continent. The dissolution of a divided
Germany is much more than merely a national procedure. Not
something exclusively German, it is closely bound to the overcoming of the political division of Europe. Nonetheless, the question
of the nation's position in the closing twentieth century will long
continue to occupy minds, perhaps even more strongly in the former
GDR than in the western part of the country. The reasons for
this are seen by Michael Bartsch, political editorialist of the Dresden
weekly *Sachsenspiegel*:

Again in 1990 national feelings are proving strongest where the greatest internal and external lack prevails — in the East. However para-
doxical it may sound, a strongly and generously accepted Germany is

consequently then most capable of integration and least susceptible to chauvinism.

But before we, in words used by people from Kohl to Jaspers, transcend the nation-State, we ought also first to become a nation. Traumatic aspects of history could otherwise easily rise again. For a year now, and explicitly in these days, we have a scarcely-valued opportunity to come to an understanding with our neighbors and above all with ourselves.

The road of Europe passes through a Germany that is a matter of course, that understands itself. It is the "Europe des patries" described by de Gaulle. Partnership with neighbors will succeed only if we love ourselves too a little — in as unconstrained and as little "heroically German" fashion as possible. It is not only the New Testament that knows that love of one's neighbor presupposes a piece of self-love.

Then it becomes idle to speculate on great-power ambitions, on a seat on the Security Council. Neither artificial "raison d' état of modesty" nor attitudes of economic giantism but naturally-growing German authority will settle these matters.

It would be wrong-headed to seek to transcend a German identity in a European one, before it is even halfway healed by its snap treatment.[93]

Never before in this century have the peoples of Western Europe been as close as they are today to the goal of political unification. In December 1990, two governmental conferences of EC countries started developing into treaty texts the twofold vision of economic and monetary union and political unification. With successful conclusion of the special summit in Rome in late October, preparations in particular for economic and monetary union have secured a surprising degree of agreement. Eleven of the twelve governments (the exception being Britain) have agreed to foundation of a European central bank system beginning 1 January 1994, provided that the internal market is completed, the necessary Treaty amendment has been ratified, the issuing banks are independent, and financing of Member States' budget deficits is ruled out.

In the case of foreign and security policy, longer negotiations will have to be expected; however, the outlines of political union can be discerned in initial preparations. The twelve countries involved wish to maintain their national identities while guided

93. Michael Bartsch, "Der Weg zu sich selbst und zum Nachbarn. Über die absurde Angst vor der Freiheit," in *Sachsenspiegel*, 12 October 1990.

by the principle of subsidiarity: the European central State is not to exist, any more than comprehensive powers for the union. This plan should meet with acceptance, particularly among Germans, as federalism, with the distribution of power over many centers, has proved itself successful for over forty years in the Federal Republic.

The Proper Approach to Sovereignty

The "speculations" mentioned by Michael Bartsch as to a permanent seat for united Germany on the United Nations Security Council had been revived a few days earlier by Nikolai Portugalov, the Soviet expert on Germany and adviser to the international section of the CC of the CPSU. His article in *Der Spiegel*, "The Thorny Path to World Power," addressed a problem being intensively discussed in those weeks:

> Germany is, then, on a very thorny path towards world power — one that demands both sacrifice and circumspection. This cannot be compared with the twice-failed German "seizure of world power": the role as world power is this time coming to Germany inevitably.
>
> The world, and above all the Germans themselves, are going to have to live with that. It is therefore advisable not, like many German politicians and commentators, to fall into feelings of inferiority or guilt, but, as so far without nationalistic upsurges, to properly invest the enormous windfall that history has unexpectedly bestowed on the Germans.
>
> Yet thought about guarantees against new German relapses into hubris, which are after all always theoretically possible, is very much needed. The pan-European system of security and cooperation would offer at least a partially comprehensive insurance here. Western European integration alone, not to speak of NATO, which is becoming superfluous, would be a rather too tight corset for united Germany.
>
> What would instead be comparable with fully-comprehensive insurance would be the tying of Germany into world responsibility — for instance through a decision by the UN General Assembly to raise it to the rank of a permanent member of the Security Council. It is, moreover, beginning to look anachronistic to see the possession of atomic weapons as the sole criterion for a great power.[94]

94. Nikolai Portugalov, "Der Dornenweg zur Weltmacht," in *Der Spiegel*, 8 October 1990.

The tempting phrase "new world power" was initiated by Green MP Antje Vollmer, who had called for a public debate on the role unifed Germany should take in Europe and the world. To her own party she issued the warning that it must adjust to the changed situation and not linger in a doubtful posture. Her attempt to reconsider her attitude with regard to the German unification process and the function of a critical opposition in these radically changed times, led to furious comments about the MP from her own ranks. In an interview broadcast by *Sender Freies Berlin* and printed in the daily *Frankfurter Rundschau*, Antje Vollmer explained her political change of heart and the notions she associates with a sovereign Germany.

Interview with Bundestag Green spokeswoman Antje Vollmer, 15 September 1990 (extracts)

My thesis is that in both German States there has come about a reshaping of the deep structure of society, including social psychic life, that has gone almost unnoticed in domestic policy but has been clearly picked up in foreign policy terms. The result is a sort of civilization of Teutondom. This has been achieved not by Mr. Kohl, but by us ... the Greens, the people of '68, the citizens' initiatives, the German intellectuals. This sudden insight that my generation had not been entirely ineffectual took one aback. Then like a shock came the next sudden recognition: now nobody any longer controls this Germany except us. Now we have to do it ourselves. This is again a piece of political growing up, if one can no longer creep along behind the back of some sort of great powers that will anyway ward off the worst. And that means that we too, the political Left, the opposition, civil rights people — have to emerge very quickly from the pedagogical provincialism of the Left, from alternative existence in a niche and from the noble role of victim. At one bound we are free and in the open. . . .

After all, we have been in this remarkable hybrid position a long time: economic giant and political dwarf. It has also meant that we have never felt ourselves fully responsible for ourselves politically. Let us consider all those arms exports, to Iraq, to South Africa; scandalous in any case, but from the great-power viewpoint doubly so. The German average citizen and average politician have not so far wanted to accept that. We too have always stiffened ourselves against it, politically and mentally. But all at once that is the way the facts are. And the question is whether I now — as opposition — set about coping with that, or else go on dreaming away in the role of infant that cannot be made responsible for controlling the giant?

The question of whether Germans want to "remain political dwarfs" has also been asked by other observers of the new political situation in Germany. In an interview with *Die Welt*, shortly after the day of German unity, Arnulf Baring, professor of Contemporary History and International Relations at the Free University of Berlin, defended the view that the new position had not yet been fully grasped in many West German circles; instead, people continued to think of Germany as remaining the Federal Republic, augmented by a rather vague addition. With this mentality of "keeping one's eyes tightly shut," in the words of Baring, author of a much-read book about the Germans' "New Megalomania" (published in 1988), no proper decision on the capital could be taken, nor the new political situation in general be properly dealt with. As to how to deal with the newly-gained sovereignty, Baring offered the following solution:

> For decades we have bewailed the fact that the Federal Republic was economically a giant but politically a dwarf. Now we cannot say what many West Germans would like to say: we want to stay political dwarfs! Of course we have to act extremely prudently, circumspectly; we ought not to have too many illusions about our present economic performance capacity or build too exclusively upon the economy....Without economic stability there will presumably be no viable common polity among us. On that we must be clear. This one-sidedness, this dominance of purely economic thinking, makes us very vulnerable as a political community. We have to rethink our priorities!
>
> Other countries have quite different priorities. Take only the USA. Considered from the outside it is a world power; from the viewpoint of the socio-political situation internally it looks rather shaky. But they have a consciousness of their responsibility for other peoples, particularly those of the free world. We are of course not a world power. But we are becoming a European great power, and we therefore cannot retreat from our European task. Being a power today does not mean power to command, domination, or fanfares. It means above all more duties: to demonstrate one's usefulness to others.[95]

A few weeks earlier, an article in *Die Welt* by Horst Teltschik,

95. Arnulf Baring, "Wollen wir Deutsche politische Zwerge bleiben?" in *Die Welt*, 8 October 1990.

Ministry Director in the Chancellor's office and until the end of 1990 foreign policy adviser to Helmut Kohl, was given the title "From 'political dwarf' to 'world power': Reflections on Germany's new role in Europe." The author himself had provided the programmatic title "The miracle of the Caucasus has a future only jointly," alluding to the Kohl-Gorbachev meeting of July 1990, which brought the breakthrough for a successful conclusion of the Two-plus-Four talks.

For Teltschik, the slogan "Germany the world power," increasingly used by foreign, political and media interlocutors, is being accepted partly because no one abroad has yet taken seriously the formula that the Federal Republic of Germany is economically a giant but politically a dwarf. According to the Chancellor's adviser, the real question is how to handle this new position responsibly: there should be an interplay between Germany's new self-image and changed expectations on the part of their partners:

> Just as the Federal Republic of Germany in the past was no "political dwarf," so will united Germany not be a "world power." But it can be seen even today that this Germany is taking on new weight and new quality in international politics. These are rooted not only in the newly acquired size and strength or in a new self-image of German politics, but also in the sometimes greatly changed expectations of us by major partners, that we should take on international responsibility and exercise solidarity more than we have done.
>
> For us Germans, accordingly, the question therefore does not arise whether we are or want to be a "world power," but how we are in future to handle our newly acquired weight responsibly....
>
> The ideological confrontation is giving way to competition between systems and rules of political, economic, and cultural action that can serve the same objectives, but need not lead to identical solutions. We ought not, therefore, to see our social systems as static, finished entities, however much they may come to be similar between East and West....
>
> All these perspectives of European integration and pan-European umbrella structures leave no leeway for great-power or world-power policy by a united Germany. What they instead call for is energetic and creative pursuit by German policy of a new European architecture within which we shall be ever less sovereign but ever more an integrated component of a community. That is how the new Germany will find its identity in Europe.[96]

96. Horst Teltschik, "Vom 'politischen Zwerg' zur 'Weltmacht' — Nachdenken über Deutschlands neue Rolle in Europa. Das Wunder vom Kaukasus hat nur gemeinsam Zukunft," in *Die Welt*, 22 September 1990.

These remarks recall a similar debate that started at least ten years ago on the question of whether the Federal Republic was already "a secret great power" (E.-O. Czempiel). In the late 1980s, examination was made of the Federal Republic's foreign policy under the title "A world power against its will" (C. Hacke). Common to both positions was the finding that a world-power role had as it were accrued to the Germans in a fit of absence of mind. In a speech published in early 1990 on the fortieth anniversary of the foundation of the Federal Republic of Germany, Tübingen political scientist Volker Rittberger held that the Federal Republic had been converted from a power-state "Saul" to an interdependency-oriented "Paul." Conceptions of great-power or world-power status corresponded to a partly exaggerated, partly outdated notion, though the Federal Republic's world-policy responsibility had undoubtedly increased with its influence:

1. The question whether the Federal Republic has the status of a world power can be answered only with an unambiguous no.
2. Despite its manifest economic superiority, it can similarly not be attributed the quality of a hegemonic European power, since the Federal Republic's international status can increasingly be defined only as a part of the European Community.
3. Taking this restriction into account, the Federal Republic above all constitutes an internationally cooperating democratic trading State. However much this identity as a trading State means a peace-policy gain over the power-State past, responsibility for the external costs resulting from that identity is very poorly perceived. West German policy and society still have to learn to internalize these costs and include the costs of failure to learn in their accounts.[97]

On 2 August 1990 Iraqi aggression against Kuwait lent a new and urgent dimension to the question of Germany's increased responsibility on the world stage. Saddam Hussein's invasion illustrated that the disappearance of the East-West conflict had not yet removed the risk of military conflicts. Instead, new challenges to peace were arising, which could be opposed in joint action by the West and by appropriate modification of capacities to prevent war; however, it requires political will and, in the case of united

97. Volker Rittberger, "Die Bundesrepublik Deutschland — eine Weltmacht? Außenpolitik nach vierzig Jahren," in *Aus Politik und Zeitgeschichte*, 4–5, 1990, 19.

Germany, the appropriate constitutional machinery for subsequent realization of intended action.

The Basic Law amendment that would make German participation in military actions under United Nations auspices possible, both in principle and constitutionally, could be tackled by the Federal government only after the first all-German elections. The debate as to whether the Germans should take on world political responsibility, however, began in autumn 1990. In the viewpoint of the *New York Times*, there is no doubt that the reticence hitherto exercised by the Federal Republic (and Japan) must be abandoned:

> Perhaps the least troublesome approach would be constitutional changes permitting force deployments abroad only as part of collective security and peace-keeping operations. That would reduce the chances of unilateral action, or inaction. It would also integrate German and Japanese forces into a larger multilateral force.
>
> Both nations have matured as democracies, and as responsible international citizens. They already play full and vital roles in virtually every sector except collective security. Now, in the post-Cold War era, they are both needed to make collective security viable, and truly collective.[98]

A few days after completion of the German unification process, Federal Chancellor Helmut Kohl, in an interview in the *Süddeutsche Zeitung*, addressed pressing domestic policy issues and Germany's future international role. In particular, he warned against yielding to the already widespread tendency toward provincialism and withdrawal from international responsibility.

Interview with Federal Chancellor Helmut Kohl, 11 October 1990 (extract)

SZ: United Germany is taking on much greater weight than the Federal Republic had to date. The drawback is that enormous expectations are being made of us. One example is our support in the Gulf. Will you bring forward the requisite constitutional amendments on this point?

KOHL: Here we are under time pressure. Outside the German national

---

98. "Germany and Japan, Too. Global Policy Recruits," in *New York Times*, 22 October 1990; here quoted from *International Herald Tribune*, 23 October 1990.

borders we can no longer convince anyone by pointing to the fact that the Constitution ties our hands. It is very injurious to our country's moral stature to be on the one hand world champions in exports and on the other to withdraw from international responsibilities. In any case, many among us are increasingly tending towards provincialism on questions of foreign policy. They think that what is happening here among us is the navel of the world, and what is going on outside is of no interest. But we are a part of one world, and that is why in New York, London, or New Delhi people are looking to see whether the Germans are meeting their responsibilities.

In the debate on how to handle the new size, most German voices stress the concept of "responsibility" as a central category; conversely, the problem of others' responsibility for successful German unity also presents itself. In a very reflective consideration of unification, the *Neue Zürcher Zeitung*, in a leading article published shortly before 3 October entitled "In a European Perspective," suggested that the solution of the German question might succeed because Germany had become greater, not "a new greater Germany," and would be fully tied into the European and transatlantic partnership. Adenauer's concept of national unity within the Western Community had essentially won; now it was a matter for the West to grant the new Germany the benefit of trust:

> Many doubts as to whether the considerably larger-sized Germany that has become sovereign can really be "trusted all along the line again" still preoccupy many minds, at any rate in Europe. That is comprehensible on the basis of the experiences made in a single generation — and probably also comprehensible to the historically-aware German. The doubts are bound up with questions of Germany's future role in European and world politics. And they have to do with certain traits of the national character, to which even the Weimar classics attributed a tendency to exaggerations, for instance a see-sawing between extremes, such as between self-abnegation and self-overestimation. Such traits were to be seen in German self-assessments, rating the country as a "political dwarf" to date, but the future "bellwether of world history."
>
> If the history and politics of the Federal Republic are taken as a basis for judgment, then there are really no substantial points justifying the fear of immoderacies of the type described. The Bonn State that the ex-GDR is joining by acceding to the Basic Law has proved itself

a stable, free democracy and has gained much trust as a loyal member of Western defense and the European Economic Community, and also in the CSCE. The view that one should or would have to keep Germany permanently under control by institutional measures, rendering it harmless, because of its sins in the Hitler period, because its essence is still always feared to be going to turn out the other way, is impracticable in the long term. Through their release into sovereign freedom, instead, the Germans are being expected henceforth to take up the normal, full measure of responsibility for themselves and of co-responsibility for Europe and the world. This responsibility would certainly not be met, as Walter Scheel once pointed out, if the country were to present itself to the world as merely an economic giant without any political memory.[99]

Germany in the New International Field of Force

But this degree of laxity in dealing with the "new giant" in Europe, as various foreign newspapers dubbed the new Germany at its birth, was far from being discernible everywhere: uncertainty, worry, and even fear were also expressed with regard to German unification. With striking frequency, observers with a historical background pointed to those weeks in the high summer of 1789 when the "Grande Peur" spread in France; a kind of mass psychosis in which fear fed on fear. What was in the background then was uncertainty, connected with the radical novelty of the situation. This may well be the case again today, as fears spread of their own accord, as if by contagion. Yet the wish also persists to trust the new; alongside many fears, there are also many kinds of hope.

In a collective volume published in autumn 1990, Ulrich Wickert, who has lived for years in Paris as a television correspondent and director of the ARD Studios, sought to track down this diffuse unease at the "star pupils" of the Old Continent and to survey contemporary witnesses from home and abroad on the topic of "Fear of Germany." His introduction attempts to locate the fear syndrome among the new framework conditions in Europe:

---

99. "Deutschlands Vereinigung im Blickfeld Europas," in *Neue Zürcher Zeitung*, 30 September – 1 October 1990.

Fear as a political phenomenon accompanies disruptions whose outcome is initially uncertain; for instance, the "Grande Peur" at the time of the 1789 revolution. And since in 1990 it is German unification that is the point around which the whirligig of European restructuring is turning, the existence-threatening feeling of being unable to locate oneself in the new system in accordance with one's own values concentrates on Germany and the Germans.

Thus, from answers to the question about the fear of Germany there emerges a fascinating contemporary portrait of the spiritual and political condition of Europe. Had it not been their own highest political value, democracy, that triumphed, with self-determination of peoples as one of its principles, the Germans' neighbors would have been tempted to exert stronger influence on the process of unification. All that is left to them are not entirely unjustified formulae of warning. . . .

The new order in Europe, starting with the change in Soviet policy, means, with German unity, above all a change in one's own status. That alone generates fear enough, especially since the culture of the 20th century demands "success." But the question whether "success" will come to an end arouses all the more fear the stronger the main competitor grows.[100]

Inflation of the German problem and German self-doubt is represented symbolically by the liberal Paris weekly *Le Point* in a special supplement for the day of German unity. The picture on the title page is the unhappy Federal Chancellor — heavily pregnant, thanks to the photographer's retouching skills — with the double title "The French anxiety. What Germany is going to be born?" In a leading article entitled "The season of suspicions," Claude Imbert arrived at the following assessment of the relationship between France and its powerful neighbor to the East:

In Europe, as is natural after a great earthquake, the eye is caught by what has been thrown up: this mountain of power, both demographically and economically, of the reunified Germany with its 80 million citizens. That mountain is throwing a shadow over France. . . . In the old landscape, France enjoyed a political, demographic and above all strategic illumination, which over forty years has become increasingly advantageous because it was increasingly deceptive. For though we were not in danger, West Germany did not wait for its renewed meeting with the East to outclass us economically and make the Deutschmark

100. Ulrich Wickert, ed., *Angst vor Deutschland* (Hamburg: Hoffman & Campe, 1990), 11ff.

shine out before the Franc in the firmament of the European currencies.

At any rate, the emergence of the German colossus is bringing under our noses what we did not like to see. Over and above that, it is moving the European center of gravity away from us, from the Rhine towards Prussia and from Bonn to Berlin. From the top of the Berlin Reichstag that has been regained, the German eagle nests equidistant from Strasbourg and from Warsaw. Germany, a big nation, is again becoming a great nation: all it lacks is the military arm. From the height of its power, its industrialists and merchants are looking far beyond the West, at the wide world. And France looks at Germany. It is the season of suspicion — thoroughly foreseeable after all.[101]

To be sure, opinion surveys were still saying, long after the opinion-formers had denied it, that the French were in favor of reunification; yet, that too had changed with the closer approach of unification. It remains an open question how far this development toward greater distancing has been partly influenced by negative assessments from segments of the establishment and from the media. Shortly before the opening of the Berlin Wall, 70 percent of the French surveyed still saw unification of the two German States as no obstacle to European unification, and 60 percent were convinced that German unity was also a good thing for France. Barely a year later, however, not much could still be seen of this relaxed attitude, as a survey published in *Le Figaro* on 1 October 1990 shows. Presently, fear of the economic dominance of united Germany (62 percent) and, causally connected with it, worry over negative effects of the European internal market on their own country (57 percent), seem to have the upper hand. The ending of Germany's division now delights only 37 percent of the French, and 27 percent of those surveyed fear disadvantages for their country. A notable 32 percent of the population on the other side of the Rhine regard the unification of the two German sub-States with indifference.

For Hungarian Andras Hajdú, head of planning in the Budapest Foreign Ministry, the new European historical landscape seems to offer no occasion for such fearful visions. Fear of the change in system, the accompanying upheavals, the economic crisis, and general fear of collapse of the international postwar system, are all recorded by the Hungarian diplomat attentively, but also with concern. The decisive difference from the perceptions of other

---

101. Claude Imbert, "Le temps des soupçons," in *Le Point*, 1–7 October 1990.

neighbors, however, lies in his view that the Germans "scarcely play any decisive part in this fear structure of the Hungarians." Hajdú even goes so far as to assert that the Germans have been "assigned the role of positive hero, the part of the one that has — so far — succeeded in everything." Consequently, in Hungary, if one looks for negative feelings toward the Germans, one could at the most meet with envy. According to Hajdú, the underlying reason for the overwhelmingly positive assessment of German unification in Hungary is based upon the fact that the Germans always meant for Hungarians their link to Europe:

> Hungary's goal today is Europe. All the hopes formulated in relation to the Germans are directed at that concept. All the parties, all the political opinions, even the opinions of simple citizens, stress and underline that our international relationships should above all serve this single primary goal: to facilitate joining Europe. German-Hungarian relationships give this element its decisive content. What we expect from the Germans is that they should smooth the path for us to the European institutions; we want to mobilize our "special relationship" for those objectives.
>
> It is perhaps seldom put so unambiguously in public, but it must be stressed on this occasion that this is one of the most important reasons why there can be no notion of fear: German unification contributes to speeding-up the process of European unification. The German-Hungarian relationship has thus, from a means, become an end....
>
> For while it is first of all the East Germans who are going through the cleansing fire of integration, the Central and Eastern Europeans will be following them. Just as the GDR would not like to be the poorhouse of Germany, so the Eastern Europeans want to avoid the same thing in relation to the whole continent. And here the Germans too will have a decisive part to play. And their responsibility is correspondingly great.[102]

The temptation and hazards of special German roads, aside from the economic and security-policy communities of Europe, thus seem to have been banished at the outset. One may also presume similar motives behind Moscow's agreement to NATO membership for a sovereign Germany. If the Soviet price for peace had yesterday been the division of Europe and the Wall in Germany,

---

102. Andras Hajdú, "Systemwandel voller Tücken," in Ulrich Wickert, ed., *Angst vor Deutschland, op. cit.,* 257f. (note 100).

what Gorbachev was now seeking was a link to Western European integration. This does not mean Soviet abandonment of the search for a special relationship with the new Germany, to which the Soviet leadership plainly entrusts, or from which it expects, a key role in providing financial, economic, and technological aid and access to the Community internal market. Behind this, one may also presume a perception that the Soviet Union's fear of Germany's relapse into aggressive tendencies are much less likely given full integration into the Western partnerships, rather than a special position. In an article written for the collective volume "Fear of Germany," Hans-Dietrich Genscher also sought arguments to help to get rid of the potential for fear undoubtedly present among many neighbors. In his capacity as Federal German Foreign Minister, Genscher had always been concerned with foreign sensibilities toward Germany and sought to include others' preoccupations in his considerations. It is indubitable that he played a very decisive part in generating the image of a European Germany instead of a German Europe, thereby also dispelling fears.

We want a European Germany, not a German Europe. Essay by Federal Minister for Foreign Affairs Hans-Dietrich Genscher, September 1990 (extracts)

It is only in this historic dimension that German unification will become possible — without German neutralization: with united Germany as a member of the European Community and of the changing Western alliance, and through our active part in building a European system of peace in the context of the CSCE.

I think all our neighbours ought as far as Germany too is concerned to think in European and not nation-State terms. Is, after all, an efficient German economy a ground for concern in a Europe that is growing together? Is it not instead a gain for the whole of Europe? Whom in Europe would it help if the German economy were weak? Is it even possible at all to speak of the economic strength of a country in a nation-State sense, when we are growing together into the common internal market, when we are creating the European economic and monetary union? I hope that all those who have reservations over European economic and monetary union recognize this political dimension. One cannot feel the economic efficiency of one European country to be a disadvantage for Europe, particularly when the point is to overcome the economic division of the continent and contribute to the economic rehabilitation of the countries that after decades of failed economic policy are urgently in need of help. We want Central and Eastern Europe to take part in economic development and social justice. We do not want ideological and power-policy causes of tension to be replaced by economic causes of tension that again divide Europe. But for that we in the West — including Germany — need economic efficiency. And we need it to overcome the ecological challenge and promote development of the third world. . . .

The issue now is to transfer the new political culture of shared living in the European Community into shared living in the whole of Europe. Here we Germans will not forget that our position in the heart of Europe has placed us not *between* West and East but in the center of Europe — as a part of the *one* Europe. For that reason we shall also seek to ensure that West and East in Europe again become geographical expressions, ceasing to be marks of political or economic difference. It is not only our history but just as much our geographical position that confers upon us a special responsibility for the peaceful future of Europe. And it is true that our history has never belonged to us alone. But it is equally true that our actions and first and foremost our thinking are of especial importance for the fate of the whole continent. That is why the fundamentally European consciousness and European responsibility of the Germans are a gain for the whole of Europe.

For Stuttgart professor of modern history Eberhard Jäckel, who in the "historians' dispute" had vehemently taken a position against those of his colleagues who doubted the uniqueness of the National Socialist crimes, "fear of one's own strength" ought to be elevated to the guiding principle of political action in the united Germany. Even if Jäckel, who has published several works on the Nazi period, cannot with the best of goodwill discern any indications of renewed German striving for world power, he nevertheless regards it as appropriate to take measures now against the temptations facing a great power:

> In any answer, we ought not to forget that we are the most populous country in Europe. Being afraid of one's own strength must be a guideline of German policy. United Germany can become a risk for the European balance; not tomorrow or the day after, and perhaps never. But prudence should make one avert risks even if the likelihood of their occurring is slight. . . .
>
> As much federalism as possible, as little centralism as possible, must be the first answer. All superfluous concentration of power is to be avoided; for it could some time lead to temptation. For that reason

alone Bonn should remain the seat of government. Irresponsible politicians may arise. That can scarcely be prevented. At most, one can prevent or hinder them from doing damage. If Hitler had been a Luxemburger, he would have remained the fool he was. It was only from the center of the strongest central State that he could begin his march. Now and only now, we have a possibility of not letting him emerge again. The next answer has to be transferring as much sovereignty as possible to European and international institutions. For that reason alone Germany ought not to leave NATO and become neutral, since it would then regain military sovereignty. A European Central bank must be created, simply for the reason that the German Central Bank, because of the sheer size of our money supply resulting from our population figures, can cause incompatibilities.[103]

A quite different kind of inhibition is recognized by CDU Deputy District Chairman for Berlin, Volker Hassemer, who between 1983 and 1989 held office as Berlin's Senator for Culture. For him, the dispute that has persisted for months over whether Bonn or Berlin is to be the future German capital and seat of government is primarily a fear of change, which he feels is a trait of West German mentality leading Germans to ignore the new Europe in process of becoming a reality. Combined with his vehement plea for Berlin as capital is Hassemer's sharp criticism of all those politicians who believe that the Germans could, in a desperate attempt "to remain as they were," ignore the new challenges:

In the postwar epoch of limited sovereignty and imposed self-restraint, the West Germans have run their household very privately, very industriously, very successfully. One does not go around exulting over that, but one knows very well what one has, and quite decisively: it is a very special sense of value and of one's own worth, and is also externally displayed ingrown attitudes, trends in taste, usages and objectives that have here grown together into a very special quality, a specific situation. Here even the incoming of the GDR may be an irritant, or a city like Berlin — and it would be no different with Paris or London — even seem frightening . . . . That this West Germany does not get along easily with this Berlin need not therefore surprise us . . . . The no-longer divided Europe is not just the existing Western Europe, only bigger. It will be a new Europe. The wealth of the continent can now be fully plumbed. The case is no different with Germany. Early

---

103. Eberhard Jäckel, "Furcht vor der eigenen Stärke? Das vereinigte Deutschland muß Versuchungen vorbeugen," in *Die Zeit*, 1 November 1990.

on, and indeed beforehand, it was clear that united Germany would obviously not be an enlarged GDR. That was a matter of course to everyone after these forty years. Many have over time drawn from that the wrong interpretation that the new Germany is the Federal Republic of Germany, only bigger. And that is wrong. Clinging to Bonn is, my conclusion runs, an actual expression deep within of this wrong view. With Berlin as seat of government the Germans will be taking on these new issues, showing themselves to be equipped for the developments that will be decisive worldwide. The government moving from Bonn to Berlin will leave the postwar development, the West German dimension of our country, behind and at last truly open up to this new stage in German and European history.[104]

The difficulties for Germans in establishing their position in the new international field of forces and a suitable place on the world stage, are analyzed from a British viewpoint by *The Guardian*. In a leading article marked by great understanding of the German difficulties, the liberal London daily gave expression to the conviction that new problems might unexpectedly arise in connection with the Germans, even if the old German question of the postwar period was settled. It was therefore important above all not to leave Germany alone as it "strikes out into the great unknown," but to give it the feeling that this journey would be taken together:

Having encouraged and applauded Germany's (probably over-hasty) rush to reunification, the Western governments and their people should now avoid pressing for quick results or drawing too early dire conclusions . . . .The German leaders themselves are well aware that they must tread very carefully. The intention is to become a major power but not a great one. Germany is highly dependent on exports, and poor in raw materials, it is said. This is an argument for interdependence and not for empire. In the same frame of mind, a united Germany may not necessarily go on pretending that NATO is indispensable. It could easily appear to be another aspect of the confrontational past which now seems inappropriate to the more diverse needs of a larger CSCE-style Europe. All this and much more lies ahead in a new decade which almost defies prediction. In truth the Germans are striking out into a great unknown. But then, they are by no means alone.[105]

104. Volker Hassemer, "Deutschlands Hauptstadt als Brücke für ein west-östliches Europa. Wir sind mitten im Wandel oder: nur nicht stören — alles bleibt beim alten?" in *Frankfurter Rundschau*, 20 October 1990.
105. "Together into the great unknown," in *The Guardian*, 3 October 1990.

The strength of the old Federal Republic lay primarily in its relative weakness, resulting from multiple dependence. Since its foundation, its endangered position in security-policy terms, and Berlin's exposed location in particular, gave it an initially passive and later increasingly active key role in formulating Western policy. Even within larger systems like NATO, the EC, and the CSCE, united Germany, in contrast, will be an incontrollably independent economic and political factor of power. This strengthens the possibilities of influence over foreign policy but, at the same time, makes it more sensitive to external pressure and still more susceptible to foreign criticism, obliging it to be considerate.

Unification essentially came about on Western terms and that was also desired by great majorities in the GDR. It came about as integration of the GDR into the Federal Republic, not as a compromise between West and East and not as a growing together on middle ground. Above all, German foreign policy must now fulfill the promise of making the unification of Germany into the motor for European unity. Committed cooperation in the further development of the EC must dispel any doubts there may be of the Germans' dedication to Europe. The resolute reshaping of relationships with the Central and European countries, including the USSR, and contribution to stabilization in the difficult transition must, however, also prevent a new wall of economic and social differences from lastingly dividing Europe.

On the day after German unity, the weekly magazine *Stern* published an interview with Federal President Richard von Weizsäcker centering on the question of Germany's new role in Europe and the world. A remarkable point made was the assessment of the Soviet leadership's possible motives in ultimately agreeing to unification, pointing to the important role of the Germans "in their geopolitical position."

Interview with Federal President Richard von Weizsäcker, 4 October 1990 (extract)

STERN: Mr. President, you are the first Head of State of united Germany. Do you see yourself as President of a new political great power?

VON WEIZSÄCKER: The word "great power" does not properly express the historical process we find ourselves in at the moment. We have an increment of tasks in Europe and in the world and an increment of responsibility. The category of great power comes from a time of rivalries among States and imperial predominance that we in Europe are after all setting about overcoming.

STERN: Will the tasks falling to the new German State not be different from those of the Federal Republic to date?

VON WEIZSÄCKER: To understand the new role of Germany, we ought to take a look at the question of unity from the Soviet viewpoint. The central objective of the Soviet reforms and the condition for their success domestically is to overcome the distance between the Soviet Union and Europe. The Soviet leadership has recognized that this can only be achieved with decisive help from the Germans. They have understood that the division of the Germans does not serve this vital interest but stands in its way. That is why, from a Soviet viewpoint, the unity of the Germans must be promoted. You can see how important the role of the Germans in their geopolitical location is. Accordingly, the weight of the Germans has indeed grown, but so has the weight of their responsibility in Europe.

STERN: Is the restoration of unity on 3 October then a new beginning for the Germans?

VON WEIZSÄCKER: It is the first time in our history that the Germans' desire to belong together in one State has come about in accord with their neighbors. To accomplish our unity, we did not go to the Hall of Mirrors in Versailles after a war against our major neighbor. Instead, we jointly adopted the concept of German unity at the conference table along with our neighbors and allies.

Nevertheless, for a successful *Ostpolitik*, Germany's ties with the West remain the decisive precondition, and on this point there is broad consensus between the major parties. These ties are the basic condition for the German capacity to act at all. The United States and France will still be Germany's most important foreign policy partners in the 1990s irrespective of the development of relationships with the Soviet Union. And it is only jointly with France that the greater Europe can be created, building on the European Community.

A Vote for the Architects of Unity

Continuity in foreign policy is also guaranteed by the results of the first all-German Bundestag elections on 2 December 1990. At this culminating point in the year of German unification, the architects of unity and advocates of orienting the new Germany to its European connections received an impressive majority. This confirmed the course to unification steered by Federal Chancellor Kohl and his Foreign Minister Genscher in the previous twelve months, and conferred on the Christian Democrats and the FDP a clear mandate to govern for the next four years. Conversely, all those who had attacked or criticized the unification process had to accept losses.

Of the all-German votes, 54.8 percent went to the coalition partners in Bonn: 43.8 percent to CDU/CSU and 11 percent to the FDP. The Social Democrats did not manage to break through the spiral of mood against them. At 33.5 percent, they fell well behind their election objective. Things were still more bitter for the Greens in the West. Against all predictions, at 3.9 percent they failed the 5 percent hurdle and were voted unceremoniously out of the Bundestag. Their place is now being taken by deputies from Alliance 90/Greens, a citizens' movement originating in the East to which voters in the eastern part of the territory gave their approval in the form of 5.9 percent of the vote.

The Republicans, whose entry to the Bundestag was regarded by many as inevitable after the European elections eighteen months earlier, reached only 2.1 percent. Finally, the PDS owes its entry to the Bundestag solely to a judgment of the Constitutional Court, which this time prescribed separate electoral areas for East and West. In 1994, the successor party to the SED will fail because of the 5 percent clause. Its performance in the former Federal Republic (0.3 percent) cannot lead it to expect any chances, and the 9.9 percent in the East will shrink still further. The outcome is the following distribution of seats for the total of 662 deputies: 319 seats for the CDU/CSU, 79 for the FDP, 239 for the SPD, 8 for Alliance 90/Greens, and 17 for the PDS. The clear electoral victory of the existing coalition partners means that in the first all-German Bundestag there is no alternative to a Christian Democrat-led government. The Social-Liberal option of the years from 1969 to 1982, which at least hypothetically existed in the last parliament of the old Federal Republic, is now not even mathematically possible.

It is true that the Bundestag elections of 2 December 1990 were dominated by German unification and the associated image of the parties; yet, the European dimension played a very important part in both the election campaign and the programs of the parties. Challenges were felt not only with regard to the economic and social costs accompanying unity, but also from the hopes and expectations that neighbors and partners placed on Germany's capability. In observing the German situation on the eve of the elections, Mainz political scientist Werner Weidenfeld saw these connections:

> Undoubtedly the surrounding world's expectations are greater than the Germans' self-perception would like to admit. Moscow tempts with the privileged title of world power. Washington declares its German friend to be its partner in leadership. The East Europeans make their economic calculations fast to German assistance. The West Europeans see the key to progress in integration as lying in German hands. And all together fear that the Germans might start concerning themselves with themselves alone. . . .
>
> We have always said German and European unification were two sides of the same coin. We now have the opportunity of confirming the correctness of this position. The most direct interaction will lie in the acceleration of West European integration. Together with that is the fact that we Germans cannot allow any doubt to arise as to our willingness for integration, and that our European neighbours have an elementary interest in hedging Germany in through integration. It is becoming noticeable in these very days that the rate of integration is increasing. . . .
>
> The new Germany will, without any ifs and buts, have to join the group of European leading powers. It has a share in responsibility for the success or failure of the completion of Europe. Leadership is not achieved by going it alone, but through initiatives toward forming a community. "Integration" thus becomes the key concept of the new epoch in Germany, as in Europe.[106]

Looking at Europe in upheaval, Weidenfeld is concerned with the development of three different forms of community: the further development of the European Community to political union, the creation of an Atlantic community, and finally, the formation of a pan-European community. These questions were touched upon in the major parties' programs for the 1990 Bundestag election campaigns and helped to determine their foreign policy profiles.

---

106. Werner Weidenfeld, "Für Deutschland beginnt jetzt eine neue Zukunft," in *Die Welt*, 1 December 1990.

In the CDU's program, the passage on the party's conceptions of Germany's role after the upheavals in both parts of our continent begins with the lapidary statement: "Germany is our Fatherland, Europe is our future." The Christian democrats advocate "European union," which will be the "basis for the growing together of all of Europe," and stress that "Franco-German friendship will remain the motor for European unification" for united Germany as well. They further advocate strengthening the rights of the European Parliament and common EC foreign and security policy. In order to confer necessary stability on the new European security structure advocated, NATO and the Bundeswehr are as "indispensable" to the CDU as the "trans-Atlantic association" with North America.

In relations with the countries of Central, Eastern, and Southeastern Europe, the CDU hopes that in the future borders will have the nature of "open roads and the opportunity for encounter in freedom." It appeals to expellees to understand the need for definitive recognition of the German eastern frontier and asks for their contribution to "settlement, as mediators between cultures and peoples." Finally, the CDU stresses the "key role for European integration" that will accrue to German-Soviet relations.

Yes to Germany — Yes to the future. Election program of the Christian Democratic Union of Germany for the all-German Bundestag elections, 2 December 1990 (extracts)

Germany is our fatherland, Europe our future.... The CDU wants a European Germany prepared for genuine partnership in a European spirit.

A European union should be the basis for the integration for the whole of Europe. For united Germany, the Franco-German friendship will continue to be the motor for European unification. The rights of the European Parliament must be strengthened. And it is only with a common foreign and security policy that Europe can effectively represent its common interests in the world and assume its responsibility for the overcoming of the worldwide problems of humanity.

We wish to live in good-neighborliness with Poland, Hungary, Czechoslovakia, and the other countries of Central, Eastern and Southeastern Europe. We assign to the frontiers a new character, pointing toward the future: that of open roads and the opportunity for encounter in freedom.... We know that the definitive fixing of the German eastern frontier is particularly painful to those Germans who, because of war and the injustice of expulsion, had to leave their homes. We have respect for them and their feelings, and at the same time call for their indispensable contribution to settlement, as mediators between cultures and peoples. In this spirit, they are making an essential contribution to a lasting European system of peace. . . .

A key role for European integration is played by the comprehensive development of German-Soviet relations. We want to take up from the good traditions of German-Russian relationships, making a contribution here, through a labor of understanding and reconciliation, toward a lasting system of peace. We shall support the political and economic transformation in the Soviet Union to the best of our ability. In view of the immensity of this task, however, it is essential for the West to provide help jointly and concordantly. . . .

NATO and the Bundeswehr continue to be indispensable. For four decades they have guaranteed peace and freedom. The stability of an all-embracing security structure in Europe requires the transatlantic association with North America.

Germany will do justice to its responsibility for Europe. It will engage actively in building up a new European Security structure in which the European Community, the West European Union, NATO, and the CSCE complement each other.

In principle, the Liberals' election program does not differ from the Christian Democrats' on the issues addressed, though a number of accents are placed differently. The postulate of a "European Germany"— as distinct from a "German Europe" — frequently used by both parties in the election campaign and in general throughout the unification year, meant for the FDP that from German unification there must come "a contribution for a united Europe." German "responsibility for Germany as a part of Europe" is stressed as much as is termination of the "power politics" that has repeatedly thrown Germany into disaster in the past. In the Liberals' self-portrayal, the FDP is the party of Europe. It has decisively helped to overcome political obstacles on the road to the European internal market and brought leading initiatives toward democratizing the EC and creating a European central bank. Of course, political union and strengthening the European Parliament's rights are also among the FDP's demands, and it advocates extension of the unitary European foreign policy of the EC "to all aspects of security policy too."

The FDP supports "active membership by a united Germany in the North Atlantic Alliance," but goes further than the CDU, demanding that NATO redefine "its strategy, its armament and its relationship to the States of Europe not belonging to NATO." In particular, for the FDP "the CSCE process with involvement of North America is the most important framework" for cooperation in Europe as a whole. The Liberals plead for promotion of "political and economic reform endeavors" in the States of Central and Eastern Europe and stress that the USSR "must not be excluded from the processes of cooperation" that are becoming stronger in Europe. In the Liberals' view the EC must be open to all European States "that share its goals and values" and meet the necessary conditions.

Liberal Germany. FDP Program for the Bundestag elections, 2 December 1990 (extracts)

German unification must bring a contribution toward a united Europe. Germany must not be the place where European division is manifested, nor the starting point for power politics, but the pointer of the way to a single Europe. German unification should not be national egoism, with its hollow exultation, but be in responsibility for Europe, as a part of Europe. . . .

The European Community (EC) must be developed further into a European union on the basis of a democratic constitution . . . .The European Parliament should be elected in all Member States on the principles of proportional representation. It must receive comprehensive legislative powers and democratic control and budget powers . . . .The European Political Cooperation (EPC) among governments must be coupled with the Community's external relations into a unitary European foreign policy. This must extend to all aspects of security policy too. . . .

The EC is an essential structural element in the future of Europe. It must be open to all States that share its goals and values and meet the necessary conditions.

For cooperation in Europe as a whole, the CSCE process is the most important framework. . . . For the CSCE process, the involvement of the United States of America, Canada, and the Soviet Union is indispensable.

Germany and the other EC States must jointly promote the political and economic reform endeavours and the strengthening of human rights in the States of Central and Eastern Europe. . . . The USSR must not be excluded from the processes of cooperation that are intensifying in Europe. Its economic relations to the former GDR must be seen and further developed in this context. . . .The FDP supports active membership by united Germany in the North Atlantic Alliance (NATO). . . . NATO must redefine its strategy, its armament, and its relationship to the States of Europe that do not belong to NATO. All States of Europe must give each other assurances, across the old bloc frontiers, that they no longer regard each other as enemies and that they renounce the use of force. The move from the previous policy of confrontation to a policy of cooperation must be speeded up.

In contrast to the two coalition partners, the CDU/CSU and FDP, the SPD did not submit an election program for 2 December 1990. It did, however, present a government program for the years 1990 to 1994, in order thereby to document its claim to return to governmental responsibility. It is striking that the European policy positions of the party are somewhat more radical than those of the Christian Democrats and Liberals. Even on the question of Western European integration, on which there is agreement in principle among the major parties, the SPD goes well beyond other parties' proposals for reinforcing the EC. The SPD's objectives largely assume the vocabulary of the "founding fathers of Europe," particularly with regard to the central demand for creation of the "United States of Europe." With this postulate, the SPD is taking a clear position in the conceptual dispute between those who strive only for a loose "European federation of States" and those who want a firmly structured "European federal State." At the same time, with its demand to "make membership possible for the new Central and Eastern European democracies," the SPD takes up ideas current among Résistance fighters of a free, democratic, and ultimately united Europe.

Unlike the FDP, the SPD calls not only for rethinking in NATO but also for the "creation of a European security system" in the framework of the CSCE, in which the "existing military alliances will dissolve." Relationships with the United States are discussed above all from the viewpoint of equal partnership in NATO, in order that foreign forces can be "stationed on no other basis for their presence than in other NATO States."

Government program for 1990–1994. THE NEW WAY — ecological, social, and economically strong. Resolved by the SPD Party Congress in Berlin, 28 September 1990 (extracts)

The military blocs are losing their function. We aim at dissolving them. Our goal remains an agreement to create a European security system in the framework of the CSCE, in which the existing military alliances will dissolve. Equal partnership for Germany in NATO requires that foreign forces not be stationed under any other basis for their presence than in other NATO States. We reject deployment of NATO or the WEU, or additional military tasks for them, outside the area to which the Alliance applies.

Germany's national unification must not let us lose sight of the great objective of Europe. We want a United States of Europe. We want to strengthen the EC and at the same time make membership possible for the EFTA States and the new Central and Eastern European democracies. To prepare that, we have to strengthen the EC institutions and grant the European Parliament the proper rights for a freely elected representation of the people in a democracy. Anyone wishing to solve the great transnational problems such as environment protection needs a strong Europe. . . .

It is only if the new Central and East European democracies manage to find a link with the economic and ecological development of Western Europe that new social disruptions, new migrations of peoples from East to West, and relapses into dictatorial forms of rule and dangerous nationalistic disputes can be prevented. For what is true of internal peace applies to external peace too: national questions are above all social questions. . . .

The strengthening of European constitutional bodies must go hand in hand with strengthening of the provinces and regions in the States of Europe. For the great problems of our time, even great nation-States are too small — for the everyday problems on the spot, the big nation-State is not suitable. The Europe of the future, the United States of Europe, must have a federative constitution.

On 2 December 1990, Germans finally said goodbye to the old order. In their votes they were exercising their common freedom, impressively confirming the course that had in less than a year led to unification. It was a great pledge of confidence for the existing and future government coalition. If over the next four years the coalition succeeds in coping with the problems of united Germany, then this has truly been a decisive election. However, as has been shown by the results of different regional elections in 1991, as well as by the protracted debate on the financial costs of unity, the domestic situation of the FRG is somewhat unpredictable.

Chancellor Kohl and his Vice-Chancellor, Foreign Minister Genscher, must prove themselves in the new Germany, both internally and externally. Helmut Kohl had assured his Western European neighbors that the new Germany would not remain self-preoccupied. A few days after the elections, the time had come to act on this promise with a joint Franco-German advance in the cause of Europe's political union, and in time for the governmental conference of Heads of State and Government of the EC scheduled for 15 December in Rome.

In a joint message to the President-in-Office of the Council of 6 December 1990, Paris and Bonn proposed that, in order to improve the efficiency of the union, the European Council be made into a permanent institution, with increased powers. It should exercise the "function of arbitrator, guarantor and stimulator for coherent integration" on the road toward European union. Mitterrand and Kohl also advocated extending to all spheres the future joint foreign and security policy of the EC. Accordingly, decision-making structures should be patterned in such a way that in the future the Council of Foreign Ministers would both deal with Community issues and act on the common foreign and security policy of the European Council.

With the Franco-German proposal, the European Parliament would be considerably strengthened. The President appointed by the European Council and the whole EC Commission would have to be confirmed by a majority of the Parliament. The Treaty on European Union should further specify the bases and conditions for a genuine European citizenship.

Joint letter from Mr. Mitterrand and Mr. Kohl to the President-in-Office of the Council of the European Communities, Mr. Giulio Andreotti, 6 December 1990 (extracts)

For the effectiveness of the Union, we propose that the role and tasks of the European Council be confirmed and extended. It should act as an arbiter and a guarantor, and as promotor of consistent pursuit of integration along the road towards European Union. . . .

We suggest that the European Council should define the priority areas for joint action: for instance, relations with the USSR and countries of Central and Eastern Europe, implementation of the conclusions of the summit of 34 and continuation of the CSCE process, disarmament negotiations, relationships with countries on the southern shores of the Mediterranean. . . . Foreign policy will thus be able to grow into a true joint foreign policy. Development policy ought also to be part of the Union. Additionally, political union should include a genuine security policy, leading ultimately to joint defense.

Through their joint initiative of December 1990, the French President and the German Chancellor wished to demonstrate that Franco-German closeness would continue to constitute the precondition, and perhaps even the driving force, for European unification. During the year 1990, the impression might have been formed that the Franco-German tandem had lost its capacity to speak out on the great questions of Europe's destiny and to provide impetus for the unification process.

General Charles de Gaulle, whose 100th birthday was celebrated in France on 22 November 1990, best described this close connection between Franco-German relationships and the European dimension. In a talk on 10 March 1966 in the Elysée Palace with former Federal Chancellor Konrad Adenauer a year before the latter died, the French statesman sketched a picture of cooperation between Paris and Bonn that, more than any of his other statements on the topic, is better treated as a political testament.

Talk at the Elysée between General Charles de Gaulle and former Chancellor Konrad Adenauer, 10 March 1966 (extract)

France exists, it is growing again. Germany exists too. But France has not the resources to exercise leadership within Europe. Europe is the combined affair of the French and the Germans together. That is the right way. Alone, we do not have the means to lead Europe. You do not either; but together we can do it. We must march hand in hand. The fact that economic interests may not necessarily be the same does not constitute a fundamental barrier. There is the fact that you are cut in two by the Soviets. That is a special case, but someday it will come to an end. A free Europe can be organized only after deep agreement between our two countries. You and I have tried to bring that about, thanks to the Franco-German friendship treaty. Since then, different tendencies have come to play. But it will be needful always to return to that starting point or else resign oneself to the fact that Europe will not be made.

Choosing this path, however, means opting in favor of effort. While so many factors under various pretexts encourage ease, renunciation, or back-sliding, this Europe must be merited. Indeed, for forty-five years Westerners made the effort, and through their complementary merits, they managed to bring into being a Germany different from the old one: democratic, moderate, and respectful of law and human rights. Additionally, they managed to contribute to the events that have led to this extraordinary explosion of freedom in the East. It is now up to Germany to deserve a Europe whose destiny is no longer to be decided elsewhere, but is to be mistress of herself, constituting another pole of attraction and progress. In such an undertaking, why should the Franco-German tandem not maintain a privileged place? The world agreed to assign it such a place when prospects long seemed confined to Western Europe alone. If the horizon has now extended, it is possible that this same twosome could play the same driving role in this broader framework, as long as they keep the will to do so.

Conclusion

The Germans in the East and West have barely begun to come to terms with the recent unification of the country. Only very gradually do they realize what the problems and burdens of unity are going to be. Now, following the decision of the German Parliament to move the capital to Berlin, they face another decisive event, whose consequences are difficult to gauge. The vote in favor of Berlin as the seat of government, which occurred on 20 June 1991 after a marathon debate lasting eleven hours, was the first sovereign decision of the new Germany. Wolfgang Schäuble, the Christian Democrat Minister of the Interior, was therefore quite right when he said in Parliament that this was not a competition between two cities, Bonn and Berlin; what in fact was at stake was "the future" of Germany.

There had been unanimous approval when Lothar de Maizière, the last Prime Minister of the GDR, admonished his countrymen in the year of German unification that the new task was to "overcome the division by mutual sharing." But it was only during the debate on the location of the capital that all Germans saw with full clarity that sharing was not an act of mercy on the part of the old Federal Republic; rather, it signified that the changes, which unification had brought with it, were to be borne jointly. The eastern parts will find it easier to adapt when learning that the western parts, too, will have to make adjustments. This in turn will help to complete the inner unity of the nation, which has yet to be achieved.

It was from the ranks of the smaller parties, and in particular from those of the Free Democrats, that the decisive votes were cast in favor of the motion to move government and Parliament to Berlin. This emerges from an evaluation of the votes for the two motions that had been put by the protagonists of Bonn and of Berlin respectively. In the evening of 20 June, a small majority of 18 votes tipped the scales in favor of the Berlin motion. Of the 662 deputies, exactly 660 cast their vote; one vote was void and one deputy abstained. Of the remaining 658 votes, 338 were cast in favor of Berlin, while 320 deputies wanted Bonn to remain the seat of government and Parliament.

No parliamentary decision, since the unsuccessful vote of no-confidence against Chancellor Willy Brandt and his *Ostpolitik* in 1972, has aroused such deep emotions as this one. But unlike the vote of 1972, the rift cut straight through all the different parliamentary parties. Up to the last minute, the decision remained contested to abandon Bonn as a postwar provisorium on the western fringes of the Federal Republic and to make a fresh start in Berlin, the former capital of the Reich, on the eastern periphery of Germany. On the other hand, it is important to remember that the Bundestag decision might not have come about, if twelve of the sixteen Federal Länder had not spoken out earlier in favor of Berlin as the actual capital, rather than the capital to be used only for purposes of representation. Moreover, it is not expected that the Bonn bureaucracy will move to Berlin overnight. An extended deadline — there is talk of ten to twelve years — will enable Berlin to prepare itself thoroughly for its new task, just as Bonn will have time to adjust to its role as the second largest administrative center of the Federal Republic.

The move to Berlin is thus not the founding stone of German unity, but its capstone. In the meantime, politicians and ordinary citizens in East and West will have to make even greater efforts and sacrifices if the building of German unity is not to collapse beforehand. Similarly, the political debate concerning the future of Germany and its role within Europe and the world will continue. The old Federal Republic could consider itself well taken care of within the walls of a capital that had a low profile and was invariably thought of as provisional. And yet, this provisorium became a success story that lasted for forty years. Now that it had unexpectedly been absorbed by a "united Fatherland," traditional certainties and ways of doing things have been shaken.

The argument, which arose in connection with German unification, that the Federal Republic would became more "eastern," is untenable, if only because Eastern Europe after forty years of imprisonment is trying very hard to move westward politically and economically. Germany will not be more "eastern" as a result of unification; it is the European Community, hitherto the only part of Europe capable of concerted action, which will move into the center of the Continent. There is, however, one important consequence of the vote for Berlin that concerns the relationship between East and West within Germany directly. Berlin as the German capital and seat of government is designed to counter the sense of abandonment, of distance, and of a lack of sympathy that, apart from their economic plight, has had a depressing effect upon many of the citizens of the former GDR.

As long as Bonn was the capital and seat of government, no economic energies emanated from it. Berlin, and even more so the political transformation in the whole of Europe, will change this. Berlin is to be a bridgehead for Central and Eastern Europe. Does this mean that it will be no more than the first stop-over for many people who are on their way from the economically backward regions in the East to prosperous Western Europe? Berlin, with its 3.5 million inhabitants, is still the largest city in Germany and the only one that has the character of a metropolis. But there are marked economic differentials between it and its hinterland that cannot easily be levelled out.

The question of Germany's future capital has been a political one from the start. Economic consequences had to be considered, but they could not be of crucial importance.

Berlin, the multi-cultural metropolis in the East, can anticipate a boom similar to the *Gründerjahre* after 1871. On the other hand, the Bundestag vote is a dramatic setback for the Bonn region, as no new roles are available to it that could act as a realistic substitute. Some 42,000 people in this region are employed in government or government-related positions. On the assumption that each one of them supports an average of 1.5 family members and that eight employees provide employment for one additional person, the total number of people in the Bonn region directly or indirectly dependent on Bonn as the former capital, comes to 175,000. Depending on where one draws the regional borders, this amounts to between 25 to 35 percent of the total population.

The protagonists of the move to Berlin, as the capital of the former Reich, highlighted above all the city's tradition and its role during the past forty years as the symbol of the unity of the German state, to which innumerable speeches and resolutions had pointed. It is forty-two years ago that Bonn was declared the interim-capital to stand in for Berlin. At that time, on 3 November 1949, the Bundestag ratified, with an overwhelming majority, a vision that for a long time remained an illusion: "The leading organs of the Federation will move their seat to the capital Berlin as soon as universal free, equal, secret, and direct elections have been held in the whole of Berlin and in the Soviet Zone of Occupation. The Bundestag will thereafter reassemble in Berlin." Since the resolution was never rescinded, the credibility of earlier professions was also at stake. Thus, Chancellor Kohl stated in his speech that Berlin had been the "focal point of Germany's division and of the longing for German unity;" it was, therefore, the natural seat of government and Parliament. The advocates of the status quo countered that Bonn was the symbol of a working federation. There existed at the beginning of the debate, a compromise proposal that, pointing to the costs of a move, pleaded for a separation of government and Parliament.

Rita Süssmuth, the president of the Bundestag, commented in the wake of the majority vote in favor of Berlin that "experience and rationality" had been juxtaposed by "emotion and visions of the future." Manfred Stolpe, the Minister President of Brandenburg, explained his relief at the pro-Berlin vote with the argument that in this period of irritations and worry among the people of the five new Länder the "psychological aspect" was of decisive importance. In the view of some younger deputies, holding on to Bonn and rejecting the move to Berlin was above all a generational question. In the West, people had grown up with the Bonn democratic system, while young people in the East associated all the negative elements of former Communist rule with Berlin. In the end, the question of the credibility of earlier declarations in support of Berlin and consideration of the state of mind of the people in the five new Länder, all of whom, according to the polls, had opted in their large majority for Berlin, appear to have tipped the scales.

Will the move of the capital now turn the Bonn Republic into a Berlin Republic within the new Europe, and does this mean that the "Bonn modesty" of the Germans will be abandoned? The pro-Berlin faction in Parliament promoted their solution as the "completion of German unity." Meanwhile, the protagonists of Bonn campaigned for a "federal solution." On the day after the Bundestag vote, however, voices could also be heard in the Berlin

Chamber of Deputies pleading for "a capital devoted to modesty;" a capital that was capable of sharing and would not try to centralize everything. Basically, the dispute over the capital is in many ways the political correlate to the discussion on the proper role of the Germans within Europe and the world. This debate had preoccupied historians and experts in the months following the unification of Germany.

At the same time, the debate confirmed the results of a representative poll, conducted by the Infratest Institute between October and the middle of November 1990 and published in *Süddeutsche Zeitung* on 4 January 1991. According to the poll, "Germany 2000: the state we wish for" will be a different state from that of the present-day Federal Republic — a state with different domestic priorities and with a different image abroad. The population wants the united Germany to present itself to the rest of the world as a peaceful partner and to refrain from assuming a role as a world power. Some 75 percent of those polled expressed a desire that Germany should "rather more keep out" of international conflicts. A mere 25 percent favored the alternative that Germany should "rather more involve itself" in such conflicts. On this point the differences between East and West Germans were but small.

A mere 6 percent regarded the United States as a great power and nation that could serve as a model for a future Germany. Nor did more than 10 percent of those polled wish to emulate the economic power of Japan. Most people (40 percent) opted for Switzerland and the values of "prosperity and independence" associated with that country; "Welfare State Sweden" came second place (29 percent). Some 71 percent advocated the formation of a European Federal state during the 1990s. Forty percent of those polled expressed indifference as to where the first European head of government would hail; another 40 percent hoped to see a German politician at the top. There was a broad consensus with regard to national consciousness. A majority of Germans in East and West (52 percent) thought it was just about at the right level of intensity; 18 percent believed that there was already too much of it; 29 percent thought there was too little.

This picture of the new Germany, which is shaped by a need for harmony, gives no grounds for anxieties that the skeptical and negative attitude toward power, which is so clearly shaped by German history, might be reversed. The pro-Berlin vote does not call into question a political consensus that there will be no return to classic power politics in Germany. Nor will the new location of Germany's capital in the geographical center of Europe change the fact that the country is rooted in the Western system of democracy and of the free market — the most important legacy of the Bonn Republic.

Indeed, with the changes in Eastern Europe and the end of the Cold War, the Federal Republic is no longer the easternmost country of the West. The former communist states are transforming themselves into democracies. The Soviet Union, too, is striving to narrow the gap with Western Europe. Hence, the choice of Berlin is not only indicative of a turn toward the five new Länder inside Germany; it also stands for the country's special responsibility in helping to make the transformation of east central Europe a success. It is the task of a united Germany to promote, together with its partners in the European Community, the newly gained liberties and to contribute to their vitality.

Chronology

1944

12 September	Protocol of the European Advisory Commission on the division of Germany into zones
14 November	Decisions of the European Advisory Commission on the control machinery in Germany

1945

4–11 February	Yalta Conference (Roosevelt, Stalin, Churchill)
7–8 May	Unconditional surrender of German forces at Rheims and Berlin-Karlshorst
5 June	Declaration regarding the defeat of Germany and the assumption of supreme authority by the victorious powers
17 July–2 August	Potsdam Conference (Truman, Churchill, then Atlee, Stalin)

1946

21–22 April	Forced amalgamation of KPD and SPD in Soviet zone to form SED
25 April–15 May, 15 June–12 July	Foreign Ministers' Conference of victorious powers in Paris

1947

1 January	Economic administration in American and British zones combined (Bizonia)
10 March–24 April, 6–9 June	Foreign Ministers' Conference in Moscow Conference of German *Land* Prime Ministers in Munich
25 November–15 December	Foreign Ministers' Conference in London

1948

| 24 June | Start of the Berlin Blockade |
| 1 August | French zone of occupation joined to the Bizone to form one economic area (Trizone) |

1949

4 April	North Atlantic Treaty, creating NATO
12 May	End of the Berlin Blockade
23 May	Basic Law of the Federal Republic of Germany (FRG) comes into force
23 May–20 June	Foreign Ministers' Conference in Paris
21 September	Occupied Status for the FRG comes into effect
7 October	Establishment of the German Democratic Republic (GDR)

1950

9 May	Robert Schuman proposes European Coal and Steel Community (ECSC)
25 June	Start of the Korean War
5 August	Charter of the Germans expelled from their homelands (*Heimatvertriebenen*)
26 October	René Pleven proposes formation of a European army with participation by the FRG

1951

15 March	Reestablishment of the (West) German Foreign Office
18 April	Signing of the European Coal and Steel Community Treaty in Paris
20 September	Interzonal Trade Agreement between the FRG and East German authorities

1952

10 March–23 September	Exchange of Notes between the Soviet Union and Western powers over a Peace Treaty with Germany
26 May	Signing of the Germany Treaty in Bonn between the FRG and the three Western Allies
27 May	Signing of the European Defense Community (EDC) Treaty in Paris

1953

| 17 June | Popular uprising in the GDR and East Berlin |

1954

| 25 January–18 February | Foreign Ministers' Conference of the Four Powers in Berlin |

| 25 March | The GDR acquires further sovereignty rights |
| 23 October | Western Allies end occupation (Paris Treaty) |

1955

25 January	Soviet Union declares the ending of the state of war with Germany
5 May	The FRG regains its sovereignty under the Paris Treaty
9 May	The FRG joins NATO
14 May	Founding of the Warsaw Pact (GDR a member)
14–23 July	Geneva Summit Conference (Eisenhower, Bulganin, Eden, Faure)
9–13 September	Visit by Chancellor Adenauer to Moscow: resumption of diplomatic relations with USSR
17–20 September	GDR Premier Grotewohl in Moscow: GDR acquires sovereignty

1956

| 18 January | Founding of East German National People's Army |
| 7 July | West German Parliament passes military conscription law |

1957

| 25 March | Signing of Rome Treaties establishing the Common Market and Euratom |

1958

| 27 November | Berlin Ultimatum: the Soviet Union gives notice to terminate occupation and Four Power status in Berlin |

1959

| 11 May–20 June, 13 July–5 August | Foreign Ministers' Conference of the Four Powers in Geneva, attended by delegations from FRG and GDR |

1960

| 16–17 May | Failure of Paris Summit Conference |

1961

| 3–4 June | Kennedy and Khrushchev meet in Vienna |
| 13 August | Building of the Berlin Wall |

1962

| 22–28 October | Cuban missile crisis |

1963

17 December | First agreement on transborder travel between the GDR and the West Berlin Senate

1964

12 June | Agreement on mutual military support between Soviet Union and GDR

1969

28 October | Chancellor Brandt's government statement on readiness to negotiate on equal terms with the GDR ("Two states – one nation")

1970

19 March | Meeting between Brandt and Chairman of GDR Council of Ministers Stoph in Erfurt, East Germany
21 May | Brandt-Stoph meeting in Kassel, West Germany
12 August | Signing of German-Soviet Treaty in Moscow
7 December | Signing of German-Polish Treaty in Warsaw

1971

3 September | Signing of the (Four Power) Quadripartite Agreement on Berlin
17 December | Signing of Transit Agreement between FRG and GDR

1972

21 December | Signing of the Basic Treaty between the GDR and FRG

1973

18 September | Both FRG and GDR become members of the United Nations
11 December | Signing of the Prague Treaty between FRG and Czechoslovakia

1975

30 July–1 August | Concluding phase of Conference on Security and Cooperation in Europe (CSCE) in Helsinki

1979

12 December | NATO Twin-track decision taken in Brussels

1981

11–13 December | Meeting between West German Chancellor Schmidt and East German Premier Honecker at the Werbellinsee (GDR)

1984

4 September	Honecker postpones his visit to the FRG scheduled for October

1985

26 April	Warsaw Pact renewed for twenty years
1–6 May	U.S. President Reagan's trip to Federal Republic
4–5 May	Summit of industrialized countries in Bonn

1986

19–22 February	Visit to Bonn by the President of the East German Parliament, Horst Sindermann
17–21 April	11th Congress of the SED, in presence of Mikhail Gorbachev
6 May	Signature of FRG-GDR Cultural Agreement after twelve years of negotiations
11–13 October	Reagan-Gorbachev summit meeting in Reykjavik

1987

12 June	Reagan visit to West Berlin
6–11 July	Official visit to USSR by Federal President Richard von Weizsäcker
27 August	SPD and SED draw up a joint theoretical document
7–11 September	Honecker becomes first East German President to visit FRG
11 December	Meeting of Warsaw Pact leaders in East Berlin
8–12 December	Soviet-American agreement in Washington on elimination of INF

1988

11 February	First meeting in East Berlin between West Berlin Mayor Diepgen and East German President Honecker
24–27 October	Visit by Chancellor Kohl to Moscow

1989

2 May	Hungary begins dismantling the "Iron Curtain"
12–15 June	Official visit to FRG by Soviet President Gorbachev
10 September	Budapest authorizes East Germans present in Hungary to leave for "the country of their choice"
30 September	Some 6000 East German refugees are authorized to leave the FRG Embassy in Prague for the Federal Republic
7 October	GDR celebrates its 40th anniversary, in the presence of Mikhail Gorbachev
9 October	Monday demonstration in Leipzig by around 70,000 people

18 October	Erich Honecker ousted and replaced by Egon Krenz
4 November	One million people demonstrate in East Berlin
7 November	GDR government resigns
9 November	Opening of Berlin Wall and intra-German frontier
11–12 November	Two million East Germans spend weekend in West
13 November	Hans Modrow becomes new GDR Prime Minister
28 November	Chancellor Kohl presents his ten-point plan to the Bundestag
8–9 December	Strasbourg meeting of European Council deals particularly with the German question
19 December	Kohl-Modrow summit in Dresden
22 December	Opening of Brandenburg Gate
24 December	Complete freedom of movement between FRG and GDR for German nationals

1990

7 February	FRG proposes monetary union to GDR
10 February	Gorbachev recognizes the Germans' right to decide their own future
13 February	The Two-plus-Four process, bringing together the two German States and the four victorious powers to define the external conditions of unification, is proposed at Ottawa (Ottawa Group)
18 March	First free general elections in GDR
12 April	Grand government coalition formed of "Alliance for Germany," the Liberals and the Social-Democrats, led by Lothar de Maizière
28 April	European Council special session in Dublin on German unification
5 May	First meeting of Ottawa Group in Bonn
6 May	Local elections in GDR
18 May	Signature in Bonn of State Treaty on FRG-GDR economic, monetary, and social union
10 June	The Three Western Powers lift their reservations regarding representation of Berlin in Bundestag and Bundesrat
22 June	Second meeting of Ottawa Group in Berlin
25–26 June	European Council in Dublin
1 July	Entry into force of monetary union
5–6 July	NATO summit in London
16 July	Kohl-Gorbachev meeting in Zheleznovodsk in the Caucausus
17 July	Agreement on German-Polish frontier at Ottawa Group meeting in Paris

31 August	Signature in Berlin of Treaty of Union between the two Germanies
12 September	Signature in Moscow of Treaty on the Final Settlement with respect to Germany
3 October	German unification by accession of the GDR to the Federal Republic of Germany
14 October	Regional elections in the five Länder reconstituted in the ex-GDR
27–28 October	European Council in Rome
9 November	Signature in Bonn of German-Soviet Treaty initialled on 13 September in Moscow
14 November	Signature in Warsaw of German-Polish Treaty on the frontier
19–21 November	Conference on Security and Cooperation in Europe in Paris
2 December	First all-German general elections
14–15 December	European Council in Rome
15 December	The two Intergovernmental Conferences of the Twelve on Economic and Monetary Union and on Political Union begin their work

Documents

Introduction

Speech by Federal President Richard von Weizsäcker at the Hour of Remembrance of the German Bundestag for the 40th Anniversary of the End of the War in Europe, 8 May 1985
Source: Weizsäcker, Richard von: *Von Deutschland aus*. Berlin, Corso bei Siedler, 1985, p.11ff.

Chapter 1

For Our Country, appeal of 26 November 1989
Source: *Neues Deutschland*, 28 November 1989

Ten-Point Program to overcome the division of Germany and of Europe. Speech by Federal Chancellor Kohl to the German Bundestag on 28 November 1989
Source: *Bulletin. Presse- und Informationsamt der Bundesregierung*, No. 134/1989, p. 1141ff.

Government statement by the Chairman of the Council of Ministers of the GDR, Hans Modrow, given before the Volkskammer in East Berlin on 17 November 1989
Source: *Neues Deutschland*, 18–19 November 1989

National Anthem of the German Democratic Republic
Source: *Einigkeit und Recht und Freiheit. Nationale Symbole und nationale Identität*. Bonn, Bundeszentrale für politische Bildung, 1985, p. 31

National Anthem of the Federal Republic of Germany
Source: Ibid. p. 23

The Germans in Europe. Berlin Declaration of the Social Democratic Party of Germany, resolved at the SPD Party Congress on 18–20 December 1989
Source: Vorstand der SPD. Bonn, Referat Öffentlichkeitsarbeit, 1989

Federal President Richard Freiherr von Weizsäcker's interview with GDR television on 13 December 1989
Source: *Bulletin. Presse- und Informationsamt der Bundesregierung*, No. 143/1989, p. 1213ff.

Speech by European Commission President Jacques Delors to the European Parliament in Strasbourg on 17 January 1990
Source: *Debates of the European Parliament*, No. 3/385, pp. 108ff.

Article by Soviet Foreign Minister Eduard Shevardnadze "On Foreign Policy"
Source: *Pravda*, 26 June 1990

Speech by Hans-Dietrich Genscher, Minister of Foreign Affairs of the Federal Republic of Germany, to the World Economic Forum in Davos on 1 February 1987
Source: *Pressemitteilung des Auswärtigen Amts*, No. 1022/87, 1 February 1987

Chapter 2

Report on the Future Tasks of the Alliance (Harmel Report), 14 December 1967
Source: Renata Fritsch-Bournazel: *Confronting the German Question.* Oxford/New York/Hamburg, Berg, 1988, p. 34

FRG's agreements with East European countries (*Ostverträge*)
Source: Ibid. p. 35ff.

Treaty between the Federal Republic of Germany and the Union of Soviet Socialist Republics (Moscow Treaty), 12 August 1970

Treaty between the Federal Republic of Germany and the People's Republic of Poland on the basis of the normalization of their mutual relations (Warsaw Treaty), 7 December 1970

Quadripartite Agreement on Berlin, 3 September 1971

Treaty on the Bases of Relations between the German Democratic Republic and the Federal Republic of Germany (Basic Treaty), 21 December 1972

Treaty on Mutual Relations between the Federal Republic of Germany and the Czechoslovakian Socialist Republic (Prague Treaty), 11 December 1973

Final Act of the Conference on Security and Cooperation in Europe (CSCE), 1 August 1975 (Helsinki Final Act)
Source: Ibid., p. 40

Interview with Federal Minister for Foreign Affairs, Willy Brandt, on the Deutschlandfunk, 2 July 1967
Source: Bulletin. Presse- und Informationsamt der Bundesregierung, No. 70/1967, p. 604

Press conference by French President Charles de Gaulle, 4 February 1965
Source: de Gaulle, Charles: *Discours et Messages,* Vol. IV. Paris, Plon, 1970, p. 35ff.

Speech of Federal Minister for Foreign Affairs Hans-Dietrich Genscher on the occasion of the SIPRI-IPW Conference in Potsdam, 9 February 1990
Source: Bulletin. Presseabteilung der Botschaft der Bundesrepublik Deutschland in Paris, No. 15/1990, 9 February 1990

Speech by Federal Minister for Intra-German Relations, Dr. Dorothee Wilms, 28 April 1990
Source: Bulletin. Presse- und Informationsamt der Bundesregierung, No. 49/1990, p. 385ff.

New Year message by French President François Mitterrand, 31 December 1989
Source: La politique étrangère de la France, Textes et Documents, November-December 1989. Paris, Ministère des Affaires Etrangères, 1990, p. 227f.

Declaration by French Foreign Minister Robert Schuman, 9 May 1950
Source: Gerbet, Pierre: *La Naissance du Marche Commun.* Brussels, Editions Complexe, 1987, p. 162ff.

Declaration of the European Council in Strasbourg on Central and Eastern Europe, 8/9 December 1989
Source: Bulletin of the European Communities, No. 12, 1989.

Speech by Dr. Erhard Eppler in the German Bundestag on 17 June 1989
Source: Stenographischer Bericht des Deutschen Bundestages, 11. Wahlperiode, 17 June 1989, p. 11296ff.

Speech by U.S. Secretary of State James A. Baker to the Berlin Press Club on 12 December 1989
Source: Europe documents – English edition. Agence Internationale d'information pour la presse, Luxembourg, December 1989

Speech by Soviet Foreign Minister Eduard Shevardnadze to the Political
Affairs Committee of the European Parliament in Brussels, 19 December
1989
Source: European Parliament, Political Affairs Committee, duplicated
typescript

Chapter 3

Protocol on the zones of occupation in Germany and the administration
of Greater Berlin, 12 September 1944
Source: Fritsch-Bournazel, *op. cit.*, p. 7

Agreement on the Control Machinery in Germany of 14 November 1944
Source: Fritsch-Bournazel, *op. cit.*, p. 8

Declaration at Yalta, 11 February 1945
Source: Royal Institute of International Affairs (ed. Beate Ruhm von Oppen):
Documents on Germany under Occupation 1945–1954. London/New
York/Toronto, Oxford University Press, 1955, p. 4

Berlin Declaration regarding the defeat of Germany and the assumption
of supreme authority with respect to Germany, 5 June 1945
Source: Ibid. p. 29ff.

Communiqué on the Three Power Conference in Berlin (Potsdam Agreement) of 2 August 1945
Source: Ibid. p. 48f.

Speech by U.S. President George Bush to the NATO council, 4 December
1989
Source: *American Foreign Policy Current Documents 1989*. Washington,
Department of State Publications, 1990, p. 297

Press conference by French President Mitterrand at the conclusion of his
state visit to the GDR, 22 December 1989
Source: *La politique étrangère de la France*, *op. cit.*, p. 212ff.

Report of GDR Prime Minister Otto Grotewohl to the GDR Volkskammer, 20 May 1955
Source: *Dokumente zur Außenpolitik der Deutschen Demokratischen Republik*, Vol. II, Berlin (East) 1955, p. 246

Declaration by Federal Chancellor Helmut Kohl on the outcome of the
talks with President Gorbachev of 16 July 1990
Source: *Informationen. Bundesminister für innerdeutsche Beziehungen*,
No. 13/1990

Treaty on Relations Between the German Democratic Republic and the

Union of Soviet Socialist Republics of 20 September 1955
Source: *Gesetzblatt der DDR 1955*. Part I, p. 918

Declaration by the Government of the USSR on the granting of sovereignty to the German Democratic Republic, 25 March 1954
Source: Royal Institute of International Affairs, *op. cit.*, p. 597f.

Warsaw Pact Treaty of 14 May 1955 (translation of extract from the German version)
Source: *Dokumente zur Deutschlandpolitik* III/1. 5 May–31 December 1955. Bonn/Berlin: Bundesministerium für gesamtdeutsche Fragen, 1961, p. 37ff.

Constitution of the German Democratic Republic of 9 April 1968, amended 7 October 1974
Source: Münch. Ingo von, ed.: *Dokumente des geteilten Deutschland. Quellentexte zur Rechtslage des Deutschen Reiches, der Bundesrepublik Deutschland und der Deutschen Demokratischen Republik*. Vol. II, Stuttgart, Alfred Kröner Verlag, 1974, p. 463ff.

Convention on Relations Between the Three Powers and the Federal Republic of Germany (Germany Treaty), as amended on 23 October 1954
Source: Royal Institute of International Affairs, *op. cit.*, p. 619ff.

Resolution of the NATO Council on the outcome of the Four and Nine Power Conferences, 22 October 1954
Source: *Foreign Relations of the United States 1952–1954*, Vol. V, Washington 1983, p. 1365f.

Convention on the Presence of Foreign Forces in the Federal Republic of Germany, 23 October 1954
Source: Royal Institute of International Affairs, *op. cit.*, p. 635

Treaty on the Final Settlement with respect to Germany, 12 September 1990
Source: Press and Information Office of the Federal Government: *Documents of German Unity*. Hamburg, Friedrich Reinecke Verlag, 1990, p. 3ff.

Resolution of the Two-plus-Four Conference in Paris on the "definitive nature of Germany's frontiers," 17 July 1990
Source: *Informationen. Bundesminister für innerdeutsche Beziehungen* No. 13/1990, 17 July 1990

Charter of Germans expelled from their homelands, 5 August 1950
Source: *Erklärungen zur Deutschlandpolitik. Eine Dokumentation von Stellungnahmen, Reden und Entschließungen des Bundes der Vertriebenen, Vereinigte Landsmannschaften und Landesverbände*. Part I, 1949–1972. Bonn, Kulturstiftung der deutschen Vertriebenen, 1984, p. 17f.

Agreement between the Republic of Poland and the German Democratic Republic on the demarcation of the established and existing Polish-German national frontier (Görlitz Treaty), 6 July 1950
Source: Royal Institute of International Affairs, *op. cit.*, p. 498f.

Note from the Federal Government to the Three Western Powers, 19 November 1970
Source: *Dokumentation zur Entspannungspolitik, op. cit.*, p. 223f.

Talk by the Minister for Foreign Affairs of the Republic of Poland, Prof. Dr. Krzysztof Skubiszewski, on 7 February 1990 in Bonn
Source: *Europa-Archiv* 6, 1990, p. 195ff.

Speech by Foreign Minister of Czechoslovakia, Jiři Dienstbier, on 16 May 1990 at Harvard
Source: *Europa Archiv* 13–14, 1990, p. 397ff.

Chapter 4

Speech by Kurt Schumacher to leading representatives of the SPD, 31 May 1947
Source: *Acht Jahre sozialdemokratischer Kampf um Einheit, Frieden und Freiheit*. Bonn, Vorstand der SPD, 1953, p. 26f.

Speech by SPD Deputy Chairman Herbert Wehner to the German Bundestag on 30 June 1960
Source: Haftendorn, Helga/Wilker, Lothar/Wörmann, Claudia: *Die Außenpolitik der Bundesrepublik Deutschland*. Berlin, Wissenschaftlicher Autoren-Verlag, 1982, p. 190ff.

Speech by Parliamentary State Secretary to the Federal Minister for Intra-German Relations, Ottfried Hennig, to the Evangelical Working Group, Cologne, 27 April 1989
Source: Bulletin. *Presse- und Informationsamt der Bundesregierung*, No. 41/1989 p. 375ff.

Address by Consistory President Manfred Stolpe at the joint German commemoration in East Berlin, 17 June 1990
Source: *Das Parlament*, 22 June 1990, p. 2f.

Declaration of Principle by Federal Chancellor Konrad Adenauer in Moscow, 9 September 1955
Source: *Dokumente zur Deutschlandpolitik* III/1, 1955, *op. cit.*, p. 305ff.

Speech by French Defense Minister Jean-Pierre Chevènement to graduates of the Institut des Hautes Etudes de Défense Nationale, 21 May 1990
Source: Chevènement, Jean-Pierre: Evolution du Monde, Rôle et Politique de Défense de la France. *Défense Nationale* 7/1990, p. 9ff.

Contribution to debate by Ambassador of the Republic of Hungary to Switzerland, János Hajdú, in the Berlin Reichstag, 10 November 1989
Source: Fischer, Alexander, ed.: *Vierzig Jahre Deutschlandpolitik im internationalen Kräftefeld. Berlin Kolloquium für Deutschlandforschung in Verbindung mit dem Bundesminister für innerdeutsche Beziehungen,* 8–10 November 1989. Cologne, Edition Deutschland-Archiv, 1989, p. 73ff.

After-dinner speech by GDR Prime Minister Lothar de Maizière in the Quai d'Orsay, 19 June 1990
Source: Embassy of the German Democratic Republic in Paris, duplicated typescript, 19 June 1990

Treaty on the creation of a monetary, economic and social union between the Federal Republic of Germany and the German Democratic Republic, 18 May 1990
Source: Bulletin. Presse- und Informationsamt der Bundesregierung, No. 133/1900, p. 1379ff.

Treaty on good-neighborliness, partnership and cooperation between the Federal Republic of Germany and the Union of Soviet Socialist Republics, initialled on 13 September 1990 in Moscow and signed in Bonn on 9 November 1990
Source: Bulletin. Presse-und Informationsamt der Bundesregierung, No. 133/1900, p. 1379ff.

Speech by City Councillor Ernst Reuter on Republic Square, Berlin, 9 September 1948
Source: 40 Jahre RIAS Berlin. Tondokumente aus Politik, Musik, Unterhaltung, Literatur und Hörspiel. Berlin, 1986.

Speech by US President John F. Kennedy before the Schöneberg Town Hall in Berlin, 26 June 1963
Source: New York Times, 27 June 1963

Speech by Czechoslovak President Václav Havel at the Brandenburg Gate, Berlin, 2 January 1990
Source: Frankfurter Rundschau, 3 January 1990

Speech by governing Mayor Walter Momper before the Schöneberg Town Hall, Berlin, 10 November 1989
Source: Auswärtiges Amt, ed.: *Umbruch in Europa, op. cit.,* p. 76ff.

Speech by Federal President Richard von Weizsäcker on the occasion of conferment of the Honorary Citizenship of Berlin in St. Nicholas's Church, 29 June 1990
Source: Dokumentation Berlin. Presse- und Informationsamt des Landes Berlin und Presseabteilung des Magistrats von Berlin, 1990, p. 11ff.

Chapter 5

Presidency Conclusions of the Special Meeting of the European Council, Dublin, 28 April 1990
Source: Bulletin of the European Communities, Supplement No. 4/1990.

Interview by British Minister for Trade and Industry Nicholas Ridley with Dominic Lawson
Source: "The Spectator," 14 July 1990

Article by Italian Foreign Minister Gianni de Michelis
Source: NATO Review 3, May–June 1990, p. 8ff.

Interim report of the Temporary Committee of the European Parliament to consider the impact of the process of German unification on the European Community, 9 July 1990
Source: European Parliament Session Documents, No. A3–183/90/Part B: Explanatory Statement, 9 July 1990.

Speech by Federal Chancellor Kurt Georg Kiesinger for the day of German unity, 17 June 1967
Source: Bulletin. Presse- und Informationsamt der Bundesregierung, No. 64/1967, p. 541ff.

Speech by Federal President Walter Scheel on the 25th anniversary of the day of German unity on 17 June 1978
Source: Reden der deutschen Bundesprasidenten Heuss/Lübke/Heinemann/ Scheel. Munich/Vienna, Carl Hanser Verlag 1979, p. 268ff.

Statements by Federal Chancellor Helmut Kohl and GDR Prime Minister Lothar de Maizière on signature of the State Treaty in Bonn on 18 May 1990
Source: Informationen. Bundesminister fur innerdeutsche Beziehungen, No. 10/1990, 18 May 1990

Speech by French Foreign Minister Roland Dumas to the National Assembly on 7 November 1989
Source: La politique étrangère de la France, op. cit., p. 13ff.

Press conference by French President François Mitterrand in Strasbourg, 9 December 1989
Source: Ibid. p. 149ff.

Speech by Federal Chancellor Helmut Kohl on "The German Question and European Responsibility" in Paris, 17 January 1990
Source: Bulletin. Presse- und Informationsamt der Bundesregierung, No. 9/1990, p. 61ff.

For a common future. Declaration by the leading German bishops, 1 July 1990
Source: *Berliner Sonntagsblatt*, 1 July 1990

Interview with Czechoslovak President Václav Havel, 10 March 1990
Source: *Die Welt*, 10 March 1990

Speech by Federal President Richard von Weizsäcker in Prague, 15 March 1990
Source: *Europa-Archiv* 9, 1990, p. D 237ff.

Chapter 6

Speech by Saarland Minister-President Oskar Lafontaine (SPD) to the German Bundestag on 23 August 1990
Source: *Das Parlament*, 31 August 1990, p. 3

Interview with Bundestag Green spokeswoman Antje Vollmer, 15 September 1990
Source: Jetzt kontrolliert niemand mehr dieses Deutschland außer uns. Ein Doppelschock, die Großmacht Bundesrepublik und die Rolle der linken Opposition. Matthias Greffrat im Gespräch mit Antje Vollmer. *Frankfurter Rundschau*, 15 September 1990

Interview with Federal Chancellor Helmut Kohl, 11 October 1990
Source: Wir stehen vor einem gewaltigen Kraftakt. Der Bundeskanzler beantwortet Fragen nach den vordringlichen innenpolitischen Aufgaben und der künftigen internationalen Rolle Deutschlands. *Süddeutsche Zeitung*, 11 October 1990

We want a European Germany, not a German Europe. Essay by Federal Minister for Foreign Affairs Hans-Dietrich Genscher, September 1990
Source: Wickert, Ulrich, ed.: *Angst vor Deutschland*. Hamburg, Hoffmann und Campe, 1990, p. 317ff.

Interview with Federal President Richard von Weizsäcker, 4 October 1990
Source: Es wird schon gelingen. STERN interview with Richard von Weiszäcker. *Der Stern*, 4 October 1990

Yes to Germany – Yes to the future. Election programme of the Christian Democratic Union of Germany for the all-German Bundestag elections, 2 December 1990
Source: Material zur Bundestagswahl am 2.12.1990. Bonn, CDU-Bundesgeschäftstelle, November 1990

Liberal Germany. FDP Programme for the Bundestag elections, 2 December 1990
Source: Material zur Bundestagswahl am 2.12.1990. FDP-Bundesgeschäftsstelle. St. Augustin, liberal-verlag, 1990

Government programme for 1990–1994. THE NEW WAY – ecological, social and economically strong. Resolved by the SPD Party Congress in Berlin, 28 September 1990
Source: Material zur Bundestagswahl am 2.12.1990. Vorstand der SPD. Bonn, Referat Öffentlichkeitsarbeit, 1990

Joint letter from Mr. Mitterrand and Mr. Kohl to the President-in-Office of the Council of the European Communities, Mr. Giulio Andreotti, 6 December 1990
Source: *Bulletin. Presse- und Informationsamt der Bundesregierung*, No. 144/1990, p. 1513f.

Talk at the Elysée between General Charles de Gaulle and former Chancellor Konrad Adenauer, 10 March 1966
Source: Maillard, Pierre: *De Gaulle et L'Allemagne. Le rêve inachevé*. Paris, Plon, 1990, p. 256

Index